Drafting and Assessing Poetry

A Guide for Teachers

Drafting and Assessing Poetry

A Guide for Teachers

Sue Dymoke

P·C·P
Paul Chapman
Publishing

First published 2003

Apart from any fair dealing for the purposes of
research or private study, or criticism or review, as
permitted under the Copyright, Designs and
Patents Act, 1988, this publication may be
reproduced, stored or transmitted in any form, or
by any means, only with the prior permission in
writing of the publishers, or in the case of repro-
graphic reproduction, in accordance with the terms
of licences issued by the Copyright Licensing
Agency. Inquiries concerning reproduction outside
those terms should be sent to the publishers.

 Paul Chapman Publishing
A SAGE Publications Company
6 Bonhill Street
London EC2A 4PU

SAGE Publications Inc
2455 Teller Road
Thousand Oaks, California 91320

SAGE Publications India Pvt Ltd
B-42, Panchsheel Enclave
Post Box 4109
New Delhi-100 017

Library of Congress Control Number: 2002106581

A catalogue record for this book is available from the British Library

ISBN 0 7619 4854 6
ISBN 0 7619 4855 4 (pbk)

Typeset by Dorwyn Ltd, Rowlands Castle, Hants.
Printed in Great Britain by Athenaeum Press, Gateshead.

Contents

List of Figures

Acknowledgements

I would like to thank the following copyright holders, who have kindly granted permission for reproduction of their work.

Moniza Alvi for 'How Thought Accompanied the Traveller' drafts and commentary; Ann Atkinson, Liz Cashdan, Livi Michael and Ian Pople for 'Creative writing in higher education: criteria for assessment of portfolios of writing' (first published in *Writing in Education*, 21, Winter 2000–01) Richard Bain for 'Hypertexting' (first published in *Secondary English Magazine*, 2 (3), February 1999); Ian Baker for 'The Magical Garden'; Debjani Chatterjee for 'A Winter's Morning in Tirmapur' and commentary; Carly Forrest for 'A Midsummer Night's Dream'; Sean Gibson for 'The Magical Garden'; Jean Hayhoe for 'City Blues' by Mike Hayhoe; Tom Hopkins for 'Bird Flight' and GCSE coursework commentary; Henry Ives for 'My Garden'; Jackie Kay for her responses on drafting; Ekaterina Krylova for *The Torrent Raged* and GCSE coursework commentary; Ian McMillan for 'The Destiny Girls' (first published in *The Invisible Villain*, Macmillan, 2002) and commentary; Brian Moses for 'The Ssssnake Hotel' (first published in *Welcome to the Ssssnake Hotel*, Macmillan, 2001) drafts and commentary; Jane Murphy for *Raindrops* and her commentary on demonstration; Charles Nicholls for 'Going to Bed'; Jack Samuels for 'The Magical Garden'; Tim Shaw for 'My Garden'; Tom Short for 'The Tornado' and GCSE coursework commentary; Chelsea Clarke Smith for 'Friends'; Caroline Stanley for 'Leave me Alone'; Myfanwy Thomas and the British Library for the draft manuscript of 'Adlestrop' by Edward Thomas (ADD, 44990 f 10v–11r); Paul Violi for 'Appeal to the Grammarians' and commentary; Clive Wilmer for 'Bottom's Dream' (first published in *Around the Globe*, 20, Winter 2001–02) and commentary: Cliff Yates for 'Leaves are Just Thin Wood' (first published in *The North*) and commentary.

Every effort has been made to trace the copyright holders, but if any have been inadvertently overlooked I would be pleased to make the necessary arrangements at the first opportunity.

I also thank the poets featured in Chapter 3 who have responded to my many questions with encouragement and enthusiasm; the teachers who have given of their time so willingly and allowed me to visit them in their classrooms; the English departments at The Minster School and West Bridgford School, Nottinghamshire and Philippa Goad for tirelessly locating pupils for me; David Belbin, Christine Hall, Bernard Harrison, Mark Pike and Morag Styles for their advice and support.

For my poetry teachers

Introduction

The Moon is dark and silent
and always still.

There are rocks upon her surface
like a hill.

There are craters and sand there.
Beware astronaut beware.

The above poem was the first and only piece of writing I can remember completing at infant school. Although it may not be a memorable poem in itself, its significance for me has been far reaching. When I was seven years old I was encouraged to write this piece in the summer Neil Armstrong took his first steps on the moon. My teacher, who read poems by Robert Louis Stevenson and Walter de la Mare to the class, instilled in me a lifelong fascination with poetry. The arrangement of the words on the page and the way poems like de la Mare's 'Silver' sounded, when she read them aloud, had a mesmeric effect. Margaret Atwood describes the magic of poetry in its 'verbal attempt to accomplish something desirable' (Levenson, 1992: 22). Seamus Heaney states a desire to celebrate 'the surprise of poetry ... its given, unforeseeable thereness, the way it enters our field of vision and animates our physical and intelligent being' (Heaney, 1995: 15).

It was these intangible yet distinctive qualities which suddenly caused poetry to demand my attention and to permeate my early experiences as a reader and writer. In moving through school and into higher education, it became very clear that there were some teachers for whom poetry formed a regular feature of their classroom practice. They encouraged experiment, redrafting and sharing responses to texts. There were other teachers who preferred the novel or developing comprehension skills and appeared to be avoiding poetry. Nevertheless I knew that writing poetry was somehow becoming an essential activity for me and I was frustrated when not encouraged to further this developing interest.

The ideas behind this text have developed from my early forays into poetry along with a number of professional starting points including teaching and researching English at higher and secondary level, providing inservice training and my experience as a published poet and poetry workshop leader. In interviewing secondary English teachers I have found that many wanted to support their students to make progress with poetry writing. However they felt wary of taking over a student's drafting and intervening to the extent that the student's ownership of a poem might be in doubt. Often teachers were also reluctant to make final assessments of their students' poetry, believing they lacked guidance or a supportive framework. It was evident that the assessment of students' poetry was a contentious issue which needed to be explored. English teachers identified writers' drafts as a potentially valuable teaching tool for discussing the writer's craft and the choices which writers make but they remained uncertain about how to obtain or to use such material. Some practitioners were reluctant to use information and communications technology (ICT) in the poetry classroom other than for presentational purposes. Inviting published poets into the classroom was an infrequent occurrence. I also found that, in critical texts on the writing process, specific detailed references to the theory and history of writing poetry within educational contexts were very limited. It was difficult to gain a satisfactory overview and those texts which did exist, such as Koch (1970), Hull (1988) and Yates (1999), tended to focus on one poet's practical approaches.

As a result of the research I uncovered a need to explore the above issues further and to support teachers in developing this central aspect of their English teaching. *Drafting and Assessing Poetry* is therefore a theoretical text with a practical dimension. It engages readers in critical debates about poetry teaching and its place in an assessment driven curriculum. The book offers a range of teaching strategies for developing students' poetry writing skills and guidance about assessment approaches. Critical commentaries combine with illustrations of successful classroom practice in examining this essential but under explored aspect of English teaching.

The National Curriculum was first introduced into England and Wales in 1990 and revised over the next decade. When it was first introduced poetry was in an uncertain place within the Orders for English. Chapter 1 explores the place of poetry (especially writing poetry) within this overarching framework and the subsequently developed National Literacy Strategy.

In Chapter 2 the focus is directly on drafting poetry in the classroom. It takes a closer look at the terminology used in the National Curriculum to define elements of the writing process. With the emphasis on thinking skills in the classroom (in the UK especially), it is important to recognise the contribution which drafting poetry can make to the development of a child's thinking. Bereiter and Scardamalia's research on the psychology of the writing process is considered alongside teachers' reflections on their own drafting and practical suggestions to support the development of a thinking environment. The work of Donald Graves, Robert Hull, Pat D'Arcy and the current workshop practices of Cliff Yates have all been influential in developing pupils' and teachers' understanding of what constitutes drafting. Their relevance to the classroom context is explored here. Specific advice is offered on the use of drafting books and portfolios; diagramming and other planning strategies; modelling/teacher as writer; interventions; drafting partners and other strategies for encouraging critical reflection on the process of writing poetry. This chapter also provides examples of successful practice from the drafting classroom, including a newly qualified teacher's account of modelling poetry and pupils' commentaries on their own drafts which were completed during the study of poetry examination texts.

Young writers must be encouraged to prize their own developing voices, but they must also learn how to effectively shape their words so that they can convey their intended meanings to audiences. Debra Myhill's research for the Qualifications and Curriculum Authority (QCA) on what young writers need to do in their narrative writing underlines the importance of a more explicit focus on the craft of writing (QCA, 1999). Closer consideration of the different drafting processes of published poets, together with their final published or performed poems, is an essential element of this focus. The move towards shared drafting within the Literacy Strategy and the Key Stage 3 Strategy, in which the relationship between reading and writing can be actively cemented, is an extremely positive step. However gaining access to the drafts of published writers is not always so easy. In Chapter 3 published poets Moniza Alvi, Jackie Kay, Debjani Chatterjee, Ian McMillan, Brian Moses, Paul Violi, Clive Wilmer and Cliff Yates discuss their drafting techniques and offer powerful insights into the development of specific poems. Advice is also given on accessing and working with other draft manuscripts, including 'Adlestrop' by Edward Thomas and the work of John Keats and Wilfred Owen.

W.H. Auden scorned the idea of publishing drafts. He disapproved of the publication of drafts of T.S. Eliot's *The Waste Land* on the grounds that there was 'not a line he left out which makes one wish he'd kept it ... this sort of thing encourages amateurs to think "Oh, look – I could have done as well"' (Newman, 1973: 292). In stating his case Auden seems to be missing the point: drafts let readers into the writing of a poem in ways which a final published piece never can. Through close reading of a draft they can unravel some of the mystique of how a poet works with language.

Information and communications technology in its many forms can be a very powerful tool in poetry teaching. Chapter 4 considers the different ways in which ICT can support the teaching of poetry writing. These include: drafting on screen; using e-mail and conferencing; using CD-ROM packages and other software; strategies for teaching the fast developing subgenre of text message poetry; accessing websites; using overhead transparencies (OHTs) as well as audio and video materials. Details of recommended classroom resources and websites are provided.

Bringing a poet into the classroom is the ultimate way of breathing life into the drafting process. If the visit is to be a success and to have a long-lasting impact on students' perceptions of poetry, then it must be carefully planned. Chapter 5 explores good practice for working with visiting professional writers to create a productive writing workshop environment in classes across the secondary age range. Contact details for those wishing to plan poetry visits in and out of the classroom are given. It also outlines how teachers can build on the workshop experience to develop the poetry curriculum further by referring to the development of a scheme of work on writing ghazal poetry.

Poetry is deemed by many teachers to be 'notoriously hard to assess' (Andrews, 1991: 75) but if teachers (who are not generally novelists or newspaper reporters) are able to mark responses written in prose, chosen from a range of genres such as letter, diary or narrative, then should they not be able to assess poems too? Chapter 6 investigates the reasons for perceived difficulties with poetry assessment whilst offering advice about practical approaches. If practitioners lack confidence in teaching the writing of poetry then it is inevitable that they will remain uncertain about assessment. Teachers' attitudes to assessing poetry and the assessment frameworks of both the National Curriculum for English and the UK public examinations system are considered, together with views about what constitutes progression in poetry writing. Chapter 6 draws on the critical perspectives of Carter, Benton, Driver and D'Arcy and alternative models for the assessment of writing. It argues for regular poetry assessment in the hope that such an outcome might remove the mystery surrounding the genre and establish it on an equal footing with prose text types.

Chapter 7 provides a context for the poetry classroom of the twenty-first century by looking back over the last 40 years. In the 1960s a number of the poets, teachers and educationists were gaining recognition for their work which would help to shape the kind of poetry teaching familiar in UK classrooms today. Their influence can be seen both on practical approaches to poetry teaching and on the place of the genre within the English curriculum. This chapter concentrates primarily on these key figures and movements who have contributed to debates about the teaching of writing poetry. However it also acknowledges the inevitable and fertile links between writing, reading, performing and listening to poetry – links which are strongly reinforced throughout this text.

I hope that teachers will find *Drafting and Assessing Poetry* a thought-provoking and practical book which will inspire them to light the fuse of poetry in their own classrooms.

Sue Dymoke
April 2002

1

The Place of Poetry within the National Curriculum Orders for English

In the advent of the National Curriculum poetry was in an uncertain position, heralded by some teachers and critics as central to the English curriculum and treated with suspicion by others whose own educational experiences of poetry had not made them favourably disposed towards the genre. The National Curriculum was first introduced into England and Wales in 1990 and revised over the next decade. This chapter explores the place of poetry (especially writing poetry) within this overarching framework and the subsequently developed National Literacy Strategy.

The Cox report

The Cox report's proposals for a new assessment driven curriculum in English and Welsh schools with five attainment targets for: Speaking and Listening; Reading; Writing; Spelling; Handwriting and Presentation underpinned the development of the National Curriculum for English. This report attempted to impose a linear model of development on the subject of English. According to the proposals, students would move through four Key Stages during their compulsory 5–16 education and 10 assessment levels.

The report contained a number of references to poetry. Cox acknowledged that one of an English teacher's greatest joys could be to foster a love of literature in one's students. There was also a recognition of the need for constant nurturing of a young child's 'instinctive pleasure in rhythm, pattern and rhyme' if this was to be developed into an appreciation of the 'richness of poetry' (DES, 1989: 7.1). Cox recommended the crucial link between language and literature should be consolidated by activities such as writing in different poetic forms.

Wade and Sidaway perceived a 'crisis of confidence' (Wade and Sidaway, 1990: 75) about poetry in the curriculum at this time. However they remained optimistic that the proposals of the Cox committee would 'foreground poetry' (Wade and Sidaway, 1990: 83). In their investigation into the attitudes of middle school students to poetry, and a subsequent comparison with teachers' views, they established that 'a chasm' existed between interested and receptive students and teachers who 'revealed concern for poetry allied to lack of confidence' (ibid.). They identified a need for further work on curriculum guidelines and examples of good practice.

The National Curriculum

The practical implementation of the National Curriculum Orders (1990) found favour with many English teachers. The main reason for this was the way it built on heavily supported models of English teaching which were learner centred and based on personal growth (including those models which had been discussed at the 1966 Dartmouth conference and are described in Chapter 7) together with a focus on cultural analysis and the study and recognition of a literary heritage (Protherough and King, 1995). The Orders adopted the five attainment targets and Key Stage structure suggested by Cox. The attainment targets were supported by Programmes of Study (PoS) which indicated both 'general' and 'detailed' provision required for compliance with the Orders. The PoS included very specific references to listening to, performing, reading and writing poetry.

For example for Writing at Key Stage 2 (pupils aged 7–11):

Pupils should:
   … have opportunities to create, polish and produce individually or together, by hand or on a word processor, extended written texts, appropriately laid out and illustrated, *e.g. class newspapers, anthologies of stories or poems, guidebooks etc.* (DES, 1990: 37)

For Writing at Key Stage 3 (pupils aged 11–14):

Pupils should have opportunities to:
   … build on their experience of reading and hearing a wide range of poetry, and write both individually and in groups, using poetic features such as rhythm, rhyme and alliteration in verse forms such as jingles, ballads, haiku etc;
   … organise and express their meaning appropriately for different specified audiences, *e.g. their peers, their teacher, known adults … a road safety officer, a novelist or a poet.* (ibid.: 39)

And for Writing at Key Stage 4 (pupils aged 14–16)

Pupils should have opportunities to:

... select verse forms appropriate for their own choice of subject matter and purposes through experience of a wider range of poetry. (Ibid.: 41)

It is interesting to compare these references to providing opportunities for writing poetry with later revisions of National Curriculum. Subsequent documents offer less detail on this aspect and non statutory illustrative examples are pared down. It not until the emergence of the National Literacy Strategy in 1998 that this level of detail (couched in much more prescriptive language) returns.

Discussions about pedagogy

The period surrounding the development and inception of the National Curriculum was a fertile time for discussion about the nature of English and many aspects of pedagogy including those directly pertaining to poetry teaching. One focus was on the purpose and nature of literature teaching (particularly on ways of responding to poetry). Marsh (1988) was concerned about the current state of literature teaching. He portrayed teachers as being faced with a muddle of analytical, humanist, aesthetic, cultural and purely practical purposes when teaching literature. He considered that the system of practical criticism used in examinations led to a focus on passing judgements on or extracting meanings from poetry. In adopting this inappropriate approach, the experience of immersion in reading the texts was bypassed (Marsh, 1988). Michael Benton had also long been concerned about the ways in which literature, and particularly poetry, was taught in schools: 'far too often we imply that poems are riddles with single solutions which we, the teachers, happen to know rather than objects crafted in a medium of riddling wordplay, yielding a range of meanings' (Benton and Fox, 1985: 19).

The notion of poetry as a puzzle is, sadly in my experience, a common perception among students (and their teachers) who engage in a hunt for the missing clue which will help them solve the poem. Too often the students believe that the teacher is keeping the clue from them which causes discussion about poetry to turn into a closed guessing game when it should be a shared exploration of the words on the page.

For Benton, literature teaching needed to be grounded in a coherent methodology centred on the reader and the notion of a plurality of meanings. He was hopeful that the development of a methodology based on reading and response rather than 'conventional narrowly conceived ideas of comprehension and criticism [was beginning to] give poetry back to its readers' (Benton, 1990: 31). He urged this process to continue, citing as good practice examples of a student's annotations from a 'mental walk' around a poem (Benton, 1990: 32).

The metaphor of a journey of meaning making was a central focus in *Developing Response to Poetry* (Dias and Hayhoe, 1988) which explored the potential use of reader response theories, including those of Riffaterre, Iser and Rosenblatt (1978), to inform classroom practice. Rosenblatt argued that the same text could be read both efferently and aesthetically. With efferent reading, a summary of text would suffice whereas with aesthetic reading the text itself was of central importance. In her view a paraphrase of a poem did not equate to reading the original. 'Accepting an account of someone else's reading or experience of a poem is analgous to seeking nourishment through having someone else eat your dinner for you and recite the menu' (Rosenblatt, 1978: 86). She considered that readers, respecting the limitations set by verbal clues within a text, drew on their own resources to fill in the gaps and thus 'realise[d] the blueprint provided by the text'. In her view, the key role of poetry, or any other literary text, was to serve as 'a stimulus to the creativity of the reader' (Rosenblatt, 1978: 88). Rosenblatt's work in particular was considered to have implications for the teaching of poetry in schools which 'unwittingly demand that pupils adopt an efferent stance' (Dias and Hayhoe, 1988: 22). The writers also suggested that if students were continually taken on 'packaged tours' of poems, conducted by their teachers (masters of texts who will enlighten them en route) then they were 'unlikely to learn to travel on their own' (ibid.: 7) or to make sense of a poem for themselves. Such imagery marked a move away from the focus of the reading as the poem/product and towards an investigation of the processes involved in reading/making meaning. Michael Benton described this shift as being 'not the discovering of meaning (like some sort of archaeological dig) but the creation of it.' (Benton, 1995: 334).

Dias and Hayhoe wrote with an urgency about the need to 'present a coherent basis for response-centred teaching' (Dias and Hayhoe, 1988: 7). The impact of critical theory on poetry teaching was, for them and their four contributors, the main cause of the unpopularity of poetry in the classroom. Their analysis of new criticism, structuralism and post-structuralism concluded that the role of the teacher had not been sufficiently addressed by these movements. While some knowledge of theories might have been helpful, these needed to be adapted 'pragmatically in the constantly slippery context of the classroom' (Hirst in Dias and Hayhoe, 1988: 115). In the reading of any poem and the development of one's attitudes to poetry a person's 'reading history' (Dias and Hayhoe, 1988: 35) should be considered to play a vital part.

Michael Benton's endorsement of this developing 'response centred methodology' (Benton et al., 1988: 202) and observations from Marsh (1988) on the importance of understanding a writer's craft were included in Cox (DES, 1989). It is interesting to note that by 1995 Benton was becoming more sceptical about the ill-defined nature of reading and response which he saw as often leading to very open ended tasks in the classroom (Benton, 1995).

Revisions: 1993

The Conservative government also had concerns about Literature. Their proposed revisions to the Orders in 1993 were 'grounded in quite a different philosophy' from that of Cox (Protherough and King, 1995: 1). Driven by a desire to define 'basic skills' (DfE, 1993: 71) and to reassert the place of what the government perceived as the English 'literary heritage', the proposals recommended the insertion of lists of 'suitable' poetry and fiction which, it claimed, would give students access to the 'richness of great literature' (DfE 1993: 72–3). The lists caused controversy even among 17 of those writers who appeared on them (Harrison, 1994a). A reading anthology of poems and extracts of 'high quality' texts for use in standard tests at Key Stage 3 was introduced and greeted with 'despondency' (Berliner, 1992: 4) by secondary English teachers. For Frater, writing from the standpoint of a retired member of Her Majesty's Inspectorate (HMI), the anthology was: 'part of the price which pupils and schools must pay for an unedifying concoction of blind dogma and contingent, quick-fit decision making' (Frater, 1993: 51).

During the establishment of a National Curriculum in 1990 many English teachers became politicised and saw 'the control of the subject was at stake' (Ball, Kenny and Gardiner, 1990: 83). This power struggle was taken one stage further with the dispute over the Statutory Assessment Tests (SATs) which pupils were to sit at the end of Key Stages 1–3. The 1993 Key Stage 3 English SATs were boycotted by the majority of state secondary schools and the proposed use of an anthology at Key Stage 3 was eventually abandoned.

Revisions: 1995

Following the intervention of the Dearing committee in 1993–94, the number of attainment targets was slimmed down from five to three: Speaking and Listening, Reading and Writing. Assessment levels were reduced to eight (plus exceptional performance). The Key Stage 3 tests (taken by pupils aged 14) were modified to include teacher assessments and opportunities for students with special educational needs to complete alternative classroom tasks. However other changes, namely the reduction of coursework limits at GCSE and A-level and the inclusion of pre-twentieth-century and twentieth-century reading lists, were to have a real impact on poetry teaching.

Positive reactions to the 1995 Orders were limited. Protherough and King considered the new Orders approached the flexibility teachers desired in that they 'abandoned any pretence of being a syllabus and simply offers a basis or broad checklist for departments' own schemes of work' (Protherough and King, 1995: 14). Within the attainment target for Writing, use of poetic models was still recommended in the revised curriculum (together with writing of poetry based on the student's own experience) although the written outcomes were to be in each student's 'own distinctive style' (DfE, 1995: 23). This phrase was, at the very least, an ambiguous one as a 'distinctive style' was more unlikely to be found in imitation than in any other kind of writing (Knight, 1995). The phrasing used here did however appear to echo an earlier DES document which encouraged teachers to distinguish between students' individual voices and those which had been 'rented for the occasion' (DES 1987: 29). Many of the detailed references to forms (such as haiku and sonnet) and specific literary techniques found in the 1990 Orders were replaced by a broader instruction to give students opportunities to write in 'a range of forms'. While arguably this might have made the curriculum more flexible for teachers, one could, *pace* Andrews (1991), question whether the vagueness of this instruction lessened the guarantee that poetry would be taught in depth and by all teachers.

The impact of the 1995 Orders on poetry teaching was most keenly felt in the Reading attainment target (En2). Here poetry was written about in terms of 'quality' (DfE, 1995: 19). Poets were selected in the light of their 'established critical reputations' and teachers were forcefully told that their students' reading 'should include' writers from specific lists (ibid.). Texts from other cultures and traditions formed a major element of the reading programmes of study. Teachers, who had previously chosen to use pre-twentieth century poetry where they considered it appropriate, were now obliged to include it at Key Stage 3 and Key Stage 4 (Atkinson, 1995). The National Curriculum Programmes of Study stressed that, in engaging with these listed works, teachers need to use activities which emphasised the pleasure and interest of the texts for their students 'rather than necessitating a detailed line by line study' (DfE, 1995: 20). As these texts were shortly to feature in revised GCSE terminal examination papers, this recommendation would present teachers with a real challenge.

The Department for Education (DfE) position was not universally accepted in the profession. Knight, for example, argued it would be impossible to appreciate the likes of Donne and Pope 'without close study' (Knight, 1996: 124). He scorned the plethora of materials (such as those by Bleiman, 1995) which were being published at this time. Many of these included DARTs (Directed Activities Related to Texts, *pace* Lunzer and Gardner, 1984) to encourage readers to participate in their own meaning making. For Knight such activities had more of a place in a laboratory than a literature classroom in that they took students away from the author. Conversely others commended the worth of such innovative approaches because they enabled students to recognise the structures within the formal patterns of poetry (Stibbs, 1995). There was a publishing boom in resources based on the DfE's pleasure principle and designed to support teachers in their new obligations to teach texts for written examinations at GCSE.

Along with the increased focus on written examinations, coursework was deigned not to be 'sufficiently rigorous' (Poulson, 1998: 126). In spite of a vigorous and widespread 'save hundred percent coursework campaign' initiated by English teacher, Mike Lloyd, GCSE coursework was reduced from 100 to 40 per cent for English and 30 per cent for Literature. At A-level, coursework was reduced to 20 per cent maximum by the Schools Curriculum and Assessment Authority (SCAA). A-level syllabuses were 'forced to return to the old "stand and deliver" modes of examining' (Harrison, 1994a: 104). Students were no longer able to submit their original writing assignments unless these were accompanied by commentaries linking them to approved texts. A restriction on the choices of published texts from specific periods and on coursework approaches led to a move away from using poetry texts and students' own poetry writing for coursework. During this period I was an A-level Literature coursework moderator. It was very clear to me, and to other colleagues, that the study of the novel began to dominate and the number of traditional essay assignments about prose texts submitted by students dramatically increased.

Since the revised National Curriculum Orders of 1995, poetry teaching in secondary schools has increasingly focused on the reading of poetry and the writing about that reading. In 1997 a poem, *In Memory of My Grandfather* by Edward Storey, was included for the first time in the Key Stage 3 SATs Paper 1. Students were asked to consider: 'How does the poem suggest the grandfather changed the boy's life at home when he visited?' (SCAA, 1997: 7). They were given bullet points of issues to comment on in their answers. The inclusion of a poem in this examination provoked much informal discussion among English teachers, some of whom felt their students had not been prepared to respond to poetry in this way. The report on the 1997 National Curriculum assessments commented on the slight drop in performance at level 4 compared with the 1996 results for this question, which were written in response to a media text. A tendency to copy out lines from the poem, without providing a linking comment, was also observed. Even successful candidates found this question the most challenging on the paper, although results at level 7 were more consistent with those of previous years (QCA, 1998). Poulson argued that even prior to this date 'Teachers were beginning to teach to the test in order to maximize pupils' chances of getting higher grades' (Poulson, 1998: 128).

At GCSE level, syllabuses continued to include a large poetry content in the form of anthologies for study. The most popular of these was the NEAB Anthology (NEAB, 1996). The material in the anthologies was informed by a prescribed list of pre-twentieth century poets in the National Curriculum Orders and the requirement for reading of poems from other cultures and traditions. Opponents of the introduction of the examination board anthologies argued that they restricted teachers' opportunities to make connections between texts and contexts, and distanced students from cultural experiences by emphasising 'difference' (Rose and Scafe, 1997: 129). The selection limited personal engagement, demanding that students 'translate and respond to it as if they were responding to a comprehension exercise' (ibid.).

Poems in the anthologies could lend themselves to a range of assessed activities. However, the writing of poetry still struggled to find its place in the official curriculum. This was exemplified by a GCSE Chief Examiner's report which expressed surprise at some students' decision to write poetry in response to a question that asked them to describe a given place 'in such a way that it can be easily imagined by your reader' (NEAB, 1998b: 4). Although the candidates were not penalised for writing poems the report noted: 'by adopting a form generally not suited to an examination of this kind, some candidates clearly limited their own personal achievement' (NEAB, 1998a: 25). In this case poetry was considered inappropriate as a form of writing under examination conditions. This consideration highlighted a specific view of the place of poetry within the curriculum and also raised issues about its assessment which will be returned to in Chapter 6.

Individual practitioners

Carter claimed that poetry was 'not in the minds of those who composed' the revised orders (Carter, 1998: 1). The emphasis was firmly with transactional writing and poetry was perceived as 'a kind of fair-weather visitor' (Carter, 1998: 2) to the curriculum. His impassioned plea for the sustained place of poetry in developing literacy skills in the primary classroom and the power of dreaming in poetry writing has many resonances for secondary English teaching. Carter's framework of 'eight modes of encounter between children and poetry' (ibid.: 5), which formed the basis of the Clwyd Poetry Project, provided structured routes into poetry teaching and the issue of progression in poetry, for those teachers lacking in confidence. His ideas about assessing poetry are explored in Chapter 6.

From the mid-1990s individual practitioners, such as Dennis Carter and Cliff Yates began to have an impact on classroom practice. Cliff Yates, a deputy head at Maharishi School in Skelmersdale, was the Poetry Society's Poet in residence for Secondary Education in the UK. Like Jill Pirrie (whose work is described in Chapter 7), many of his students have had considerable successes in poetry competitions over a number of years. Examples of their work frequently appear in the *Times Educational Supplement* (*TES*) Young Poet column. During Yates's residency The Poetry Society asked him to share his poetry teaching methods with others. In *Jumpstart* he provides an anecdotal and entertaining insight into his classroom – a place where reading and writing are 'related activities' (Yates, 1999: xii) and teachers as well as pupils are always required to have a notebook at hand to record their experiences. (His workshop methods are analysed more fully in Chapter 2.) Yates does not link his activities with the National Curriculum or mention GCSE (although he considers some of his more demanding activities suitable for Year 10). Unlike Brownjohn (1980), to whom Yates acknowledged his indebtedness, *Jumpstart* is not a manual or a recipe book but a portrait of a working teacher/poet. Many of the activities included can be found in one form or another elsewhere (such as in Brownjohn [1980] and Koch [1970]). Despite the publisher's declared intention to show that 'poetry is teachable and everyone can get better at it' the book tends to underline that successful poetry teachers like Yates are a breed apart. The writer is clearly at ease with poetry. He draws on a personal store of poetry reading and writing routines and experiences which he can share with his students when stimulating new ideas or supporting their drafting processes.

Surveying poetry teaching

Poetry writing at Key Stage 4 was found to be in marked decline by the Poetry Research Project (Benton, 1999; 2000). The findings of the survey of poetry teaching in the secondary school reported on the responses of 100 teachers from one local education authority (LEA) and drew comparisons with Peter Benton's 1984 survey. They were published in *Oxford Review of Education* during the period I was completing research into the poetry teaching of six secondary school English teachers. Although there are obvious differences in the sample size and scale of the two research projects, it is productive in this context to compare briefly some of the key findings on: the place of enjoyment in the poetry classroom; writing poetry; the effects of the National Curriculum; the impact of GCSE anthologies on practice; professional development in poetry teaching and teachers' views of poetry.

Benton reviewed the changes perceived to have occurred since the implementation of the National Curriculum. He documented an increased emphasis on the use of poetry for the development of language and discussion skills. In contrast, enjoyment was considered less of a reason for discussing poetry than it once was. The language of poetry, including its brevity and compactness, was viewed by five of my sample as being a key reason for studying poetry. Anna liked the way poems could achieve 'extraordinary things in a very small space' while for Bruce poems could address 'all the qualities of language that we want to address in English but in a small package' (Dymoke, 2000a: 226). Among these teachers, enjoyment was frequently thought to be an achievement of a poetry lesson sequence and might exhibit itself in a number of different ways. All six shared a commitment to a 'response centred methodology' (Benton et al., 1988: 202) but considered that this was being severely tested by the plethora of poems that they were expected to teach to their GCSE pupils.

Benton argued that teachers had greater confidence about the place of poetry in the curriculum than previously and they were more likely to intervene in the writing process, even if, in reality, poetry was an infrequent activity. There was a belief among the teachers questioned that poetry was an aspect of English in which all students could make achievements. This belief, echoed by all the teachers in my own sample, has a significant bearing on the place of pupils' own poetry within the assessment framework and will be addressed in Chapter 6. As far as intervention was concerned, there was a marked gender divide among my own sample about the appropriate approaches to use. Male teachers felt more able to help young writers polish their drafts while female teachers' approaches were tempered with concerns about pupils' ownership of their drafts. The drafting of poetry was largely restricted to Year 7 classes although it did continue less frequently in Years 8–12. With all six teachers, writing poetry almost always occurred in response to reading and discussion of a poetic model. There was little evidence of teachers modelling the drafting process themselves. The volume of poetry reading to be covered at GCSE was seen to be squeezing out opportunities for poetry writing at this level, even though the teachers appeared to recognise its value and were anxious to reclaim this activity with future groups (Dymoke, 2000a).

In Benton's 1984 survey (explored in Chapter 7) he noted the limited amount of in-service training (INSET) time devoted to poetry teaching. Although he does not comment directly on this with his second cohort, one could argue that the situation has not significantly changed. In interviewing my own sample it was clear that their professional development in poetry teaching had occurred in a haphazard way. None had experienced any systematic poetry training which could have focused in on gaps in subject knowledge or enabled them to reinforce/refine their skills. During a period of rapid change in English teaching, which included new methods of examining poetry at GCSE, they were reliant on chance, self-orchestrated encounters with new poems or poetry publications or teaching colleagues who happened to have an interest in poetry. Even with the advent of the National Literacy Strategy, it was evident that this pattern of omission was set to continue.

Benton noted that poetry teachers were more concerned about the genre itself and the constraints they were under to deliver poetry in an over-loaded curriculum than how they should teach it. Forty-nine per cent of the teachers he surveyed disagreed with the prescriptive lists of pre-twentieth century writers in the National Curriculum while 40 per cent considered that the National Curriculum had had no impact on their poetry teaching. Although poetry remained at the centre of the curriculum with its 'overwhelming list of canonical writers' (Benton, 2000: 87) this was now less of a spiritual position and more of a 'geographical location' (ibid.).

For teachers in my sample, the 'hard slog' to deliver the content-heavy Key Stage 4 curriculum dominated. They did welcome the fact that poetry at GCSE was no longer a 'blind spot' which could be avoided by those teachers who were uncomfortable with poetry. However they were concerned about restrictions on their personal choices of poems – and, in several cases, their deliberately limited selections of 'major poets' from the National Curriculum lists endorsed the desire for more choice. All six teachers were concerned that teaching poetry should not become a reductive process, solely geared towards preparing examination responses. During the course of the research, I sensed that they were constantly working to overcome the impositions of the poetry element of the GCSE specifications and to consider its impact on their own pedagogy. They remained determined to generate regular sustained excitement about the genre among their students rather than take them on occasional field trips to its shrine.

The National Literacy Strategy (Key Stages 1 and 2)

At the same time as secondary English teachers were coming to terms with the demands of the first examinations for the new GCSE specifications, the National Literacy Strategy (NLS) was being introduced into primary schools in England. Established by the new Labour government in 1998, its stated purpose is to provide a framework for teaching literacy in primary schools (at Key Stages 1 and 2) in order to push up literacy standards and to enable more children to leave school 'equipped to enter a fulfilling adult life' (DfEE, 1998: 1). The teaching usually takes place in a structured daily 'literacy hour' which usually follows a four-part structure. This includes opportunities for whole-class work (focusing on shared reading and writing of texts), guided and independent work at word, sentence and text level, and culminates in whole-class plenary session. The theoretical underpinning of the NLS is not made explicit in the documentation provided for schools. However teaching and learning are intended to move at a brisk pace. Teachers are encouraged to demonstrate both a confidence and ambition in their literacy instruction while using a wide range of teaching strategies including direction, demonstration, questioning, modelling, scaffolding and guiding explorations (DfEE, 1998: 8).

For Pirrie, Dennis Carter's work challenged teachers coping with the NLS to adopt a reflexive approach to their poetry teaching, to learn to be adaptable and to draw on their own resources in order to 'reclaim their autonomy' (Pirrie, 1999: 207). When the strategy was first introduced, primary teachers were divided in their view of its usefulness. During its introductory year, I was working as a Head of English in a large comprehensive school in Nottingham. The English department had close links with the feeder schools in the 'family'. Regular meetings were held with primary language co-ordinators (who were shortly to be transformed into literacy co-ordinators) to share planning strategies and practice, and to begin to make sense of the framework together. It was clear that many primary colleagues felt overwhelmed by the content of the NLS and uncertain about its impact on the primary curriculum as a whole. There was an evident tension between the desire to retain their established units of work and the need to redevelop the language curriculum in a more rigid format which would ensure compliance by all staff.

Although the strategy is not a compulsory curriculum requirement, it has gradually been adopted by the majority of primary schools. It is widely credited with having raised literacy standards in reading particularly (Furlong, Venkatakrishnan and Brown, 2001). However, the structure has clearly been unsuited to developing extended writing skills and concerns about standards in writing remain.

The Literacy Strategy is closely allied to the National Curriculum statutory requirements for English. However, it is considerably more detailed and, many would argue, more prescriptive in its outline of both the learning objectives and curriculum content to be 'delivered' by the teacher. Some primary advisers and teacher educators perceive that the NLS has provided the many primary teachers who are not English specialists with a structure which enables them to teach previously acknowledged difficult curriculum areas like poetry with greater confidence, particularly if they are provided with very detailed plans, resources and support from language specialists in their team. Although teachers may now be more aware of certain elements of the 'poetry curriculum', it does not necessarily follow that they will be more confident about teaching poetry. The thorny issue of subject knowledge will remain unless teachers are encouraged to develop their expertise in this area by reading and writing poetry for themselves.

Year 1:	Rhymes used as models
	Substitution or elaboration of own words/phrases in existing poems
Year 2:	Use of simple poetry structures
	Writing own poems from initial jottings
	Class anthologies
	Use of humorous verse
	Riddles
	Tongue twisters
	Alliterative sentences
	Collecting words for use in poems
	Word patterns
Year 3:	Calligrams
	Shape poems
	Performance poetry
	Rhythm
	Repetition
	Onomatopoeia
Year 4:	Poems based on personal/imagined experience
	List poems
	Experimenting with use of powerful and expressive verbs in poetry
	Use of choruses
	Rhyme patterns
	Similes
	Experimenting with different styles and structures
	Use of figurative language
	Producing polished poetry
Year 5:	Conveying feelings and moods
	Use of metaphor
	Additional verses
Year 6:	Personification
	Active verbs in poetry
	Using different genres as models
	Writing a sequence of poems (e.g. Haiku calendar)

Figure 1.1   *Specific references to poetry writing in the National Literacy Strategy (Key Stages 1 and 2)*

The specific requirements for poetry taught in the NLS are extensive. They present increasing demands both on class time and teacher expertise in the latter stages of Key Stage 2 especially. Activities centred on the reading and writing of poetry are outlined termly in word, sentence and text level headings in each school year of the strategy ranging from the Reception Year (ages 4–5) in which pupils should 'experience a variety of traditional, nursery and modern rhymes, chants, action verses, poetry ... with pre-dictable structures and patterned language ... [and use this experience] as a basis for independent writing e.g. re-telling, substitution, extension, and through shared composition with adults' (DfEE, 1998: 19), 'to the final term in Year 6 (ages 10–11) in which pupils should be taught 'comparison of work by significant children's author(s) and poets … to describe and evaluate the style of an individual poet … to write a sequence of poems linked by theme or form' (DfEE, 1998: 55).

Approximately 35 different poetic forms are referred to in the strategy (for specific references to writing refer to Figure 1.1). The document also contains broader references to poems linked by setting or theme and groups of poems by 'significant children's writers' and 'longer classic poetry' (DfEE, 1998: 68). It is extremely doubtful that even the most conscientious primary teacher would be able to cover all of these forms without devoting every literacy hour to poetry. This total represents a real pressure to race through a number of forms. There is a definite need for teachers to be selective in their approach and to take time to explore the forms they choose. A teacher quoted in Robert Hull's article 'What hope for children's poetry?' (Hull, 2001: 13) envisages a situation where 'Children will know 1001 forms and yet never know a poem'. Teacher Vivienne Smith guards against such an eventuality. In her inspiring account of creating a sense of community through rhyme with a Reception/Year 1 class, she emphasises that teachers need to involve pupils in the making of meaning rather than approaching poems in a fragmented way. For her it is essential to 'allow the poem to speak … to work with poems rather than against them' (Smith, 2000: 27), in order to retain the magic of poetry.

Clearly if all primary teachers are to support pupils so effectively in their learning about poetry, they need support themselves. Riley and Reedy argue that the implications for in-service training in this curriculum aspect have been underestimated. They point to the limited amount of supporting material on poetry teaching in the INSET packs used to develop teachers' understanding and skills in teaching literacy (Riley and Reedy, 2000: 95). Their conclusions closely mirrored my own findings (Dymoke, 2001) about the *Grammar for Writing* materials produced by the DfEE to 'improve writing' (DfEE, 2000: 9). The supporting training video, intended for Key Stage 2 teachers, begins promisingly with a young girl reading from her poem, which describes weather using the imagery of a game. However, it is soon apparent that this is a concession to poetry writing: all the teacher demonstrations which follow concentrate on writing different prose forms. The heavy emphasis on prose in assessment of writing is an issue which is returned to in Chapter 6.

National Curriculum 2000

The most significant changes in the revised National Curriculum Orders for English (introduced into schools in England and Wales in September 2000) focused on Drama teaching and language study. For the first time Drama has been given a discrete strand within the Speaking and Listening attainment target (En1). One outcome has been an increased focus in publications on the use of drama techniques to explore poetry texts; for example, *Cracking Drama 5–16* (NATE Drama Committee, 2001) suggests drama strategies to explore nursery rhymes and pre-twentieth century narrative poetry. The emphasis on language study has been heightened in the revised curriculum. It includes explicit requirements for the teaching of sentence grammar and whole-text cohesion which are further detailed in the learning objectives for the National Literacy Strategy and the Key Stage 3 National Strategy Framework for teaching English: Years 7, 8 and 9. The core lists of major writers and poets remain the same in this revision although they are now labelled as 'published before 1914' (DfEE and QCA, 1999: 36). The number of examples of post 1914 and contemporary writers was expanded. Following the trend begun in the 1995 revisions, direct references to reading and writing poetry (including the use of particular poetic forms and devices) have again been lessened in favour of broader headings focusing on Understanding Texts (encompassing reading for meaning and understanding the author's craft), Composition (including writing to imagine, explore, entertain) and Planning and Drafting.

The Key Stage 3 National Strategy – Framework for teaching English: Years 7, 8 and 9

In September 2000 the National Strategy was extended into Key Stage 3. Its arrival coincided with the introduction of National Curriculum 2000. First implemented in a draft form as a two year pilot in 17 LEAs across England, the Framework was subsequently 'recommended' (DfEE, 2001a) to all secondary schools in England halfway through the pilot before any wide-scale evaluation had been completed. Ironically, it was only with the arrival of the strategy in Key Stage 3 that there was official endorsement of 'flexible' interpretations of the strategy. Sue Hackman, then Director of the National Literacy Strategy, speaking at 'Creativity under Threat?' – a conference for Heads of English at the University of Nottingham in spring 2001 – was at pains to reassure teachers they would be able to adapt the Framework and to use creative and flexible approaches in their classrooms. However, this view was in contrast to that expressed by some LEAs which appear to expect a more faithful interpretation of the framework in their schools (Furlong, Venkatakrishnan and Brown, 2001). The survey of 30 pilot schools carried out by the three researchers at King's College highlights the dilemma of English teachers who have found themselves faced with a framework. Although they recognised the ways in which the structure had helped to clarify aspects of the revised National Curriculum Orders, a number of teachers surveyed commented on the speed with which the Framework had been introduced and the increased planning burden it brought with it. Furlong et al. comment on the change of emphasis in the English curriculum observed by many teachers they surveyed. Their respondents were divided between those who simply noted the change of focus and those who expressed concerns 'that Literacy was not the whole of English' (Furlong, Venkatakrishnan and Brown, 2001: 10). The latter felt that the technical aspects of the writing process now appeared more important than the development of sustained creative, personal responses.

Late in the summer term 2001, secondary teachers in England (both of English and all other subjects) participated in training to prepare them for the arrival of the Framework in Key Stage 3. The training materials, intended for secondary English departments, like those for primary teachers, made scant reference to poetry teaching. The main thrust of these materials would appear to be on teaching different types of narrative and non-fiction forms and understanding grammatical terms. Within a large ring-binder manual (and additional handouts) four poetry units were briefly summarised in a section containing exemplars of long-term planning (DfEE, 2001b: 19–20 and handouts 3.1 and 3.2). These units were not commented on specifically. Teachers were also asked to consider effective ways to deploy a teaching assistant in the teaching of 'hard poems' (DfEE, 2001b: 98–9). Finally, a quotation from the poet Ted Hughes concerning the writer's conscious manipulation of syntax was used to endorse the value of understanding grammar within the creative process (DfEE, 2001b: 133). An 'additional comment upon creativity' (DfEE, 2001b: 131) included in the section on teaching grammar indicates an awareness of criticisms previously levelled at NLS: there is an anxiety that the English curriculum should not appear to have been placed in a straitjacket.

When compared with the detailed list of poetry writing references in the strategy document for Key Stages 1 and 2, the references to writing in the Framework seem rather thin (see Figure 1.2).

It is essential that teachers are supported and given the confidence to use the medium of poetry when they are focusing on non-text specific objectives and/or those which refer to teaching writing processes. None of the 'key objectives' in the framework (DfEE, 2001a: 12), identified in bold type and deemed to provide critical indicators of progress, refer directly to poetry. These objectives have been selected 'as a focus for assessment' (ibid.) and illustrate how poetry is being marginalised from the formal assessment processes – an argument which will be returned to in Chapter 6. However, if pupils are to continue making progress with their work on poetry and (one would hope) developing an interest in writing and reading poetry which will be sustained in adult life, there is a need for teachers to build on what has been achieved by their pupils at primary school. This development will include: taking opportunities to revisit poems and forms

---

Year 7: Text level – Writing
Pupils should be taught to:
8. experiment with visual and sound effects of language, including the use of imagery, alliteration, rhythm and rhyme;
9. make links between their reading of fiction, plays and poetry and the choices they make as writers;   (DfEE, 2001a: 24)

Year 8: Text level – Writing
Pupils should be taught to:
9. experiment with presenting similar material in different forms and styles of poetry;   (ibid.: 28)

Year 9: Text level – Writing
Pupils should be taught to:
8. write within the discipline of different poetic forms, exploring how form contributes to meaning, e.g. *different types of sonnet.*   (ibid.: 32)

Figure 1.2   *Key Stage 3 National Strategy Framework for teaching English: Years 7, 8 and 9 – specific references to poetry writing*

they have previously encountered; experimenting with their own forms, styles and choices of subjects for poetry; developing an understanding of the ways in which poets work in order to inform their own writing.

GCSE specifications for 2004

With the introduction of new GCSE English and English Literature specifications in England and Wales, for first examination in 2004, poetry seems to be increasingly pigeon-holed as a genre for efferent reading. The study of poetry, using anthologies provided by the examination boards, remains the order of the day. The popular NEAB anthology, described earlier in this chapter, has been replaced by the AQA A anthology (which continues to be the market leader). This consists of two selections of poetry from different cultures and traditions (for GCSE English) together with pairs of poets (Carol Ann Duffy/Simon Armitage and Seamus Heaney/Gillian Clarke) whose work is to be compared with a group of pre-1914 male poets (for GCSE English Literature) in a series of highly structured examination questions. Other specifications seem to offer slightly more flexibility and choice in their poetry selections. For example, the Edexcel examination board has pre-1914 poetry as a coursework option within its Literature specification. This enables students and teachers to choose their own poems within thematic or stylistic groupings and could lead to imaginative writing tasks centred, for example, on the use of a particular form such as the sonnet.

Poetry as a means of stimulating original writing continues to be in decline at this level, in part because of seemingly prose-biased writing assessment criteria. This represents a missed opportunity. Writing poetry at GCSE level, whether as an initial way into exploring a poem or for final coursework, is still a viable option. It should be encouraged more widely so that students can engage with poetry in a personal way and gain a fuller appreciation of how the poets they are studying draft their work. Examples of GCSE poetry coursework are explored in Chapter 3 and further information on the assessment of students' poetry for GCSE coursework is provided in Chapter 6.

This chapter has demonstrated the mixed fortunes of poetry since the implementation of the National Curriculum. It has been shown that the increasing prominence of critical responses to poetry within the examinations system coupled with an assessment focus on students' prose writing have caused poetry writing to be perceived as a low priority for many secondary schools. Although the National Literacy Strategy at Key Stages 1 and 2 places considerable emphasis on poetic forms, there is a need to ensure greater flexibility in interpretation. Teachers (and pupils) should not be overwhelmed or daunted by poetry but able to share in its pleasures. There is also a need to cement a stronger link between primary and secondary practice if pupils are to make progress in their writing. Exploring ways in which teachers and pupils can work together to draw on their reading and to write poetry with cognisance of, but not confined by, curriculum frameworks is the key purpose of rest of this book.

2

Drafting poetry

Following Chapter 1's overview of poetry's place in the English curriculum, this chapter focuses on drafting poetry in the classroom. First, it takes a closer look at the terminology used in the National Curriculum to define elements of the writing process. In the light of the emphasis on thinking skills in the classroom (in the UK), it is important to recognise the contribution which drafting poetry can make to a child's cognitive development. Bereiter and Scardamalia's research on the psychology of the writing process, which is central to the discussion of drafting, is considered alongside teachers' reflections on their own drafting and practical suggestions to promote a thinking environment.

Pirrie, disappointed, notes that poetry in the National Curriculum serves 'little more than a cognitive purpose' (Pirrie, 1999: 204). She is right to serve a note of caution: the genre could be solely used with this aim if practitioners do not adopt more flexible interpretations. Although writing poetry can have a role in the development of cognitive skills (as is demonstrated in this chapter), pupils should also experience poetry for many other reasons, including: the insights it can provide on human experience; the sound of the words in one's head; and, most importantly, the sheer pleasure of playing with language in its most charged state, of lighting the 'fuse' of a poem, as Miroslav Holub (1987) describes it, and waiting to see what happens. This view of poetry has influenced the drafting strategies I have chosen to outline in this chapter.

The work of Donald Graves, Robert Hull and Pat D'Arcy, together with the workshop practices of Cliff Yates, have all been influential in developing pupils' and teachers' understanding of what constitutes drafting. The relevance of their work to the classroom context is explored here. Specific advice is offered on the use of drafting books and portfolios; diagramming and other planning strategies; modelling/the teacher as writer; interventions; drafting partners and other strategies for encouraging critical engagement with the process of writing poetry. Successful practice from the drafting classroom is outlined both by a newly qualified teacher's reflections on demonstration and examples of pupils' commentaries on their own drafts which were completed during the study of poetry examination texts.

Planning and drafting in the National Curriculum

A discrete section on Planning and Drafting is contained in the En3 Writing Programmes of Study across all four Key Stages within the National Curriculum document. The teacher's role in the drafting process at Key Stage 1 is directly referred to:

> working with the teacher and with others, in order to develop their writing, pupils should be taught to:
> a) write familiar words and attempt unfamiliar ones
> b) assemble and develop ideas on paper and on screen
> c) plan and review their writing, discussing the quality of what is written
> d) write extended texts, with support [for example, using the teacher as writer]. (DfEE and QCA, 1999: 20)

The teacher is seen as a guide, support and even a scribe at this stage in the development of drafting skills. As pupils become more independent writers (in Key Stage 2) references to the teacher are replaced with a series of baldly defined drafting stages which are intended to teach pupils to develop their writing. These encompass planning, drafting, revising, proofreading, presenting, discussing and evaluating their own and others' written work both on paper and on screen. Interestingly a reference to the term 'editing' is only made within the accompanying non-statutory guidance (DfEE, 1999: 28). The emphasis within the Planning and Drafting section at Key Stage 2 is on making changes and improvements which will result in a 'neat, correct and clear final copy' (DfEE, 1999: 28). This sterile conclusion seems to indicate that drafting is being perceived as a purely technical process which should lead to a satisfactory, unblemished output. The language of the programme of study gives no hint of the creativity involved in production. Furthermore, it addresses neither any notions of originality in the written piece nor the piece's impact on its eventual reader. Is it, one might ask, unrealistic to encourage Key Stage 2 writers to be original?

At Key Stages 3 and 4 the emphasis is on improving and sustaining writing, although the non-statutory guidance does acknowledge that at this point pupils will be developing distinctive styles. The drafting stages have been telescoped into one statement: 'plan, draft, redraft and proof read' and the focus shifts towards critical analysis of pupils' own and others' writing and making judgements about the necessity of using any of these processes. There appears is an in-built assumption here that pupils will no longer require such explicit teaching of the different drafting stages and greater concentration is placed on composing texts to suit different purposes.

At each Key Stage, alongside Planning and Drafting under the umbrella of 'Knowledge, Skills and Understanding', is a discrete section on Composition. This section focuses on young writers learning to make choices of form, structure, vocabulary and content to suit particular purposes and readers. It also encourages pupils both to make explicit links with reading and draw on models to inform their own written work. In the very way that it is structured, the Writing Programme of Study separates planning and drafting processes from composing. Such a separation is an extremely artificial one. It distances the intensive decision-making and selection processes from the physical act of drafting. If young writers are to appreciate an author's craft they need to learn that these occur simultaneously throughout the process. Whether typing a newsletter directly onto a screen or jotting down ideas in a notebook for the first lines of a poem, writing choices and decisions are being made as the draft is constructed, not on an entirely separate occasion. For Donald Graves, composing 'refers to everything a writer does from the time first words are put on paper until all the drafts are completed' (Graves, 1983: 223). Drafting is an integral element of composition and one without which composition cannot occur.

Composing and thinking

In their influential text *The Psychology of Written Composition*, Bereiter and Scardamalia (1987) offer two models of the composing process which are extremely helpful for teachers to consider. Both models perceive composition as a mental process which cannot be analysed solely through written outcomes.

With their 'Knowledge Telling' model, composition is a natural task which makes maximum use of existing cognitive structures and minimises the extent to which novel problems within the developing text have to be sorted out by the writer. Its distinct features are:

- a composing process which depends on evoked memories and emotions plus external assistance (in the form of some kind of stimulus) for its direction;
- a close correlation between a novice writer's knowledge telling processes and what appears on the page;
- progression from notes to completed text as a movement from one linear text to another. The transition primarily involves secretarial editing.

With their 'Knowledge Transforming' model, composition is a task which expands in complexity to match the expanding competence of the writer. This method is not restricted solely to those people who are highly talented writers, but to any writers who participate in an active reworking of their thoughts while they are writing. Its distinct features are:

- thoughts that come into existence through the composing process itself;
- transformation of the text often revealed in redrafting process;
- progression from notes to text often involves the writer in movement from a multi-level/non-linear structure towards the creation of a linear text. (adapted from Bereiter and Scardamalia, 1987)

Bereiter and Scardamalia do not perceive one model as being superior to the other, preferring instead to suggest they are 'discrete models of different design concepts' (ibid.: 29). However they do recognise differences between the text generation of children and that of expert writers. Children are perceived to:

- experience difficulties in discovering appropriate content for their texts;
- plan in a more limited and 'local' way which refers only to the immediate context;
- be able to carry out some revision processes but to lack an 'executive scheme for running the process as a whole' (ibid.: 48);
- be unable to adopt a reader's view in order to carry out effective evaluations of their own writing.

In contrast expert writers can be characterised by their considerable planning, both before and during writing. Much of their thinking aloud about a text will not be reflected in the actual written composition.

Bereiter and Scardamalia's work draws on analyses of narrative texts and graduate students' 'thinking aloud protocols' (ibid.: 18). However, their findings are pertinent to the discussion of drafting poetry. If pupils are to become confident and independent writers, able to draft poems on a range of subjects, in different forms and/or styles, then teachers need to consider what kind of thinking might take place at different drafting stages as well as to harness and develop what I shall call pupils' thinking while drafting skills. Researchers such as Bereiter and Scardamalia (1987), Smith (1982) and D'Arcy (1989) have all commented on the difficulty of accessing the thinking which takes place while writing. When leading poetry workshops and INSET events with secondary English teachers and primary language specialists, I have informally asked them to try to describe their thinking processes at the early stages of writing. In this way they can begin to explore what their pupils might experience in a similar situation. At the pre-writing stage (in this instance defined as the initial moments after a trigger word had been introduced and before a free writing activity begins) teachers identified that they were experiencing the following thoughts:

- mental blanks;
- feeling speedy or buzzy;
- making links with specific memories growing in their minds;
- exploring the impact of the trigger word on themselves;
- questioning – have I got anything to say?
- forming and/or repeating images;
- responding to sounds in their heads;
- being aware that they might be 'thinking outside the box';
- feeling liberated;
- wondering what they should write down;
- listing words or pictures;
- beginning to organise mental images;
- trying to make sense;
- waiting.

Once they put pen to paper and began free writing these thoughts changed to:

- questioning which words they should choose:
- feeling they had lost themselves in words;
- realising they were risking language;
- considering safe and non-safe areas to focus on;
- thinking about what might fit;
- being aware of influences and context in which they were writing;
- feeling wary.

As they pressed on with the draft some teachers said they were:

- experiencing a rush or feelings of energy;
- considering 'what's different?';
- beginning to think about combinations – 'that word and that word?'
- hearing sounds very strongly;
- questioning – does that work? does it matter?
- exploring context, narrative or events;
- being indulgent.

Inevitably their responses have been influenced by those of other participants and their own previous experiences. However, what is conveyed strongly, in this anecdotal evidence, is the marked contrast between descriptions of creative release, energy, making connections and risk-taking with language experienced by some teachers and those of uncertainty and anxiety experienced by others.

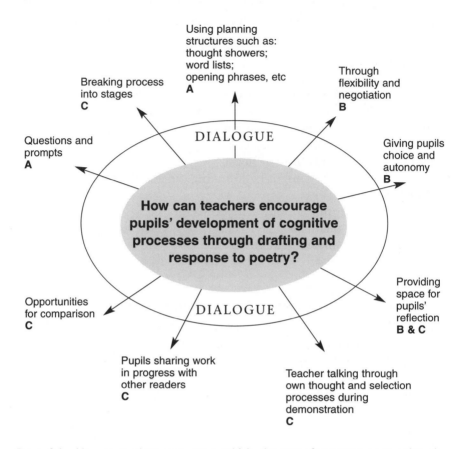

Figure 2.1 *How can teachers encourage pupils' development of cognitive processes through drafting and response to poetry?*

In Sheenagh Pugh's (1999) poem 'Tutorial' a tutor tells her students how 'words came flooding into your head and you just wrote them down'. The narrator confidently urges the writers to 'look again;/work out what you really wanted to say,/and how you failed to say it. Then you can'. In the remainder of the poem the speaker offers extensive advice about choice of words, viewpoints, structures and creating an element of surprise in writing in order that the students will outdo the tutor with their artistry. Not all English teachers are poets and not all teachers will be so confident that their students can make such swift progress with their drafts. If teachers want pupils to engage positively in their drafting, to develop their cognitive processes and drafting skills, how can they create an environment in the classrooms which enables them to do so? Figure 2.1 outlines a range of strategies which are loosely grouped into three types, namely those which are concerned with:

A) providing frameworks and structures for drafting which can gradually be removed;
B) providing an openness in the classroom which creates opportunities for independence and for choices to be made:
C) providing opportunities for young writers to take a reader's view.

Many of these strategies are demonstrated in analyses of work by Donald Graves, Robert Hull, Pat D'Arcy and Cliff Yates, and the descriptions of classroom practice which follow.

Donald Graves

Graves's investigation of young children's writing in New Hampshire, USA, had a great influence in the 1980s on the emergence of a process model of writing and informed the Writing Programmes of Study in the National Curriculum Orders for English. His book *Writing: Teachers and Children at Work* (Graves, 1983) remains an essential and energising text for all teachers who face the day-to-day reality of trying to teach writing. His work primarily concentrates on the writing of prose texts. However, his approaches are equally applicable to poetry and continue to influence writing practices in the early twenty-first century.

Graves saw the teaching of writing as the teaching of a craft consisting of a number of stages from rehearsal through drafting and revision (which involved conferencing) to publication. The students were 'apprentice authors writing for real audiences' (Maybin, 1994: 188) who would increasingly learn to control their writing in order to understand themselves and their intentions. The writing would need to occur regularly (ideally four times a week) within a literature-rich environment. He was very concerned that students should be encouraged to develop their own voices as 'most writers rent their pieces and their teachers own them' (Graves, 1981: 7). It is interesting to see how these metaphors of ownership occur in a later HMI document on *Teaching Poetry in the Secondary School* (DES, 1987). The question of ownership is one which some critics have found contentious, believing that Graves's methods can lead to the production of writing which is inappropriate for the classroom context or mainstream society (Lensmire, 1994, and Delpit, 1988, as cited in Smith and Elley, 1998).

For Graves, writing could begin with what he called 'unconscious rehearsal' (Graves, 1983: 221) which might, for example, take the form of notes, doodles or lists before a particular topic demanded attention to be written about. For me this term brilliantly describes the earliest stages of writing a poem. So often these rehearsals can be tentative, incomplete and even aimless: it is difficult to see why a particular idea has become an obsession as the words or ideas begin to repeat themselves. Then, suddenly, you might strike an unexpected link between two words or events or one particular idea will tug that bit harder at your brain and you know you have to run with it, to move into a first draft. While recognising the importance of pupils making their own choices of subject matter, Graves acknowledged that it is impossible for young writers who may not be writing every day to rehearse and stimulate choices in this way. This lack of opportunity ultimately decreases the range of writing topics on offer. Neglection of the pre-writing/initial thinking stage can significantly diminish pupils' understanding of the writing process. However there are strategies teachers can use to build rehearsal or pre-writing time into the drafting process, as is explained later in this chapter.

Graves advocated modelling of writing, believing that this 'help[ed] teachers understand their own writing' (Graves, 1983: 50) and developed a community spirit among the writers in the class. He suggested several approaches to modelling such as:

- an initial five minute period where the teacher would write alongside the children and explain to them what she was writing about and why;
- writing directly onto large sheets of pinned up paper or OHTs so that the children could watch as the teacher's words were gradually revealed.

This latter strategy is one that teachers and pupils have become increasingly familiar with, following the arrival of the NLS in primary and secondary schools. The *Grammar for Writing* videos (DfEE, 2000), designed for training in a range of NLS teaching strategies, demonstrate the use of such approaches for teaching prose texts including suspense and letter writing. It would be interesting to ascertain how many teachers feel sufficiently confident about drafting first lines of poetry directly in view without prior preparation. Examples of teacher modelling are explored towards the end of this chapter.

Graves was sensitive to the fact that some children perceived revising a draft as a considerable chore which would mess up their writing. This feeling could be exacerbated if the first draft has been written all over in red ink by the teacher. (When and where a teacher should intervene in a draft are key questions to be returned to.) However, Graves promoted revision as an active way of changing perceptions about a text, as an adjustment of vision in writing or refocusing through the tangle of words on the anticipated future shape, argument and overall movement of a piece. The link between revision and carpentry which he uses to describe this process is helpful in enabling young writers to visualise the process and its ultimate purpose:

The carpenter planes, sands, varnishes and sands again, all in *anticipation* of running the hand over the smooth surface, the pleasure to the eye of gently curving lines, the approval of friends. The carpenter has been there before, knows what will be coming, and trusts his ability to solve the problems along the way. (Graves, 1983: 160)

To support pupils' developing drafts, Graves described 'scaffolding conferences' (ibid.: 280) held between teacher and student-writer(s) which could focus on any element of the writing (including punctuation and selection for publication) and provide invaluable bridging points in the writing process. The importance of making space for young writers to reflect on their work and the certainty that, given the chance, they will have something to say about it are central principles for the conference approach. In describing these conferences Graves acknowledged the leap from conversation to composition which young writers needed to make (Bereiter and Scardamalia, 1987). Very specific advice is offered about seating arrangements, timing and duration of conferences (which are often very short) and the types of questions which might be used. These include questions to:

- initiate the process;
- keep the children talking;
- help the young writers remain oriented within the writing process and 'become conscious of how they function as writers' (Graves, 1983: 110);
- explore development of the written piece;
- deal with basic structures;
- cause a deliberate and temporary loss of control in order to set strong writers challenges and draw attention to aspects of their writing to be explored outside of the conference context;
- focus pupils on final reflection.

Graves urged teachers to use simple, straightforward approaches involving active listening and demonstration which would enable young writers to make sense of the unpredictable and often complex nature of their writing (Graves, 1983: 105). He believed that the conferences worked best when the children were able to ask their own questions. Like Baldwin (1959), Stibbs (1981) and others before him, he also believed that teachers had a kind of moral obligation to write themselves. He went so far as to suggest that a teacher should keep her or his own writing folder in the classroom along with those of the pupils. Graves's influence is undeniable. Nevertheless the process method is not without its critics who argue that a model based on the way adults write is not applicable to young writers. If young writers are to learn about how poets, dramatists, journalists or any other kind of writers create their texts, they need to gain insights into their methods and experiences which are modelled on genuine practice.

Others voice concern that the methodology is centred on enlightened classroom practices rather than individual writers' cognitive structures and relies heavily on strong teacher commitment to ensure its success (Smith and Elley, 1998). Effective teaching does rely on strong teacher commitment to pupil learning together with informed selection of the most appropriate methods which will ensure learners can make progress. In advocating the use of Graves's approaches, I think they should be used flexibly and not in isolation. There is a need to integrate successful elements of the process method with those offering both linguistic and cognitive standpoints instead of adhering rigidly to one approach. While prizing their own developing voices, young writers need to learn how they can effectively shape their words to convey their intended meanings to audiences. Debra Myhill's research on what young writers need to do to improve the quality of their narrative writing underlines the importance of a more explicit focus on the craft of writing (QCA, 1999). Closer consideration of the drafting processes of published poets (as discussed in Chapter 3) is an essential aspect of this focus.

Robert Hull

In his text *Behind the Poem* (1988) Robert Hull offers teachers a very personal poet-teacher's eye view of his poetry writing classroom. He firmly believes that 'teaching children how to write poems is often less about what the teacher does than about what he is able to notice that the children themselves are doing' (ibid.: 85).Making the time to 'notice' with 30 pupils in an hour lesson is extremely difficult. However by providing regular opportunities to write poetry (rather than making it an occasional termly exercise) it is possible to build a stronger picture of a child's strengths and their writing habits. Confidence is also an issue for the teacher in this respect: if to teach poetry writing is to notice how children are writing, one has to be able to draw on one's own experiences of reading and writing poetry. When I have interviewed experienced and trainee teachers about their reading there has frequently been a divide between those who read poetry for pleasure and those for whom poetry remains purely a work-related experience. When we turn to poetry writing, the division is even more marked. While it is unlikely that all teachers will ever be poets, attention to the writing process should include reflection on one's own. (Readers might find it useful at this stage to ask themselves when they last drafted a poem and what they can remember about their own drafting techniques.)

Another essential element of drafting, for Hull, is that it should take place in a classroom environment which promotes openness. He notes that 'openness cannot just be offered; it has to be worked towards' (Hull,

1988: 22). An atmosphere of trust and mutual support is vital if pupils are to progress. Teachers do not want to drive their pupils to lonely garrets but, instead, to ensure that they can learn from each other and enjoy their engagement with words. Having stated this ideal, it is important to acknowledge that creating a classroom environment, where children feel able to share their writing and comment on that of other pupils, is a gradual process in which the teacher must show herself or himself to be as honest and as accommodating as the pupils. Hull recommends building in time for sharing drafts as a pair, small group or a class as a useful step in establishing such an environment (Ibid.: 125). If this system is well handled it should naturally provide opportunities to explore the nature of poetry itself. Fleming also advocates that pupils should increasingly be able to address questions concerning the nature of poetry through comparisons with other types of language. Such an approach could help to lessen their feelings of bewilderment about the genre: 'thus advertising jingles, song lyrics, raps, traditional poems and verses all have their place in the poetry classroom' (Fleming, 1996: 42).

Hull used models of poems in his classroom. He argues that imitating a model could be a creative process and a strategy for guiding young writers into a literary culture in which writing is created within the context of other writing (Hull, 1988: 143). The poems written in this way need not be directly linked with the model but produced after 'a period of absorption' (ibid.: 113). Allowing time for this 'absorption' to take place may seem at odds with the 'hurly-burly' of the literacy framework but flexibility is essential if writers are to genuinely develop. Teachers need to build in opportunities to revisit and reflect on previously explored poems as this is a vital element of the creative process. A drafting book or a writing portfolio can be an extremely helpful resource in developing this way of working.

Hull realised that a flexible approach could appear 'casual' (Hull, 1988: 23) to the outside observer. Both he and researchers such as Travers (1984) and Myhill (1986) present somewhat anarchic visions of poetry-writing classrooms as sites of risk-taking outside the bounds of conventional practice where pupils are given the freedom to choose their subjects and styles. Although teachers who adhere most closely to the remit of the National Literacy Strategy may baulk at such a suggestion, developing young writers' confidence to make choices about styles and forms is essential if they are going to learn to be creative for themselves rather than just to imitate the creators. I am not suggesting that they should always have complete free choice every time they write a poem. However, as they are gradually introduced to a range of forms and styles, they should regularly be given opportunities to select for themselves those which they consider appropriate for their chosen subject and audience. They should be free to devise new forms and ways of using language which build on their developing poetic knowledge. As they become more confident writers, they need to take risks in their choices and to learn from mistakes without undermining their confidence.

In his poem 'A Course in Creative Writing', the poet and writing teacher William Stafford succinctly describes this process. He asks how much direction teachers should give if they are to allow students the freedom to make discoveries which might lead to original poems:

> They want a wilderness with a map –
> but how about errors that give a new start ? –
> or leaves that are edging into the light? –
> or the many places a road can't find? (Stafford, 1986: 99)

One of the key lessons any writer must learn is that, on occasions, drafts and plans have to be put to one side, sometimes forever. Very few poems are ever written in one session and sometimes a poem can be stillborn at the planning stage. Hull describes a situation where he encouraged his pupils to write a series of notes, including collections of metaphors, on a picture of the Buddha. He then tried to explore with them how a writer might move with their collections of phrases towards drafting a poem. In the course of this process he realised that the poetry had became 'subverted' (Hull, 1988: 79) both through his use of an over-analytical approach and his failure to provide a clear context for the notes. In this instance the effect of over-extensive, decontextualised note-making proved to be an destructive process rather than constructive imaginative one.

Hull's honest recognition of the failings of this activity provides a useful lesson. Devoting too much time and energy to heavily directed planning is something that poetry teachers (and all teachers of writing) need to be wary of. In the rush to use an extensive array of diagrams, planning charts and writing frames, the creative process can be stifled unless careful consideration is given to an individual child's specific development needs.

A similar problem to that highlighted by Hull is identified by Myra Barrs and Valerie Cork. In their research on the links between the study of literature and writing development at Key Stage 2, they mainly concentrate on analysis of children's prose writing. However, they do include several samples of poetry which demonstrate an overemphasis on simile and metaphor collection at the planning stages. Barrs and Cork argue that this overemphasis causes two young writers to become diverted from closer consideration of their subjects (Barrs and Cork, 2001: 114, 134). They conclude that the children in their research sample planned their writing most successfully when they were given plenty of opportunity for 'indirect planning' (ibid.: 77–8), involving thinking and discussion, and when they used 'open structures' (ibid.: 213) which were not formulaic. These could be as simple as reading and reflection on a text.

Pat D'Arcy

The analogy of the writing process as a journey towards further understanding is also used by Pat D'Arcy in her key text on the writing process, *Making Sense, Shaping Meaning* (1989). She explores writing many different text types including poetry. D'Arcy suggests a range of practical strategies to aid pupils at the first stages in their journey towards meaning and away from the notion that 'the minute words are written down they somehow fix meaning forever, like a fly in amber' (ibid.: 26). These include brainstorming for personal memories, clustering, mapping (as influenced by Tony Buzan's *Use Your Head*) instant pictures and the wonderfully Star Trekian 'mental teleporting'. D'Arcy advocates giving time for free writing. She suggests that after this has taken place, other pupils might also listen to the results of free writing and teachers might want to ask open questions in order to discuss the writer's intentions and meanings rather than to engage in detailed critical analysis of the words on the screen or page. Free writing is a strategy I frequently use at the beginning of poetry workshop sessions to help the creative juices to flow.

For D'Arcy drafting is the next stage in the journey. It is a solitary and continuous event, delightfully called 'burst writing' (D'Arcy, 1989: 61) by Sally (an 8-year-old pupil whose work she includes) during which writers learn to keep alert to their own thought processes and push steadily forward as the words roll out. She is keen that pupils do not become distracted at this stage by the overall 'landscape' (ibid.: 48), the minute or mechanical details of meaning: they should concentrate on the flow. In my experience, first drafting is a very precious element of the process. Time for such undistracted work must be both carefully carved out and preserved. It does not necessarily have to be a lengthy period of time: depending on the age and ability range of the class, between 10 and 15 minutes should be adequate. Ten minutes is usually ideal as it can lead to an intense writing experience and most children will respond well to the resulting pressure this brings. Whatever your timescale, it is important to establish expectations about how pupils should work during this section of the lesson early on in your developing relationship with a class and to remind pupils regularly of what has been agreed.

Inevitably some pupils will be very keen to disturb the writing silence. Try to ensure that someone is able to work directly with them on their draft. Aim to support pupils who have difficulty concentrating, or for whom difficulties with expression can become a distraction, by writing down their continuous drafts for them and reading them back together.

This strategy frees up children to pour out their words and simultaneously develops their understanding of/interest in the shaping and revision stages. Mini tape recorders and laptop computers can also be successfully used to enable children to record their drafts efficiently without interruption. While some children will find writing the first draft difficult, equally teachers can also be very tempted to intervene far too quickly and break the concentration. Be strict with yourself! Ensure that you have given pupils all the prompts and information they might need beforehand. If you are not going to be supporting a child (as described above), take the opportunity to work on a draft yourself and make it clear that you do not want to be disturbed while drafting either.

After the initial draft D'Arcy states that further opportunities for reflection are needed. Ideas previously rushed on to paper can now be clarified, developed and reshaped. Editing for meaning is the most important aspect at this stage. This will involve the pupils in listening to their thoughts and the developing rhythm of the piece – aspects which they may only be subconsciously aware of when they first began to transfer thoughts into words. When taking D'Arcy's writing journey, proofreading should take place once the piece has been shaped and should be followed by decisions about presentation or publication.

Cliff Yates

One teacher whose pupils have become extremely adept at presenting their work is Cliff Yates. In *Jumpstart* he provides an anecdotal and entertaining insight into his classroom – a place where reading and writing are 'related activities' (Yates, 1999: xii) and teachers as well as pupils are always required to have a notebook at hand to record their experiences. Many of the poetry activities included are drawn and adapted from Yates's reading of Kenneth Koch's and Sandy Brownjohn's work as well as his own experiences of adult workshops at the Cheshire Poetry Project. He regularly runs workshops and INSET sessions for teachers and for *poetryclass* (The Poetry Society initiative). Characterised by an atmosphere of good humour, shared experience and mutual respect, they are to be highly recommended.

Yates suggests that pupils should be immersed in as much drafting as possible in order to release their attachment to their first drafts. He favours working in a pacy, interactive way and recommends:

- teacher demonstration of drafting with a talk through of the decisions as they are made;
- drafting with a class, taking votes on word choices etc if there are disputes;
- giving everyone a first draft of a poem which they then work on redrafting individually or in groups (Yates, 1999).

He wants young writers to savour the challenge of 'taking risks with language and experiment' (ibid.: x) and to realise the importance which every word will have within the draft of their poems as they work towards discovering their own voices. His approach to drafting relies on using a range of lively prompt activities such as: a bag of words; structured writing; freeze framing pictures and an adaptation of the Furniture Game originally developed by Sandy Brownjohn. (An example of a Furniture Game poem, which describes a famous person in a series of metaphors is included below.)

Furniture Game poem

If this person were a bird she'd be a magnificent peacock
strutting across the lawn, displaying inky green feathers.
If this person were a car she'd be a priceless vintage sports,
dazzling red and chrome with a polished wood interior.
If this person were a flower she'd be a velvet rose,
deepest crimson, giving off a heady perfume.
If this person were an item of clothing she'd be a supple
leather boot or a fine silk kimono.
She'd be a spectacular crashing waterfall, a golden sunset
and a sleek black panther.
She'd be a complex modern painting, a vodka martini
and the coolest pair of sunglasses you've never seen.
If this person were a piece of furniture she'd be a sofa bed,
a revolving chair or a swaying hammock,
because she's forever changing her shape and identity.

Sue Dymoke

Who do you think my character is?

Yates provides access to a wide range of poems as starting points for writing. These include well-established poetry workshop favourites like 'This is Just to Say' by William Carlos Williams along with work by contemporary writers like Paul Farley, Ian McMillan and Sujata Bhatt. He believes in giving pupils time to reflect on and revisit what they read and write. Pupils keep a separate draft book for their own poetry which remains personal to them and unassessed. Examples of pupils' work can be found throughout *Jumpstart* and in *Oranges: Poems from Maharishi School* (Yates, 2001). Their poems underline just how much can be achieved if young writers are kept in regular touch with poetry and given meaningful opportunities to redraft.

Having reviewed a number of influential texts on writing, I will now consider how some of the ideas within them can be implemented in the poetry classroom.

Where to draft?

Notebooks

For any writer the notebook is a precious storehouse of potential work. In the workshop visits I have made to classrooms and writing groups, participants have always been curious about where I keep my ideas and how I use my notebook. One significant example of this was the response of a Year 8 girl who, in between my visits, bought and started to use her own notebook regularly with powerful results. I like to show pupils how to use the notebook for jotting down single words, phrases, potential lines, thoughts and gobbets of information, as well as to complete initial and early drafts of poems before transferring them on to the screen. When planning to bring published writers into your classroom it is always worth asking them if they could bring along notebooks to show students. Any materials which can help to make the drafting process more immediate are invaluable.

On a practical level you can replicate the writer's notebook by issuing each pupil with a separate drafting book. It is very important to establish early on how this book should be used:

(a) Be clear with pupils that a writer's notebook might contain all of the following (and more): tentative scribbled notes, a space for 'rehearsals' (Graves, 1983) of ideas, crossings out, circled words, arrows linking phrases together, incomplete phrases, sketches, mind maps, diagrams, writing in different coloured pens, occasional blocks of prose such as journal entries, first drafts and redrafts, and so on.

(b) Discuss with them who might write in this book, besides its owner, and in what circumstances. For example, drafting partners might jot down their comments. A teacher or other reader might help to line out a poem or make suggestions about such aspects as word order or structure. However, summative assessment comments should not be found in the draft book: although drafts might be used as evidence to support a final assessment, the work written here is in progress.

(c) Stress that this book is private and personal to them, and that others should ask permission to read its contents. English teachers can find that pupils choose to reveal very private feelings or experiences in such notebooks. In such instances they will have taken you into their confidence and this situation will need handling sensitively. In a tiny minority of cases their drafting could include fictionalised accounts or

Sherwood School
English department

This is ....'s drafting book.

My drafting partner is............................

WARNING: DRAFTING IN PROGRESS

This book may be filled with: diagrams; plans; lists of words;

arrows; circled, numbered and reordered phrases; lively ideas;

notes written in different colours; crossings out and incomplete

pieces. Don't worry - that's what drafting is all about!

(Final drafts and assessed written work are all stored in a

separate folder.)

Figure 2.2   *Example of a guidance note for inclusion in a drafting book.*

suggestions of child abuse. If you have the slightest suspicion that this may be the case you do have a duty to report your concerns as soon as possible to the named person in your school and to maintain strict confidentiality.

As well as establishing points (a), (b) and (c) with pupils, their parents and carers also need to be aware of how the drafting book is being used. Ensure that they have access to the school's or department's writing policy. A further practical suggestion to prevent any misunderstandings is to paste a brief guidance note on the inside cover of the drafting book which clarifies (for both pupils and any adults who happen upon it) how it should be normally be used (Figure 2.2). This could also be a convenient place for pupils to record the name of their drafting partner.

The book can be used in many ways and the fewer rules the better. Some writers use a double-entry system with blank left-hand pages so that they can work further on a particular draft at a later stage. A4 notebooks are now cheaply available and are very appropriate as drafting books because there is more space for annotating drafts than in the traditional A5 exercise book. It is a good idea to ask students to date their drafts as this can make reference back so much easier. Many poets date work in progress. The poet Philip Larkin not only dated the drafts in his hardback A4 notebooks, but he would also number them and write reminders to himself about the state a particular poem had reached.

Whiteboards

The arrival of the National Literacy Strategy must have heralded a boom time for the manufacturers of mini whiteboards and dry-wipe markers. When these items first made their appearance, comparisons were made with the dreaded slate and chalk – essential equipment of Victorian classrooms, which children lived in fear of breaking. Mini whiteboards can be invaluable for quick word and sentence-level activities and other poetry 'starters'. (For some examples of these refer to Badger Year 7, 8 and 9 Word Level starters [Dymoke, 2001a and 2002a]). They can also facilitate collaborative poetry writing work. Each group can draft a line or a couplet of a class poem on their whiteboards. These can easily be swapped and commented on by other groups and followed by whole-class discussion of the ordering of the lines. The jury is still out on the usefulness of whiteboards for drafting lengthier texts. By its very nature, text written on whiteboards is ephemeral. Although this can be a good thing (as it enables children to wipe away any feeling of failure and to start completely afresh) all records of their positive achievements are also lost and, along with them, *evidence* of their developing craft as writers.

When working with Year 6 Summer School pupils I sometimes begin the initial warm up activity on whiteboards. This might be word-level work such as collecting synonyms or devising short introductory metaphors about themselves. I then ask the pupils to begin writing in draft books or on paper as soon as I want them to build on what they have written and retain a record of what has gone before. Having said this, it is important to recognise that not all writers keep their drafts. Some, who work on paper, never do, while others, working entirely on screen from the beginning of the process, will only keep the final draft on record.

Computer screen

Drafting on a computer screen can be a very different experience from using whiteboards and notebooks. Students with good word-processing skills may prefer to be liberated from pen and paper, whereas those who are less confident with technology may find that the computer can frustrate their attempts to draft. As can be seen in Chapter 3, many poets leave working on the computer until a poem is nearing completion. The poet and critic Clive Wilmer considers that a draft can be 'objectified by print'. He feels that this helps him to view a draft 'just as an artefact made by another person' and see how well his layout represents what he hears in his head. This is an example of a writer finding ways to distance himself from his work, to take a reader's view. Young writers, who are still developing their critical skills, can find it hard to move beyond the notion that a printed text does not always constitute a completed publishable text. Strategies for developing drafting skills through word processing and other programs are specifically addressed in Chapter 4.

Portfolios and folders

A portfolio or a loose-leaf folder is a necessary item to use alongside the notebook. Here pupils can store final drafts along with printouts of drafts of poems which they are writing on screen. Encourage them to index or at least date their work here too. At least once a term they should reflect on development issues in their writing and identify the poems they are most satisfied with. The portfolio is a more public storage space than the notebook. Students should regularly be encouraged to read other students' work as well as to take portfolio work home to show parents and carers. Folders are of most value if they are kept over a number of years. They provide an excellent introduction to a student's work for a new class teacher and a powerful aid for pupil reflection and target-setting.

Once a range of poems have been written, the students can use their folders as a starting point for anthology work. Too often this activity can be treated as a mass copying exercise. However, if managed carefully, compiling an anthology can be an extremely rich opportunity for pupils to engage with reading and writing poetry in a more independent way. When compiling their own poetry anthologies, pupils will need to be able to read each others' work and browse through a wide range of published poetry texts (for recommendations of some titles refer to Appendix 2). The most successful anthology work is tightly focused: pupils work to strict publishing deadlines and submit a previously agreed number of poems and/or pages. In order to develop their critical skills and to take a reader's view, pupils should be expected to:

- make links between the poems they choose (for example, by comparing ways in which different poets handle similar subjects or forms);
- select some poems they have discovered as potential models for their own further writing (and explain why they have chosen them and how they have drafted their own poems);

- make decisions about the illustration and overall design of their anthologies which demonstrate an understanding of the poems included;
- provide an introduction to their anthology in which they explain their choices and comment on what they have learned about poetry.

You may want to invite an anthologist to visit your classroom. He or she can talk about the processes involved in choosing poems for particular anthologies. You can even invite an anthologist to work with your class to refine their selections. Well-known anthologists include Morag Styles, Brian Moses, Andrew Fusek Peters, Fiona Waters and Anne Harvey. I once invited Anne Harvey, the editor of many highly regarded collections including *The Language of Love* (1989) and *Criminal Records* (1994), to work with our Year 9 and Year 10 students. She shared her insights about editorial processes with the pupils and offered advice on types and titles of poems they might want to select for their own anthologies. This event really informed the pupils' developing understanding of poetry and its publication.

How to begin drafting?

There are many different strategies a teacher can use to initiate drafting. Variety is the key here. Children should be given access to as many different types of poem as possible. Although the use of a good quality literary model seems to be the preferred approach suggested in the Key Stage 3 National Strategy training materials, teachers should not feel that they always have to start by reading a poem.

Free writing

As already suggested, when used in a quick initial burst free writing can be a good strategy for kick-starting creative thought processes and beginning unstructured play with language. After five minutes pupils can be asked to read through their work and highlight or circle any combinations of words or ideas which strike them as being interesting. These can either be used as starting points for a first draft or stored as ideas to return to later in the lesson.

Spider diagrams and mind/memory maps

Spider diagrams can be used to record initial responses to a given topic. Individual pupils' ideas can be pooled on the whiteboard. Although this sharing can be a useful way of opening up the possibilities for writing on a particular theme or topic, words need to be recorded quite briskly and the activity should be used sparingly. Encourage pupils to focus on the aspects of a given topic which interest them as soon as possible, and to pick out words and phrases which seem relevant to them.

Mind or memory maps as demonstrated by Tony Buzan in *Use Your Head* (1974) and Alistair Smith in *Accelerated Learning in the Classroom* (1996) can enable students to begin to structure and group their personal thoughts about a potential subject. Such maps use words, highlighting, capital letters, arrows, links, colour, symbols and other visuals, in different ways. This powerful approach utilises both right and left brain functions to make patterns. It has primarily been promoted as a revision or summary tool. However, I have observed it being used most productively by Year 7 and 8 groups, to explore initial responses to a poem by T.S. Eliot and record potential ideas for poetry writing about a school garden. The groups in question were both from a school which had enthusiastically adopted other visual, auditory and kinaesthetic (VAK) learning techniques described by Smith. These included using brain gym (to reinvigorate the mind at key transition points during a lesson by connecting left and right brain functions) and music. When classes were drafting poetry, some English teachers would put on a music tape to create a particular mood in their classroom. The calming effect of this strategy and the way it helped some students to concentrate on their writing were very evident.

Stimuli – poems as models

The range of stimuli which can be used for writing poetry is endless and, of course, includes poetry itself. When using poems as models, try to avoid creating a situation where pupils are expected to slavishly reproduce the original. Encourage them to think for themselves, to take from the poems ideas about working with words which they can then adapt. The poet James Fenton describes how Michelangelo destroyed a young Flemish sculptor's model of his own original design which the young man had completed 'coll'alito' – to the utmost care. The master sculptor remodelled the piece to produce a work which was completely the opposite of what was expected, saying 'now go learn the art of modelling before you learn the art of finishing' (Fenton, 2001: 1).

Stimuli – other materials

Materials I have successfully used include: a rainstick; an empty box; photographs of people; sherbet lemons; a button tin; a bag of words; a selection of different art postcards; adverts; tiny newspaper stories; packets of seeds; a sound effects tape; random lines from a poem and a cage of locusts. The stimuli could be chosen because of its link with a particular

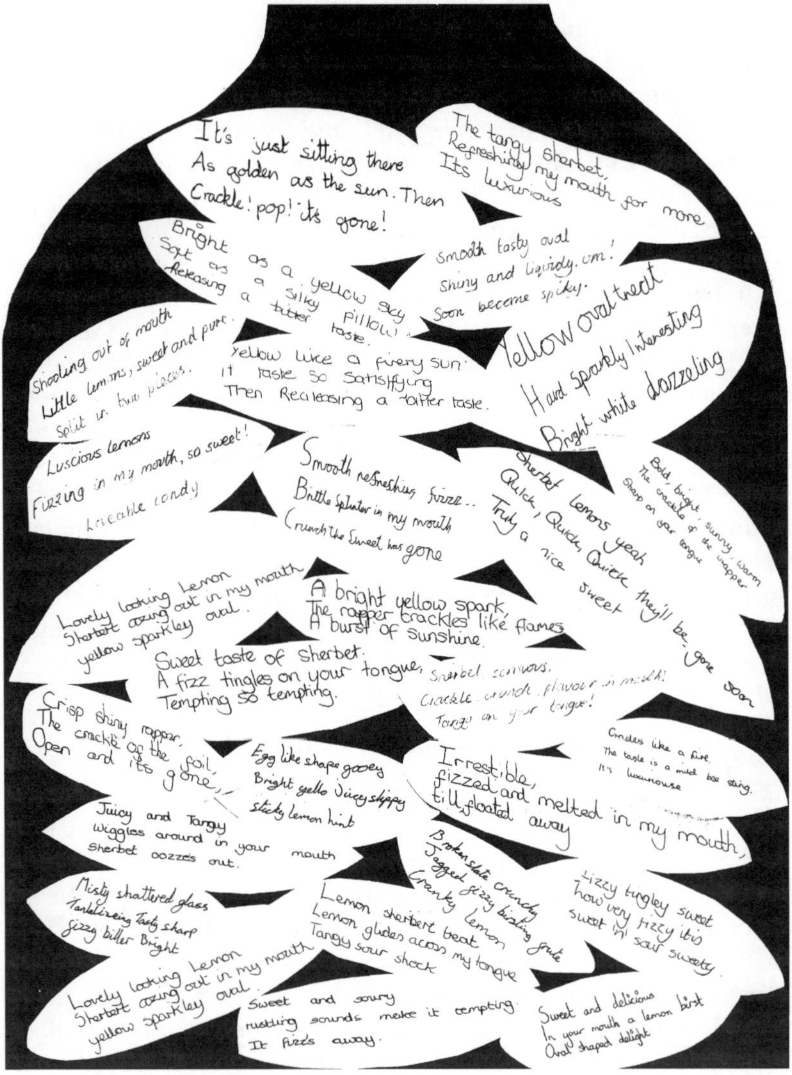

Figure 2.3   *A sherbet lemon haiku jar*

theme or because of a particular aspect of the poet's craft which pupils are to learn about. Although the material itself should be carefully selected, ultimately what is chosen is not so important as how it is used. A stimulus can help to trigger thoughts and enable writers to focus on/begin to shape their ideas. However further structures will need to be put in place if the students are to develop their skills in writing poetry.

I regularly use sherbet lemons with younger pupils to introduce them to the idea of writing precisely and originally about an event using the haiku form. The haiku, being a very short form with a tight syllabic structure that captures a tiny event or moment in time, is not unlike the sherbet lemon, a glowing brittle, oval-shaped sweet whose outer casing suddenly cracks to surprise the sweet eater with a fizz of sherbet on the tongue. Asking pupils to jot notes to question prompts and to eat at the same time has always made this a popular lesson! Once they have captured their own tiny sherbet haiku moments, and begun to grasp the purpose and construction of the form, they can go on to draft bags, packets or jars (Figure 2.3) full of sweets (not necessarily sherbet lemons). In these poems they can use a range of other Japanese forms such as rengas and tankas and experiment with their own inventions.

Although pupils need to be given time to react to what they see, hear, feel and read, and to immerse themselves in the stimuli, try reasonably quickly to move them on with their note making. When they are at this first response stage, pupils can write everything down rather than edit out responses – explain that there will be time later for that. However, it is crucial that they are aware of the context in which they are working: the intention that their notes will lead them to writing a poem. While I would never prevent someone writing down ideas in full sentences at this stage, it can be helpful to encourage writers to think in words and phrases. Also tell them not to worry about where on the page they write. (This can be very liberating. It can cause interesting juxtapositions of ideas and prevents too much of a prose narrative developing.) Many students respond well to short periods of reflection interspersed with semi-structured questions or prompts. Take no longer than 10 minutes for questioning and allow for a few minutes of extra time at the end, when pupils can review what they have written and/or add further notes.

One of many valuable lessons I learned from attending workshops at The Poetry Business in Huddersfield was to think about how you are looking at an object, then to place yourself almost on the outside of the experience and to try to look at yourself looking. For example, in a workshop which used postcards of famous paintings as a stimulus, the workshop leader, Peter Sansom, encouraged us to think about the card in different contexts and first asked what we identified with in the painting. He drew us in and out of the painting in many different ways (for example, by focusing on the light, the movement, the context in which the work might have been produced). At this stage we were not allowed to look at the title of the painting or any other information on the back of the card. Towards the end of the questioning he asked how our attention to the details in the postcards had changed the longer we looked. As a result of this intense process we had made our own meanings from the paintings. We were able to move beyond straightforward descriptions of the stimuli which had provided a starting point for individual work.

Using cloze to introduce choices when drafting

The DARTs activity of cloze is a very popular technique used in studying poetry at GCSE level. With cloze, certain lines, phrases or words of a poem are blanked out and pupils are asked to complete the blanks with words of their own or words chosen from a selection provided. If used sparingly it can be a helpful tool for focusing a reader's attention on particular words, rhythms and structures chosen by a writer. However, it can be badly mishandled if insufficient time is devoted to consideration of these choices, the reasons for them or comparison with the choices students have made themselves.

Cloze can also be a very constructive way to explore drafting with a group. Students' ideas can be pooled, and possibly combined with original lines from the poem. Then they can all share ideas about the impact of different word choices on the draft or skeleton of the poem and make decisions about which are the most effective. I have used this strategy when focusing on metaphors with a Year 7 mixed ability group. The class worked with 'The Locust' (a Yoruba poem included in *The Rattle Bag* anthology edited by Seamus Heaney and Ted Hughes, 1982). A blanked-out cloze version of the poem was read several times as pupils observed a cage of locusts borrowed from the school science labs. They also had access to a labelled scientific drawing of the insect. Pupils observed the locusts, jotting down their own words about them against a series of prompt headings (such as how the locust moves, eats, the sounds it makes, what parts of its body look like, etc.). These notes were then further shaped and cloze lines completed individually before being discussed in small groups. Finally, the Yoruba poem was read and word choices were compared. The pupils went away from the lesson with a strong idea of the poem as a whole and a sense of how writers make choices in their push for coherence and originality in their work.

The lesson briefly outlined above was one in a sequence of lessons involving writing poetry. It is important that pupils are given the chance to write a number of poems in a short space of time. This enables them to develop a much more genuine experience of the way most writers work. As can be seen in Chapter 3, writers will seldom work on just one poem at a time: more likely they will have a number of drafts on the go at once including, perhaps, texts in other genres which will all have reached different stages of completion.

Demonstration

In September 2000 17 pilot authorities in England introduced the Framework for the Key Stage 3 National Strategy into a number of schools in their LEAs (refer to Chapter 1). One of the key strategies promoted for teaching writing is the use of models of texts coupled with shared writing by the teacher to demonstrate the writing process to the whole class. As has been previously stated, the training about the teaching of writing given to secondary staff has focused on writing narrative and a variety of non-fiction genres. Advice on the writing of poetry has been notable by its absence.

Well-delivered demonstrations can bring to life the decision-making processes that occur as writers shape meanings through their choices and combinations of words, sounds and forms. Demonstration as outlined in the NLS training videos is largely seen as a whole-class activity: the teacher drafts onto a flip chart or whiteboard, talking aloud about what she or he is writing, sharing the processes she is engaged in and questioning pupils about her or his choices. A successful demonstration requires a flexible and honest approach by the teacher. She or he does not have to be a professional writer but rather someone who is able to pay close attention to the practice of writing, to actively read like a writer. The teacher may not be confident about writing poetry, but is prepared to take risks and engage in a genuine meaning-making dialogue with her pupils.

During the pilot year I was a tutor for secondary English Post-Graduate Certificate in Education (PGCE) students. It was interesting to observe the ways in which students, a number of whom were placed in pilot schools, responded to the challenges which the Framework presented. Many students arrive on PGCE courses having avoided poetry modules on their degree courses. They are only able to draw on vague memories of studying poetry from their A-level courses and need considerable support if they are to make a success of poetry in their own classrooms. Furthermore, although they may not have ever read poetry regularly, they are even less likely to have written a poem in recent memory. If the teachers of tomorrow are to be able to demonstrate writing poetry, and other forms, they need to have opportunities to develop these skills as part of their training.

During the pilot year I observed a number of examples of demonstration. While the majority of students appeared comfortable to provide their own models of newspaper reports, adverts, letters or opening paragraphs of essays, very few felt confident enough to demonstrate poetry writing. One student, Jane, showed herself to be determined to get to grips with poetry from the very early stages of the course, and was inspired by the support of colleagues in her teaching practice school. She began to experiment with a range of reading response and writing strategies for poetry. She provided her Year 7 class with a model of review writing and also spent a lesson demonstrating how she had used the poem 'Lightning' by James Irwin as a model for her own poem 'Raindrops'.

Raindrops

I find raindrops quite exciting,
Falling, freshwater, frequent,
fading,
Greeting the ground –
Quick slick thick raindrops

Escaping from the crowded clouds,
Silently, swiftly, swirling,
Spirited,
safely reaching their destination,
Earth –
Quick slick raindrops!

Jane Murphy

Both poems were presented on OHT. During the ensuing lively discussion, in which the group identified the similarities in technique she had used, she was anxious to stress that her poem represented only one way of using Irwin's poem. The poem Jane used appeared to be at a final draft stage. While she was not yet confident enough to take out an OHT pen and ask her pupils to redraft it with her, these were the encouraging first steps.

In talking to her a year later, it is evident that she has is now strongly committed to using demonstration. She is excited by its potential and critical of her own first attempts at it. 'I used to prepare the draft in advance' she says. 'But now I think that defeats the object. I am teaching [the pupils] to be spontaneous with words. I was cheating and overplanning before. I need to show revision and redrafting are worthwhile. Writing with the pupils seems natural.' Jane recognises the classroom management issues which can arise when trying to engage pupils in shared writing. She tries to create a classroom environment in which pupils are hungry to share their immediate reactions and to spark off each others' ideas about a draft. (For an example of her work refer to the commentary in Figure 2.4.) She likes thinking and writing on her feet and will talk through thoughts and processes as she writes. Jane also uses pupils' drafts to share ideas for revisions and is keen to encourage more pupils to take her place in front of the class when their drafts are being discussed.

We read Enid Barraclough's 'Procrastination' – a poem about the demise of a friendship. Students' initial feedback included thinking about and writing down 2 or 3 'things' they liked about the poem such as: any words/phrases which caught their imagination/made them think; any images that they thought were particularly effective (what and why); comments on the structure/flow of the poem or anything else they could think of. Students' feed back was recorded on the board. I then told students this is what we all should be aiming for when we write poetry, that it will cause the reader to have some reaction. Subsequent readings of the poem included text marking poetic techniques, particularly metaphors.

The next stage involved preparation for their own writing on the broad theme of friendship. Students were encouraged to draw upon personal experience, both negative and positive. In small groups or pairs, students mind mapped (a skill they are becoming increasingly familiar with) where they could go with this and were also thinking about what they would try to communicate through their poem. Lots of lovely ideas were produced here such as: writing a poem in the style of a telephone conversation with an abrupt and awkward dialogue; visually describing an old friend seen in the distance; the discovery of a gift that reminds the speaker of the past.

Language work was also introduced at this stage in the form of Vocab Cards (a set of cards I made to trial). The words on the cards are random, different and perhaps words which year 8 students would not normally use (the aim being allowing them to play with and explore language). They have to include the word(s) in the poem, so they have to construct meaning and 'grammar' around it.

During the writing process, I too worked on ideas and wrote a poem with some of the students' help using the OHP. I had already communicated to them that, because I had enjoyed the tone of Enid Barraclough's poem, I too wanted to recreate something similar. This was the 'end' product after their suggestions (which were mainly language based):

('Title-less')
Days ebb away,
running from our clasp –
tomorrow is always
smeared
with yesterday.

continued over

Doubtful, you said,
as the promise
of a rendezvous
disintegrated
with regret.
Durable are the images,
our fleeting bond –
cemented in film
unlike
the reality.

Language input from students after much deliberation!
Stanza 1 … 'ebb', 'smeared'
Stanza 2 … 'rendezvous', disintegrated'
Stanza 3 … 'images', 'cemented'

When I thought we'd sufficiently worked on the poem, students repeated the initial process (which they had completed on Barraclough's poem) thinking about, writing down and discussing 2 or 3 'things' which they particularly like or which invoked a reaction in them. I mixed the groups around here to allow them to discuss a poem with 'new' students.

It is difficult to capture the discussions that took place on paper. Students talked about the impact of our 'new' vocabulary, eg 'images' (originally 'photos') and how 'Images' has much more depth as it can refer to memories as well as snapshots. One group liked the phrasing of 'with regret' as they said it is often what people say when they can't make something: 'It is with regret...' One student talked about the impact of 'cemented' (original words included 'trapped' and 'caught') arguing that 'cemented' made him think of death and that in a way, the friendship is dead.

Only a small number of students commented on the structure of the poem (including the alliteration of the first word in each stanza, the one word on every fourth line and the use of punctuation) even though we had focused on this when we looked at the Barraclough poem. I quickly realised (when they started writing their own poems) that structure was of little concern to them; they were more interested in the vocabulary and the different words that could play with. In terms of reading and writing poetry again with this group in the future, I now know that looking at structure and punctuation within poetry will be a higher priority for us.

Jane Murphy

Figure 2.4 *Commentary on demonstration*

Some principles for demonstration

When demonstrating drafting poetry to pupils you may like to consider the following guiding principles and practical advice:

- try to write directly in front of pupils as well as to present previously prepared material;
- talk through possible choices when writing and involve pupils in decision-making;
- to ensure there is a real dialogue about the draft, give pupils the chance to ask questions too;
- experiment with using different coloured pens to denote different types of choices being made;
- take time to read the whole piece aloud at different stages in development as well as to read out sections of it;
- ask pupils to read out the drafts (stress that this is an invaluable way of identifying whether the imagined tone and structure of a piece are successfully transferring themselves onto paper);
- present the draft as a genuine draft rather than as a polished piece;
- write 'draft' at the top of the flip chart or use your computer's printer facility to add a draft watermark onto the paper;
- number and date the draft(s);
- return to a draft for a brief period during several lessons;
- ensure that pupils see teachers drafting regularly (rather than giving 'one-off' performances);
- make sure demonstration of drafting poetry is not just a whole-class activity.

Demonstration should not just be reserved for whole-class teaching. There is considerable opportunity for purposeful, focused dialogue to take place when demonstration is used more informally in guided writing situations with small groups of children and individual writers. In this way demonstration is used as a kind of intervention.

How to sustain and develop drafting

Interventions

No passion in the world is equal to the passion to alter someone else's draft. (H.G. Wells)

The questions about when and how to intervene in a pupil's drafting processes can be particularly delicate when it comes to writing poetry. One heavy-handed teacher intervention can make a marked difference in a poem where every word can carry so much more weight than it would in a lengthier piece of prose. When interviewing secondary English teachers about this issue, it was interesting to note that female teachers were shown to be more sensitive to questions of ownership than their male counterparts. They were hesitant about their own status and concerned about 'not interfering too much' (Dymoke, 2000a: 203). For example Liz felt her own uncertainty about poetry directly influenced the nature of the advice she could give young writers. While Anna's preferences for making suggestions and experimenting with response partners reflected her overall desire not to be seen as a lecturer in her classroom. Male colleagues were less tentative. I observed, and was given, examples of how they would provide pupils with alternative words, help with syllable counts, write down potential next lines and help a student to 'buff up' (Dymoke, 2000a: 268) a poem. One could argue that they were seen to be more actively demonstrating the writing process for their students by involving themselves in the redrafting or editorial stages. However the question of ownership remains crucial. Hull suggests that the teacher needs 'to go alongside the child-as-writer in his role as teacher-as-writer in order to be responsive to the nuance of the child's attempts' (Hull, 1988: 118). In assuming this role, he should be able to make creative suggestions 'without amounting to trespass' (ibid.: 119). But what amounts to a creative suggestion rather than an act of trespass?

From their research in primary classrooms, Barrs and Cork conclude that interventions are particularly effective if they occur between drafts. They observed teachers reading children's writing aloud and discussing it in ways which enabled them to continue working independently afterwards. The final decisions were left to the children. This ensured the young writers were able to retain ownership of their work. The sensitive focus on how the texts 'sounded' was seen to have a powerful effect: 'All writers need to develop a strong sense of an internalised reader: this practice helped children to anticipate the effect their writing would have on a reader. They were learning to listen to their own texts and developing a critical ear for writing' (Barrs and Cork, 2001: 81).

Intervention strategies

The appropriacy and success of these intervention strategies depend, as always, on familiarity with the child's previous achievements and the understanding/attitude towards poetry which has been developed in the classroom.

Use of broad questions can be helpful such as:

• Have you tried placing these lines in different orders?

- Why don't you experiment with some more very short lines like these two?
- What does this section sound like when you read it aloud?
- What about a title? (It could help you to draw your ideas together.)
- Do you think you need to use 'and' quite so much? ('the', 'an' and 'I' can be heavily overused too)
- Have you thought of writing in the present tense?
- Could you give a few more details about how you felt at this point?
- How can you help your reader to imagine what that smell is like?
- Which lines do you like best in this piece? Are there any ideas or words you can use from them elsewhere in the poem?

These questions, either written or spoken, aim to focus the writer on close reading of their work in order to think about the impact that it has. Some direct the writer to particular sections of the draft. However they are intended to open up the text rather than to pass judgements on it.

Reading aloud and listening

One very simple technique is to ask the writers to swap drafts and to listen to their own draft poem being read aloud by someone else. Inevitably, when you read your own work aloud, you aim to read it in the way you want it to be heard (which may mean that pauses or emphases are added where none are indicated or words are missed out). A fresh reader may draw attention to unnecessarily repeated words, odd rhythms or strange juxtapositions of words which may have been overlooked. In many cases the readings will lead to questions and further discussion about the draft. This type of intervention is a very powerful way of distancing writers from their poems, which then enables them to move on to a further draft.

Response partners

Another key intervention strategy, which also includes careful listening, is the use of drafting or response partners. The National Writing Project (1985–89) which informed the writing strand of the National Curriculum included examples of strategies teachers could use to help pupils become more effective response partners. It was felt that development of these skills would in turn strengthen students' abilities to become independent writers who would be able to read their own work critically. Although use of drafting partners is now a well-established practice in some schools, I still come into contact with classes of children who have never worked in this way. With the arrival of the NLS in primary and secondary schools, and an increased emphasis on developing a shared understanding of the author's craft, there should definitely be a place for response partners in every writing classroom.

Some principles for using response partners:

- it is best to establish this practice early in the academic year so that pupils can really benefit from observing each others' development as writers;
- ideally, pupils should be given a choice about who they work with – some pupils may be very resistant to sharing their work at first but can be persuaded round to the idea once they see how the system works;
- continuity is important but give all pupils the chance to change partners after a term;
- twos are ideal but threes can also work well too. (On odd occasions you, or a teaching assistant, might need to be someone's partner but keep to peer responses wherever possible.) The strategy of using paired peer responses should be non-threatening for young writers. It will give them the first confidence-building step towards sharing work with a wider critical audience;
- keep a list of drafting partners so that peer responses can be acknowledged and pupils drawn into discussion of shared writing;
- stress that being a response partner is a responsibility. Response partners need to be supportive people who can be creative and receptive to ideas, honest but tactful and able to take criticism;
- negotiate guidelines for working with response partners – put a copy of these on the wall and ensure everyone has a copy in their drafting book along with the name of their partner. These guidelines should include advice on how to read and comment on the draft. As children become familiar with them they will tend to only refer to them occasionally. An example is included in Figure 2.5.

The messy draft

As has already been explained, pupils should not expect to keep their drafts in a pristine state. Encourage them to mark on ideas and potential changes and then talk these ideas through. They could use:

- colour coding (especially if working on screen);
- highlighting;
- numbering;
- circling;

- arrows;
- cutting and pasting (either on screen or on paper).

Many of these techniques are commented on by poets in Chapter 3.

How to respond to your drafting partner

- Read your draft poems aloud to each other. Listen very carefully.
  Swap your work over. Now reread your partner's work to yourself at least twice before making any comments.
- Comments can be spoken or written. (Written comments can be more useful for your partner to refer to afterwards. Write comments in pencil.)
- Find two things you like in the poem and give reasons.
- Find two things you are not so sure about and give reasons.
- Draw a squiggly line alongside any parts of the poem where the language does not sound quite right.
- If you think they might need to add something more put a ^^ sign underneath that part of the line.
- Try to comment on the title – does it do justice to the poem?
- Offer a suggestion about the poem.
- Ask a question about the poem.
- Remember you are not proof reading the poem (that's the poet's job!) but draw your partner's attention to any spelling, grammatical or punctuation errors which you think could spoil the meaning of the draft.
- Now share your comments with your partner. Be honest and supportive. Try to give reasons for any comments you make.

Figure 2.5   *How to respond to your drafting partner*

Revision cards

In their research on the role of instruction on developmental processes, Bereiter and Scardamalia concluded that writers who lacked feedback from a response partner (or who were in large classes where regular feedback from a teacher was difficult) might benefit from some kind of artificial feedback system to support their essay writing. They designed and researched the use of a series of cards which included single statements similar to those a teacher or a response partner might make. The cards contained evaluative comments such as 'People may not understand this' and directive comments such as 'I'd better give an example' (Bereiter and Scardamalia, 1982 as cited in Smith and Elley, 1998). These were tested out in two ways: first, by writers who reread draft stories, stopping at the end of each sentence to choose a card which matched the sentence and, second, by writers using the cards during the first draft stage. The researchers concluded that students would need regular practice in using the cards if they were to have a marked effect. Nevertheless such cards could be of benefit in certain situations (Bereiter and Scardamalia, 1983 as cited in Smith and Elley, 1998).

Sounds

When you read your draft aloud are there lines which sound different from the rest?

Which sounds do you like? Why? Which sounds don't you like? Why?

Have you repeated words? What effect do your repetitions have?

Do any of your lines or combinations of words sound out of place?

What's the rhythm of your poem like?

Do any of your lines seem to have too many words in them?

If you've used rhyme does the rhyme scheme work? Does it seem to fit with the subject of your poem?

Forms

What do you notice about the shape of your draft on the page?

What kinds of patterns of words and lines do the poems have? Do these work?

Is your first line the best one to open your poem with?

Look carefully at the opening and closing words on each line. What impact do they have when you read them?

Do you need to move sections of your poem around?

Do you need to add lines? Where?
Do you need to cut lines out? Where?

If you are using a form (like a sonnet, a haiku, a ballad, a shape poem or a villanelle) think about whether you have used the form effectively. Is it the best form to choose for your subject?

Figure 2.6 *Examples of conference cards*

Conference cards

Conference cards, first described by Graves (1983) and referred to by Barrs and Cork (2001) do have a link with the revision cards described above although they are possibly more user-friendly and geared to poetry. They can be used by individual pupils for self-regulation, by drafting partners or by groups of children during shared writing. Each card can focus in on a different stage or aspect of the draft. Figure 2.6 contains examples which could be adapted.

The writing commentary: combining critical reflection on drafting with examination poetry

All the intervention strategies outlined in this chapter are designed to enable pupils to approach their writing with their critical eyes and ears open. The links between reading and writing are vital but as pupils move towards public examinations these can often become too narrowly focused. For example, at GCSE level pupils are expected to study a range poetry but are infrequently given opportunities to write poetry themselves (Benton, 2000; Dymoke, 2000a). If they are ever to fully appreciate the way their examination poets write, I think it is essential for them to continue to experience these processes at first hand.

One strategy used successfully for GCSE coursework combines study of a GCSE poet with students' reflections on their own drafting processes. A Year 10 GCSE class (ability range A* – D and in the second term of their course) had been reading the selections of work by poets Carol Ann Duffy, Simon Armitage and Ted Hughes published in the NEAB GCSE poetry anthology (2000/01). Study of the poets had included a number of recreative activities and DARTs including: cloze work on Hughes's poem 'Wind'; visual representations of the contrasts in Hughes's, 'The Warm and the Cold'; hot seating of the narrator of Duffy's 'Stealing'; preparing a police report on Armitage's 'About his Person' and descriptions of their own primary school memories in comparison with Duffy's 'In Mrs Tilscher's Class'.

Once they had immersed themselves fully in the poets' work, I introduced the original writing coursework assignment, giving students the option of writing either a poem or a short piece of prose which would be accompanied by a commentary. Although I was available to comment on work in progress I stressed that pupils were to use their drafting partners for support. In writing the commentary (on completion of the final draft) they were asked to reflect on the decisions they had made during the drafting stages. If appropriate, they were to explore links/points of contrast with the poets' work or other texts of their choice. Students were given a very loose outline for this commentary and encouraged to refer to their drafting books or to word-processed printouts of each stage in their draft. A surprising number chose to write poetry. This choice was interesting in itself. Bruce, a teacher whom I had previously interviewed about pupils' choices of assignments, had commented to me that he felt pupils shied away from choosing to write poetry in assessed situations 'because of the anxiety of teachers at not being able to say how good [poetry] is ... and [the students'] anxiety at not being able to assess for themselves how good it is' (Dymoke, 2000a: 195).

The issue of GCSE assessment will be returned to in Chapter 6. However, included here are examples of final drafts and extracts from the commentaries produced. They pinpoint some of the understandings about drafting which pupils can develop through using this approach.

Tom spent a considerable amount of time on the drafting stages of 'Bird Flight'. He became frustrated with certain sections of his poem but at the same time seemed to relish the opportunity to argue with himself, his drafting partner and me over individual word choices. Of all the poems written by the group his was the most consciously written in the style of Hughes.

Bird Flight

Above the waters I glide,
With lazy wings outstretched.
But darkness wraps my world in its swathes.
Chaos replaces silence, as sky redefines its form.

Spurred on by icy blasts,
I sweep the ocean's troughs.
Boiling waters threaten up,
And grope the air for prey.

Down below, a crippled shape of black,
Is battered by waves of rebuke.
I hang pitiless, aloof,
As living flotsam is engulfed.

The space between sea and sky vanishes,
With the flair of a conjuring trick.
I swim through air that does not want me.
The singsong whine pervades my head.

Amateurs flounder and fall,
Lives stifled by the smothering silence of the deep.
A turmoil of elements, intent on destruction.
But I resist the impotent fury of the storm.

From the depths of cloud, sunlight strikes,
Severing the grip of chaos.
The destroyer vanquished in a blaze of glory.
Waters pacified to oily smoothness.

With calm restored, small minds forget.
But not mine.
Lazy wings outstretched,
Secure in my perfection.

I continue on my journey.

Tom Hopkins

Tom's commentary reflects not only his developing appreciation of Ted Hughes's work but also an understanding of his own intentions in drafting 'Bird Flight'. He gives the reader a strong sense of the choices he made concerning setting, use of a first person viewpoint, alliteration, repetition, syntax and word selection. He describes his failed attempt to use enjambement (although he does not explore why he felt a need to use it or reasons for failing to do so). In conclusion he observes how he himself seems to have seeped into the poem. He is surprised by how the writing has overtaken him.

Extracts from Commentary on 'Bird Flight'

In writing my poem, I was inspired by two pieces. They were written by Ted Hughes and were called 'Wind' and 'Hawk Roosting'. 'Wind' describes, in a brutal terrifying way, the effects of the elements on the landscape and its inhabitants. 'Hawk Roosting' deals with the hawk's perceptions of itself and its surroundings. I was particularly influenced by the way Ted Hughes used anthropomorphism to give the landscape feeling ...

In my poem I wanted an observer to describe a storm that would take place at sea. I set it at sea because ocean storms are dramatic. I needed something that was not itself in danger from the elements but would influence the poem with its personality and point of view. It couldn't be a human as it would indeed be in danger from the storm, so there weren't many life-forms to choose from. The most obvious viewpoint that sprang to mind was a 'bird's eye' view. This would give me the freedom to look down upon the storm and describe it and also to watch how it influenced other creatures.

Both of the Hughes poems deal with bleak, pitiless forms of nature. In the obituary of Ted Hughes in 'The Sunday Times', Prof. John Carey described Hughes' vision of the world as a predator, devouring all things. I wanted the pitiless nature of the animal, without the predatory instincts of the hawk.

Hughes' poems use the first person ... I decided to use this in my work to create an observer. I thought this would be the best form in which to write, as it is direct and personal. Both of Ted Hughes' poems were written in four line verses and I decided to adopt this structure, with the exception of a single finishing line. I changed this to make a final impact on the reader, and to make it memorable ...

In my draft I tried to incorporate [enjambement] but I found it too difficult. Hughes also uses alliteration to emphasise a point 'black-/Back gull bent like an iron bar slowly.' I used this technique in my poem. Here is a line from my poem: 'Lives stifled by the smothering silence of the deep.' By the repetition of the 's' sound I tried to achieve the effect of drowning under water. Ted Hughes didn't use any repetition in either of his poems, but I repeated the line 'lazy wings outstretched' to develop the idea that the bird was at rest before the storm and was not afraid of it. It would live to see the next storm and all the ones after it

Hughes sometimes used words in an unusual way. In the line 'To produce my foot, my each feather:' we might have expected him to say 'my every feather' or 'each of my feathers' and this use makes the phrase stand out. In my line 'Boiling waters threaten up' I used the word 'threaten' which is usually followed by a noun or pronoun, but instead I followed it with a preposition to make the image of the sea more powerful.

In the lines 'I resist the impotent fury of the storm.' I tried to put across the idea that the bird regards the storm with contempt, because of its emasculated lack of power over him. From above, the bird observes a sinking ship ('a crippled shape of black'), and is completely removed as it comments on the destruction of the boat ...

I was pleased with my poem. I put a lot of time and effort into it, involving many draft versions, but the end result was worth it. I think it is fair to say that, unintentionally, I have put a lot of myself into this work. For me, the poem has underlying messages. I have produced an idea of an uncaring people, in a violent world, where goodness is 'engulfed' and destroyed. I also created a feeling of rejection from those people, in the line 'I swim through air that does not want me.' The people of this new society are 'small minded' and violent without reason. But this observer refuses to bend to the 'whine' of society, merely watching and thinking. I think the poem is a partial reflection of

my views on modern society. I hope that I created a poem that fulfilled
my brief well.

Another student, Ekaterina, was still drafting until the moment the
coursework was submitted! Even during her final proofread of her poem
she was making significant changes, as can be seen in this version:

The Torrent Raged

The stream of water, first a friend;
Trusted by the fish that cruise its banks,
Probing for worms in its waves and ripples.

Then a bitter enemy;
Mercilessly uprooting plants,
That once gently swayed by the river,

Breathed in its air,
And submissively submerged
Their soul and spirit under Her influence.

the torrent's
Now they yield themselves into ~~His~~ mouth,
Fooling themselves with their beliefs in providence
And their conviction that He is always right.

The torrent, possessed by greed,
Hauls earth and boulders and lugs them along,
Only to abandon them again in crumpled heaps.

The torrent is bitter too,
There is no humanity in his wintry heart.
captures
He ~~gathers~~ a child and sweeps it along with the tide, like rubbish.

Hurrying, scurrying into every den and burrow,
There is no rhythm or rhyme in its reckless ramble.

Ekaterina Krylova

Throughout her drafting Ekaterina remained in two minds about her decision to write a poem. Extracts from her commentary show this struggle. In this commentary she is also defining what poetry means for her. Her previously established perceptions about language and poetry are being challenged simultaneously by her close reading of Hughes and her own experiences of drafting.

Extracts from Commentary on 'The Torrent Raged'

My first decision was to write a poem, but I found this rather restrictive, because I felt that I had to keep the shape and length of each verse the same. I continued to write long descriptive sentences about the torrent but when I had finished it I wanted to put the prose back into poetry. I felt that because some of the techniques I used, my piece of prose had more of a poetic feel to it.

I found it difficult to break up the prose into verses. I felt that I had to start each verse with a new idea, but I noticed that Ted Hughes did not do this in his poem.

Ekaterina refers to the influence of other readers on her draft:

Several people pointed out to me that it was quite difficult to distinguish between the torrent and the river. For this reason I edited out the first line of my poem which was originally: 'The torrent raged; injuring, destroying, killing.' as it was a very confusing contrast from the second line in which it talks about the 'gentle' river. The contrast from 'under Her influence' to 'into His mouth' was also quite confusing so I changed the phrase into 'the torrent's mouth'.

Finally, she returns to the tension she experienced in finding a form she felt comfortable with. In spite of the difficulties, she reasserts her faith in a prose to poetry approach to drafting:

I am pleased with the way that I have used descriptive language in my poem. I am not so happy with the shape of my poem as the lines are all of a different length. This is probably because I wrote the poem as prose first. Overall I think it is a good idea to write poetry as prose first because it is less restrictive. I found it easier to split sentences into verses than fitting sentences around verses.

For me this commentary underlines the importance of giving students space and opportunity to experiment with drafting approaches. At no point during this assignment was Ekaterina advised to write in prose first but she (like the poet Paul Violi who is interviewed in Chapter 3) found this to be a preferred method. The chosen approach raised a number of questions for her about writing poetry which were unresolved. Ongoing dialogue about the nature of poetry is a healthy outcome from such original writing assignment work: teachers and students should not feel under pressure to produce highly polished pieces.

The Tornado

It comes from the heavens
where the lightning bolts crash
cutting the grey sky
with a brilliant bright gash.

A stack of cloud
like a pillar of Hell
falls from the darkness
and begins to swell

It touches down
in a farmer's field
dust and soil fly
as the fences yield

It picks up speed
and heads towards town
this dark creature
will not be put down

With a mighty roar
it bounds along
too close for comfort
all mercy gone

Plucking up cars
ripping up trees
sucking them up
but its hunger doesn't ease

continued over

Into town
only wreckage behind
its mouth a vortex
just horror to find

Glass shatters in windows
masonry tears away
everything is shaking
and there's havoc to play

People are running
safety their goal
away from the beast
to save their soul

Screams of the unfortunate
as they are enveloped
but it moves after all kind
a crisis has developed

The creature moves away
off towards the ocean
away across the water
it fades and slows its motion.

Tom Short

Extracts from Commentary on 'The Tornado'

Tom appears to have a keen sense of himself as a poet. In commenting on 'The Tornado', he points out that he decided to adopt a structure he had previously used. Interestingly, he does not discuss the way the compact shape of his poem seems to mirror the 'pillar of Hell' itself. He also makes an observation about rhyming poetry which demonstrates just how literally a teacher's words can be interpreted sometimes:

The last poem that I wrote, called The Titanic, was written in a style where each verse was four lines long and the second and the fourth lines rhymed. Also alternate lines in the poem had a similar number of syllables. I found this poem enjoyable to write and quite effective, so I decided to adopt the same structure for The Tornado. We were told that rhyming poems would limit the vocabulary that we could use, but I found this helpful because I find it hard to write a poem with such a loose structure.

In reflecting on his drafting processes, Tom concentrates on decisions made about tenses, rhyme and syllabics. Finally he recognises where the poem could benefit from further development:

> Along the way I had to make one very big change to the poem because I kept on muddling up the tenses. I finally decided to write the poem in the present tense. This meant that I had to change some of the rhymes, which was awkward. I chose the present tense because it made the poem sound more dramatic and as if it was happening now, around the reader. My aim was to tell the story of the tornado from its beginning in the sky, to its end over the sea.
>
> Overall I am reasonably pleased with my poem, although certain bits of rhyming are still not quite right. Keeping to a similar number of syllables on alternate lines proved to be fairly difficult. My favourite verse is number five as I think I have caught the image of the angry animal well and I managed to get the syllable rule to work perfectly. Given more time I would add to the middle of the poem, as I think there is more scope for description here. I could describe the effect of the tornado on the ocean and make more of the tornado's death.

The three students make confident use of technical vocabulary. For the most part, poetic terms are well integrated into their commentaries. In completing this assignment, some other members of the class were more prone to 'trope spotting' in their own work, with the result that they provided checklists of the techniques used rather than exploring reasons for choices made. This can be a common failing in responses to literature, particularly when writing about a text under examination conditions. It is a real challenge for teachers to ensure that their students feel able to use terms naturally and appropriately when they are writing about their own drafting processes.

The commentary furthers the dialogue about poetry writing, which can be initiated through use of the strategies outlined in this chapter about where to draft, how to begin drafting and how to sustain the process. These have included suggestions about: beginning writing (including free writing, mind-mapping, demonstration, use of cloze and different kinds of stimuli); advice on intervention strategies (such as reading aloud, using response partners, revision and conference cards) together with critical perspectives and workshop experiences which have informed my classroom practice. I am not claiming that the use of the commentary is radical or new, nevertheless it does appear to be underused. The commentary can be a useful tool to support assessment of poetry – a feature which is explored in Chapter 6. Primarily it provides writers and teachers with valuable insights into the drafting process which they can draw on in future work.

3

Using Poets' Drafts

In order for students to develop both their own writing skills and an understanding of the craft of writing it is vital that they are given access to the draft work of successful writers as well as to their published or performed poems. Textbooks will occasionally offer examples of draft manuscripts but these often serve as token illustrations of what a draft might look like rather than genuine attempts to reveal the processes which have informed the published poem. These processes will remain secret unless teachers can be given more examples along with constructive ideas about how to use this potentially rich source of material with their students.

The move towards shared drafting within the KS3 Framework, in which the relationship between reading and writing can be actively cemented, is an extremely positive step. However gaining access to the drafts of established writers is not so easy. W.H. Auden scorned the idea of publishing drafts. He disapproved of the publication of T.S. Eliot's *The Waste Land* drafts on the grounds that there was 'not a line he left out which makes one wish he'd kept it ... this sort of thing encourages amateurs to think "Oh, look – I could have done as well."' (Newman, 1985: 292). In stating his case, Auden seems to be missing the point: drafts let readers into the writing of a poem in ways which a final published piece never can. Far from making the process seem an easy one, they can at least unravel some of the mystique of how a poet works with language. In this chapter published poets Moniza Alvi, Jackie Kay, Debjani Chatterjee, Ian McMillan, Brian Moses, Paul Violi, Cliff Yates and Clive Wilmer discuss their drafting techniques and offer powerful insights into the development of specific poems. The material is appropriate for a variety of age groups from upper primary to post-16. It is accompanied by a list of further resources and suggestions on how to use drafts in the classroom to further students' understanding of a craft which has remained an unnecessary mystery for too long. I am extremely grateful to those poets who have given me permission to use their drafts and have been so willing to contribute insights in to their working practices.

Poem(s) or draft(s)?

One poem which I have used on innumerable occasions to provoke discussion about drafting and the choices writers make is 'City Blues' by Mike Hayhoe. This poem provides a useful lead in to some of the issues which could be raised with a class when reading draft manuscripts. Hayhoe's ideas about reading and response to poetry, which he outlined with Patrick Dias in the influential *Developing Response to Poetry* (Dias and Hayhoe, 1988), have clearly informed this poem. The reader is invited to take a number of different routes through it and is offered many different permutations of words. The poem is a real 'event' in the spirit of Louise Rosenblatt (1978) and the reader makes the poem.

City Blues
Sunday dawn in a November city

the bully / light\wades in
          \ sun /
sets glass aflame
/slams\/dark\ shadows on anything
\puts/ \hard/
not big enough to take it.

The wind / strips \ trees
             \unzips/
makes them tittletattle
harsh small talk
/ puts \ their leaves into a lurch
\drives/
somewhere.

A sheet of paper

/followed\ by a coke can
\ chased /
takes ridiculously to the air
/ floats\ into the sunlight
\ flaps /
is a /swan\
     \ bird /

tumbles
knows its place

as the less fortunate should.

In the /shadow\
    \ shade /

this /miniscule\ steeple
   \small   /
comes to the point
which is more than can be said
for the big-time/corporations\
           \companies /
and their /skyscrapers\
      \sky-spoilers/
/napalmed\by that
\lit up   /
lousy sun.

Mike Hayhoe

This poem could be used in a number of different ways:

- With a new class it is an excellent stimulus for introducing or reminding pupils about some of the principles of drafting and working with drafting partners. Do the students think there is a main poem crying to get out of this piece? What is the impact of the different word choices on sound, image, overall meaning, etc.? Which choices might different writers and readers make? Why? When pupils are looking at their partners' drafts how do they read them? How can partners support one another in making effective choices?
- When discussing the nature of poetry, 'City Blues' can raise such questions as: is this a poem as it stands or is it a draft? What has the writer left the reader to do? Why ?

How do poets draft?

I asked this question of a number of published poets, many of whom regularly give writing workshops and performances in UK schools. Their responses have been combined with comments gleaned from previously published material on other writers' working methods. Together they provide starting points for classroom discussion about the processes of writing poetry and new strategies which teachers might adopt to develop their students' skills further.

The poets

Moniza Alvi: the first of her four collections, *The Country at My Shoulder* (OUP, 1993) was selected for the New Generation Poets promotion. Her latest is *Souls* (Bloodaxe, 2002). After a long career as a secondary school teacher, she now works as a freelance writer and tutor for the Open College of the Arts.

Debjani Chatterjee has published four collections of poetry including *I was that woman* (Hippopotamus, 1989) and her work has been widely anthologised. She is editor of the critically acclaimed *Redbeck Anthology of British South Asian Poetry* (Redbeck, 2000).

Jackie Kay is a poet, dramatist and prose writer. She has three poetry collections published by Bloodaxe including *Off Colour* (1998). *The Frog Who Dreamed She Was an Opera Singer* (Bloomsbury, 1998) is her latest collection for young children.

Ian McMillan is a born performer both on stage and radio. He has been writer in residence at Barnsley Football Club and in many other locations. He has five collections of poetry published by Carcanet. *The Invisible Villain* (Macmillan, 2002) is his latest collection for children.

Brian Moses is a poet, anthologist and frequent workshop leader in schools. His anthologies for Macmillan include *The Secret Lives of Teachers*, *Aliens Stole My Underpants* and *Are We Nearly There Yet?* (Macmillan, 2002).

Paul Violi is the author of 10 volumes of poetry and one book of prose. *Breakers: Selected Poems* was published by Coffee House Press (2000). He lives in Putnam Valley, New York, and teaches at New York University and Columbia University.

Clive Wilmer is a freelance writer, editor and anthologist who teaches English at Cambridge University. His collections include *Selected Poems* (Carcanet, 1995) and *The Falls* (Worple Press, 2000).

Cliff Yates is a deputy head teacher and author of *Jumpstart* (Poetry Society, 1999) and *14 Ways of Listening to the Archers* (Smith/Doorstop, 1994).

Questions and answers

When did you learn to draft poems?

Jackie Kay says she learned to draft at the same time as she started writing as a child: 'I would always rewrite and rewrite till I got them to say what I wanted them to say. I think rewriting and writing are like siamese twins, joined at the hip. You have to do both. It is not popular with kids in school but they have to learn that if they want to be writers then they have to rewrite, like Beckham practising his free kicks for hours before doing them for real.' A number of other poets refer to advice they have either been given directly or read by other writers. The American poet Paul

Violi is influenced by Ben Jonson's advice to write poems in paragraph form first: 'He informs us (through the offices of the obliging William Drummond of Hawthornden in his *Conversations*) that he wrote his poems out in prose before versifying them' (Hollander, 1961: 10). For Cliff Yates 'the best advice [he has] come across is Ernest Hemingway's; stop when it's all going well – if you go on too long, you drain the life out of it'. In his experience beginning writers have 'a debilitating tendency to be "precious" about the first draft and not to want to change it.' This tendency is something which Clive Wilmer was quick to stamp out in his own early writing. For him it was a case of observing others and learning through experience:

> I'm not sure that I ever did *learn* to draft. When I began writing, I tended to work on the assumption that the first draft would be the final one, though of course there'd be a hesitation between alternatives as I wrote. I think I pretty soon realised that, in most cases, a good poem would probably not emerge until I'd worked on a text a good deal – in other words revised. I'm talking about my late teens here. When I was about 20 I met Thom Gunn and was impressed by what I learnt of his methods. He told me that his poem 'Innocence' took six months to write and went through innumerable drafts. This convinced me that, if you wanted to do your best, you had to work really hard on your poems.

Debjani Chatterjee does not remember learning to draft poems 'in any formal way' and comments that this lack of teaching 'seems strange because we were certainly given a lot of poetry to read.' When she was a teenager she tried to study the craft of poetry more seriously 'but poetry remained for me a very solitary activity and my first poetry workshops weren't until I was an adult in England. Of course drafting poems was a valuable part of the workshop experience'. Moniza Alvi thinks she also learned to draft through attending workshops. This experience made her more critical of her own work and 'more ambitious'. She values the constructive comments made by other writers which helped redrafting: 'There are often blind spots – things that need changing that you don't recognise yourself, especially soon after writing a poem.'

How would you describe the stage *before* you write the first draft of any poem? What activities characterise this stage (e.g. carrying phrases in your head, lists)?

For Paul Violi this stage of writing can vary according to the type of poem he is writing, while Ian McMillan reveals that all of his poems 'start with a bundle of ideas and images; they pop into my head and I let them swim about for a bit before I put any kind of shape to them'. These ideas, which may seem very separate at first (as can be seen in his description of writing 'The Destiny Girls') gradually begin to mix together before he writes anything down. Jackie Kay describes a similar experience, using imagery which would be excellent to share with young writers:

> Sometimes a phrase, often a phrase spoken by somebody else, sticks in my head; sometimes an expression takes me back to my childhood; sometimes it is just an idea that buzzes around like a bee looking for the jar of honey, which is the language that will come for the idea.

Moniza Alvi describes a feeling of 'congestion, something buzzing, a very vague feeling which can become quite unsettling if it goes on for more than a day or two'. Sometimes she will begin to work out a poem in her head, if she has no opportunity to write it down. However, in contrast to Ian McMillan, she avoids this because it 'usually leads to a poem being "worked out" too quickly'.

For Debjani Chatterjee the stage before the first draft can vary 'but sometimes it is feeling a certain mood and atmosphere, and visualising the content of the poem'. She thinks that a Romantic feeling of 'recollection in tranquillity' was definitely present when she began work on 'A Winter's Morning in Timarpur' (which is included later in the chapter). She writes:

> Little things that I would notice about my rather unkempt garden in Sheffield (a black and white cat often stalks through it and is the catalyst that provided this poem) triggered associations of other times in another garden in Old Delhi and in my mind I was transported to a warmer clime and a garden that I know and love.

Clive Wilmer plays a slightly different waiting game with his ideas. He might recognise 'the potential for a poem in a particular subject' long before he writes a poem. However, before writing it down, he needs what he describes as 'some verbal spur'. This could be a phrase, line, image, device or some other trigger. He goes on to comment that 'sometimes a poem begins to happen when I see some connection between a long-cherished subject and a poetic form'. The point at which form enters the equation in the writing process is interesting to consider. For Debjani Chatterjee the form is usually determined at the first draft stage. John Foster, interviewed by James Carter, says 'the form develops from and is suggested by what you think of or write down initially' (Carter, 2001: 18). This may be true in many cases, although I can think of occasions where finding a workable form for a poem has occurred much later while drafting, and this realisation of what was appropriate has suddenly brought the poem together. In their primary and early secondary English lessons students will be introduced to a range of forms and poetic models. A mark of progression in their poetry writing will be the extent to which they can select and/or adapt forms for themselves which are appropriate for the meanings they want to make.

Most of the poets thought that ideas needed time to gestate and could not be rushed on to the page. Brian Moses is keen to grab ideas if he sees them coming, even if he might not develop them into poems until much later on. Clive Wilmer comments that often his poems will 'start' when he is engaged in an activity requiring very little thought such as walking, cycling or even having a bath. While it is not possible to install baths in every classroom or regularly allow students too much freedom to roam, these observations reinforce that students need periods of time for creative and extended thinking, writing and reading which the National Literacy Strategy with its four-part lesson structure appears not to allow for. Edwin Morgan, writing before the NLS was a glimmer in anyone's eye, argues that this reception of ideas is the 'given' element in poetry whereas the craft of writing is the variable factor:

> it is certainly true that poets have to have an apprenticeship in the craft side of their writing. What it is important to remember, however, is that the other side of their writing, the inspirational or imaginative, is equally necessary and may loom large. To meet, to woo, to tempt, to attract the inspirational and imaginative spirits, no amount of craft will help, and the mind of the would-be poet must at all costs be prepared to be open and tentative and exploratory, open above all, even at times to the edge of passiveness ... (Morgan, 1994: 58–9)

For many writers there is another dimension to this initial thinking process: in which language will they generate the ideas? T.S. Eliot thought that someone could not be a bilingual poet: 'one language must be the one you express yourself in in poetry, and you've got to give up the other for that purpose' (Hall, 1959, in Plimpton, 1985: 34). The poets Derek Walcott and Amryl Johnson have both discussed the experience of writing and thinking in Creole and English. In a BBC radio interview with Melvyn Bragg, Walcott explained how he could think and draft in English and Creole, depending on the subject of the poem. For Johnson her first attempt to draft in Creole was a conscious decision, an intense visual experience in which which she 'had only to capture the moments and translate them into an appropriate form' (Johnson, 1985: 43). The question about which language(s) one can think and write poetry in would be worth exploring with bilingual learners.

How/where do you tend to write your *first* drafts?

The notebook or hard-backed exercise book still seems to be the most common location for first drafts, although Brian Moses uses a dictaphone to record ideas when he is travelling around. Cliff Yates will 'quarry' his notebook for poems. Clive Wilmer deliberately transfers lines or notes on scraps of paper into his hard-backed lined exercise book 'leaving gaps between them'. Philip Larkin followed a similar practice. He would stick adverts, newspaper clippings, sketches and letters into his notebook. His first notebook contains an advert for Millets clothing, from which he copied out descriptions and phrases, presumably with the intention of using them in a poem, although references to such items as driving gauntlets and genuine sheepskin boots are not immediately apparent in his work. Larkin would also number and date his drafts, commenting on those which he felt were finished and suitable for publishing. Edward Thomas always carried a notebook. While on country walks or staying with friends, he made detailed jottings for future use even if he sometimes doubted their relevance (Harvey, 1999: 10). Information about notebooks is worth sharing with students, especially if they are using drafting books in the way described in Chapter 2. They should learn to see their drafting books as storehouses of separate ideas which can be sifted through, linked together and developed in many different ways.

For most of the poets, many of whom are constantly on the move between workshops, readings and other events, the location for drafting can, it seems, be anywhere. Train journeys are popular. Moniza Alvi needs to be alone when drafting and prefers to write in her peaceful attic room if she can.

At what point (if at all) do you usually begin drafting on the computer screen? Do you think using a computer causes you to draft any differently than when you work on paper? If so, please try to say how.

Ian McMillan usually moves from 'drafting in [his] head' to writing on screen without drafting on the page. He feels (and I agree) that it is important for students to be aware that all writers draft differently. By gaining experience of a variety of drafting methods students should be in a better position to decide which are the most effective methods for them. Debjani Chatterjee also feels able to move straight on to the personal computer (PC) although she does prefer the untidiness of a first handwritten draft. She writes: 'drafting straight onto the computer – even the first draft – makes the product appear very much neater. Instead of words being crossed out, it's so easy to delete them'.

Cliff Yates likes to 'draft' in his head and will work on two or three poems at the same time. He will often leave poems on his notebook page for weeks before typing them up:

When it's typed, I work quickly and intuitively, coming back to a poem again and again until it settles. The main thing I do is cut – explanations, endings. I prefer poems that don't reach conclusions or 'make a point' so resist this in my own work. As soon as I detect a lack of energy in the writing, I stop, or change direction.

Paul Violi begins to use the computer when he senses 'that an idea is about to snowball'. He, and many others, feel that the word processor is an invaluable tool – especially if they carry out numerous revisions on their work. Most of the poets begin work in longhand. Moniza Alvi likes to start by using a fountain pen 'because of the fast flow of ink which can keep up with thoughts'. Jackie Kay moves onto the computer after two or three drafts. She feels that using a computer makes her draft differently than on paper. She comments on the contrast between using a typewriter and a PC:

> I still think that the notebook and the typewriter were better for poetry (not so good for fiction) because they force you to write out the whole thing again. When you do that you notice things that you might not with the computer and you make fresh choices all over again. You ponder over every word and you are decisive about punctuation and line breaks. The computer allows you to look at your lines differently and you might break the line just because it looks symmetrical on the screen.

Clive Wilmer, who is very superstitious about changing his writing procedures, still prefers to use a typewriter after first working on a poem in longhand in his notebook. His comments on his working methods, the physicality of handwriting poems and the objectivity which print can offer would be interesting to explore with students when they are reflecting on themselves as writers:

> I think there must be some connection between the physical energy of handwriting and the rhythms of verse. I couldn't begin writing on a machine, though oddly I do precisely that with prose. I usually stick to handwriting until I have a full draft of the poem – or perhaps a draft of one section of it As soon as I've done that, I feel a need to see it objectified by print. So I type it out and read it aloud to myself over and over again. I then write corrections, emendations, possible alternatives and so on in the margins. Sometimes, if I'm working over a longish period, I will use pens of different colours to be able to remember which stage an emendation belongs to. Or I used to do that. When it feels as if I've corrected everything I need or want to, I type the whole thing out again in its new version. Then I leave it for at least a day. If the poem has any complexity I shall revise it slightly several more times.

... the use of a machine seems to me to objectify what one has written – helps one to see it as an artefact, just like an artefact made by another person. It also helps to see how well your layout represents what you hear in your head.

Colour coding elements of different drafts is a practice which other writers also use. In his first poetry notebook Philip Larkin writes in purple crayon and grey pencil along with ink to distinguish between the drafts of his poem 'Ballad of The North Ship'. James Joyce demonstrates spectacular use of colour coding in the vast wide notebook of his first draft of *Ulysses*.

What do you usually do to a poem when redrafting it?

All the poets redraft in some way, viewing this as at the heart of the creative process. Paul Violi notes: 'Some short poems present more possibilities than longer works. I enjoy making something; revision sustains enjoyment. When verbs that insinuate meaning and for that advance metaphorical notions click in, I know I'm on to something'.

Clive Wilmer focuses on greater accuracy of language, 'this word rather than that one', and is also attentive to rhythm and euphony. Other actions during redrafting include: identifying unnecessary repetitions and insignificant words; discovering an aspect of the poem is not as clear as it seemed; further correction of punctuation. Interestingly, only one poet directly mentioned using a thesaurus during redrafting. Moniza Alvi's redrafting includes questions to herself which can be asked at various stages in the process:

focus on beginning and end – does it start where it should? Is there a satisfying sense of an ending? Have the best words been chosen? Are there unnecessary words? I focus on rhythm, tone, experiment with line lengths, try different forms, look at metaphors and similes – are they apt? Does the title encapsulate the poem, say too much or too little?

Redrafting can involve letting a poem stand for a while untouched so that it can be returned to afresh. Some poets comment that they might leave a piece for a gap of a few days or even six months. Moniza Alvi sadly notes: 'sometimes a poem never seems to quite get there'. This is an important lesson for young writers to learn if they are to gain genuine experiences of the process.

Debjani Chatterjee may ask her husband (who is also a poet) to be her 'first audience' at this stage. She describes how stanzas can be removed, amended or even replaced during redrafting, and says 'it is also possible for additional stanzas to be inserted to further develop a theme/image or introduce new themes/images'. It is essential for young writers to be aware of this structural aspect of redrafting if their redrafting is go to beyond mere polishing. In her insightful book *Writings on Writing* (1995: 46) May Sarton summarises redrafting succinctly as 'a breaking down process as well as a building up process' and goes on to demonstrate this with reference to worksheets of her own poems. This image of construction would be a good one to use with students. What other similarities can they find between building, for example, a new house and a new poem?

During revision whole lines and phrases may need to be abandoned. Those 'darlings' which provided the initial inspiration for a poem are frequently the ones which are most necessary (as well as the hardest) to lose because they no longer suit the way the draft is developing. I think it is important for students to realise that, if the image or phrase is an original one, a writer can recycle it and eventually use it elsewhere. If students have been using a drafting book, they will still have a record of such lines and can revisit them at a later date. Not all abandoned lines are gems however. The poet and workshop leader Peter Sansom strongly advises: 'there is no room for the dull or inconsequential word/line/image. If something's not working *for* the poem, it is working *against* it'. (Sansom, 1994: 50)

When young writers are working on the final stages of revising their drafts, they can be loathe to part with what might be unnecessary words (such as 'and', 'the' and 'of'). It is only after shaving away some of these that they will be able to let the sound and shape of the poem finally come alive. In an informal essay on his writing processes, Douglas Dunn comments on the preponderance of such words at the beginning of lines in his earlier drafts:

> for the sake of spontaneity, getting thoughts and feelings down on paper, my habit is to leave these crudities alone for the time being. Instinct and imagination ought to be given their heads in the earlier stages of making a poem, even if the writing is shoddy and wayward as a result and the metrical pulse is all over the place. (Dunn, 1994: 93)

Eventually he edits out the 'crudities'. In doing so, he acknowledges he has learned from reading the work of poets like Robert Browning whose line openings rarely begin with 'weak words'. Dunn's observes that metrical poetry, especially of the rhyming variety, *and* free verse 'are obsessed by line-endings' and that it is apparent when 'a poet's concentration has been applied vigorously to the right-hand side of a poem, leaving the left-hand side open to a string of weak words and expressions' (Dunn, 1994: 93). In light of this observation, it would be a useful strategy, during the latter stages of redrafting, for students to focus on the words used in their line openings, and, if appropriate, compare their impact with those of openings by other poets.

At what stage(s) do you tend to revise punctuation?

Paul Violi will work on punctuation to ensure a sharper timing of a line. Jackie Kay works on punctuation all the way through her drafting. She gives considerable thought to which punctuation marks she should use where:

> A dash hurries you along more than a comma. An exclamation mark feels really OTT. I don't like question marks unless they are totally necessary because they make the reader read it the way you are and they feel a bit manipulative like Hollywood movies that set out to make people cry. If anything I like simple punctuation, not too overstated so that the poem can breathe. I probably err on the side of under punctuating my poems.

A number of poets commented that they would make some punctuation changes along the way but would pay most attention to these during the later stages of redrafting and before submitting for publication. The American poet Anne Sexton found punctuation one of the most difficult elements of writing: 'The punctuating can change the whole meaning, and my life is full of little dots and dashes'. As a result she would let her editors help her with punctuation (Kelves, in Plimpton, 1985: 271). As can be seen later in the chapter, Edward Thomas made one very significant change to the punctuation of 'Adlestrop' in the final stage of working on his poem.

How many drafts do you tend to write?

Redrafting is not an exact science: the number of drafts produced can vary enormously. Five or six drafts is not uncommon, although some poets will write 20, 40 or even more! Cliff Yates says that some of his poems 'have been through dozens of drafts, others arrive more-or-less intact, it depends on the poem'. Jackie Kay usually redrafts around 12 times. She says that ultimately 'I like my poems to appear simple and accessible, and I don't like the idea of anybody being able to see the writer sweat'. In an essay on her writing, Amryl Johnson says that she drafts poetry (unlike her prose) in pencil: 'I may need to go to a third draft before I achieve what I set out to. Only the poet knows when it is finished'. (Johnson, 1985: 44). Not all poets, however, write down their final drafts for themselves. Mary Wordsworth acted as an amanuensis for her husband William. It is her hand, with its instructions to printers and the 'I wandered like a lonely ...' error on the opening line which can be seen on the manuscript of Wordsworth's most celebrated poem 'The Daffodils'.

The distinctions between drafts can also become blurred: some poets will count all their handwritten work as one draft, while all their drafts and collaborations written on screen might be replaced by a single record of the final poem. The issue of keeping track of authors' word-processed drafts and their e-mailed literary correspondence is an increasing problem for the British Library and other manuscript collections around the world.

Using draft manuscripts and commentaries by contemporary poets

The examples and accounts of drafting included in the following pages show the development of a series of poems which would offer challenges to different age groups. When working with drafts students can get much closer to the thinking processes which are an essential element of a poem's composition. In exploring the material, I have suggested a variety of ways in which drafts like these could be used in the classroom.

The first batch of draft material included here has been written by Brian Moses. It charts some of the drafting stages for his poem 'Ssssnake Hotel' (a poem suitable for Year 6 and Year 7 pupils as well as many other readers). His 'original notes' and 'more notes', which he also labels as drafts 1 and 2 (Figure 3.1), demonstrate a number of processes and students could identify what these are. He is: collecting ideas together; listing different types of snakes; thinking about the jobs they might do as well as other associations. He is also developing a rhythm, using mainly three or four lined clusters of images, some of which rhyme. Although the final lines of the poem are already in a recognisable form, the rest is fragmented. When faced with such material pupils could be asked to decide which lines the poet might be most interested in or keen to develop (before they go on to look at the next draft).

In draft 3 (Figure 3.2) Moses fleshes out his original list of snakes to experiment with new phrases and verses involving some of the listed items (for example, the water snakes and the snakes and ladders). In a number of cases he offers alternatives. Use of rhyme including internal rhyme, has strengthened considerably. It is interesting too to see how the potential ending is also being considered as the beginning. This draft would provide a good opportunity to lead into work on openings and endings of other poems. Pupils could also make their own lists of snakes and use rhyming dictionaries to collect suitable rhyming words.

In draft 4 (Figure 3.3) the poet experiments with different ordering of his lines. He is beginning to settle on the idea of certain blocks of lines to form verses. The phrase 's-s-s-snake hotel' is reintroduced into the opening and closing sentences. Eventually this will become 'ssssnake hotel'.

<u>Original notes</u>   (1)

<u>Snake hotel</u>

An affectionate python
will welcome you
to the s-s-s-snake hotel
The snake hotel

If competition winners

Boas
Mambas
cobras
pythons
carpet snake
vipers.
Anaconda
adder
Snake & ladder

If holidays = the sun
could end up as snake dinner
it wouldn't be much fun.

He'll politely enquire
if you're feeling well
as he welcome you
to the snake hotel

Pythons & mambas eat the snake hotel

The chef is an Indian python
the waiters are carpet snakes
The desk clerk is a cobra
the porter

Your dinner off to sleep
& softly ready holes

The rooms have hidden vipers
who will seek you out in your sleep
& cover you with vipery kisses.

Spend a weekend in hell
at the snake hotel
bookings are low

& you'll thank us soon
you know very well
for our introducing you
to the snake hotel

an over-affectionate python
will hug you almost to death
squeeze out yr breath

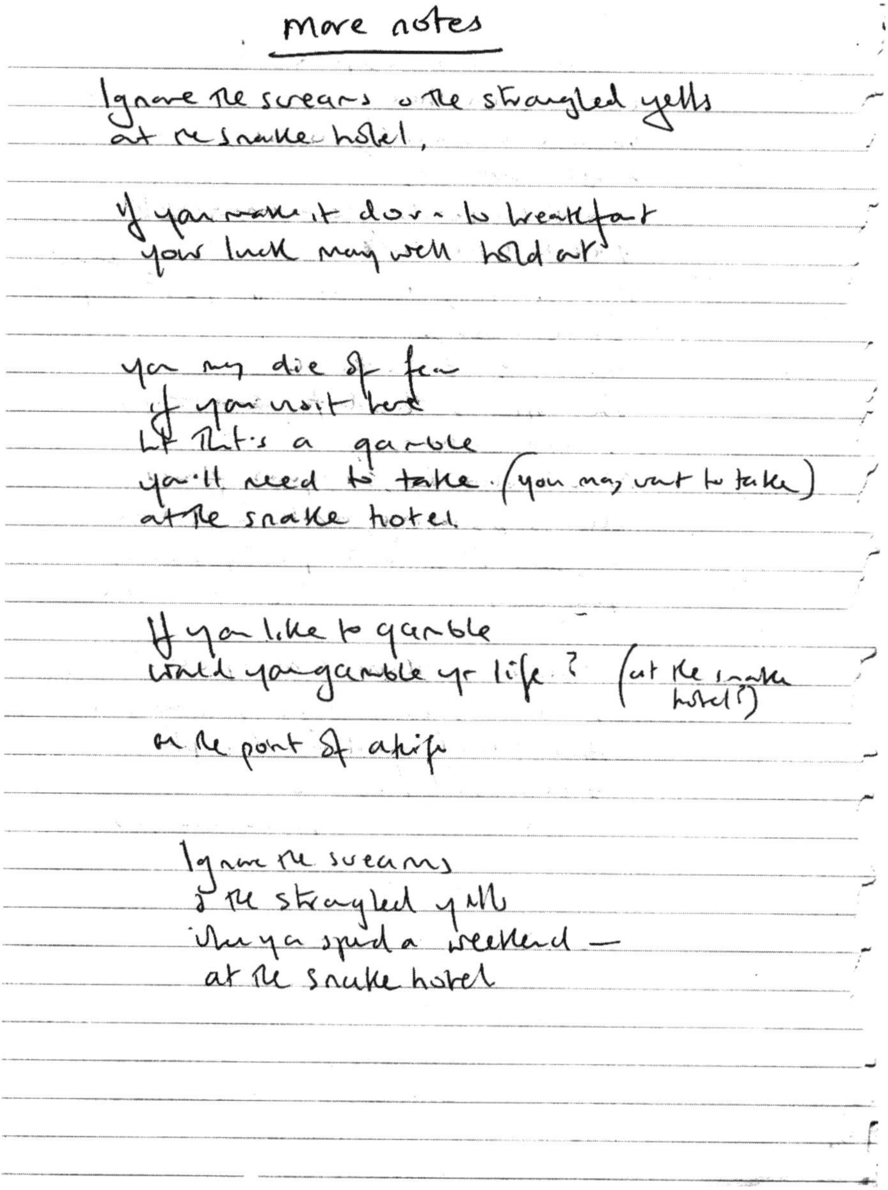

more notes

Ignore the screams o the strangled yells
at the snake hotel,

If you make it down to breakfast
your luck may well hold out

you may die of fear
if you visit bed
Lt That's a gamble
you'll need to take. (you may want to take)
at the snake hotel

If you like to gamble
would you gamble yr life ? (at the snake hotel?)
on the point of a knife

Ignore the screams
& the strangled yells
when you spend a weekend —
at the snake hotel

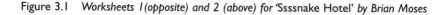

Figure 3.1 *Worksheets 1 (opposite) and 2 (above) for 'Ssssnake Hotel' by Brian Moses*

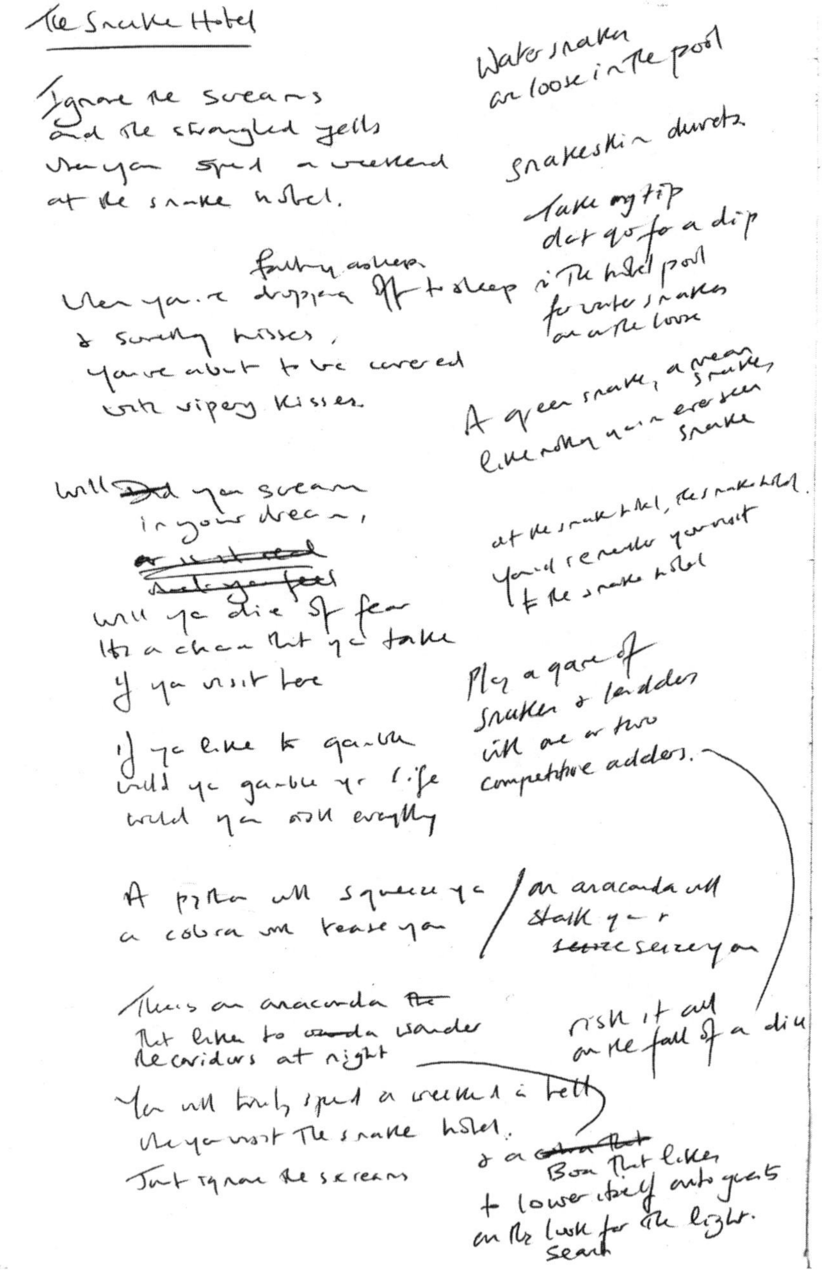

The Snake Hotel

Ignore the screams
and the strangled yells
when you spend a weekend
at the snake hotel.

When you're dropping off to sleep [fast asleep]
& sweetly kisses,
you're about to be covered
with vipery kisses.

Will [Did] you scream
in your dream,
~~or instead~~
~~make you feel~~
will you die of fear
It's a chance that you take
if you visit here

if you like to gamble
will you gamble your life
would you risk everything

A python will squeeze you
a cobra will tease you

There's an anaconda ~~that~~
that likes to ~~wander~~ wander
the corridors at night

You will truly spend a weekend & hell
when you visit the snake hotel.
Just ignore the screams

Water snakes
are loose in the pool

snakeskin duvets.

Take my tip
don't go for a dip
in the hotel pool
for water snakes
on the loose

A green snake, a mean snake
like nothing you've ever seen
snake

at the snake hotel, the snake hotel.
you'd remember your visit
to the snake hotel

Play a game of
snakes & ladders
with one or two
competitive adders.

an anaconda will
stalk you
~~seize~~ seize you

risk it all
on the fall of a dice

& a ~~cobra that~~ Boa that likes
to lower itself onto guests
on the look for the light.
search

Figure 3.2   *Worksheet 3 for 'Ssssnake Hotel' by Brian Moses*

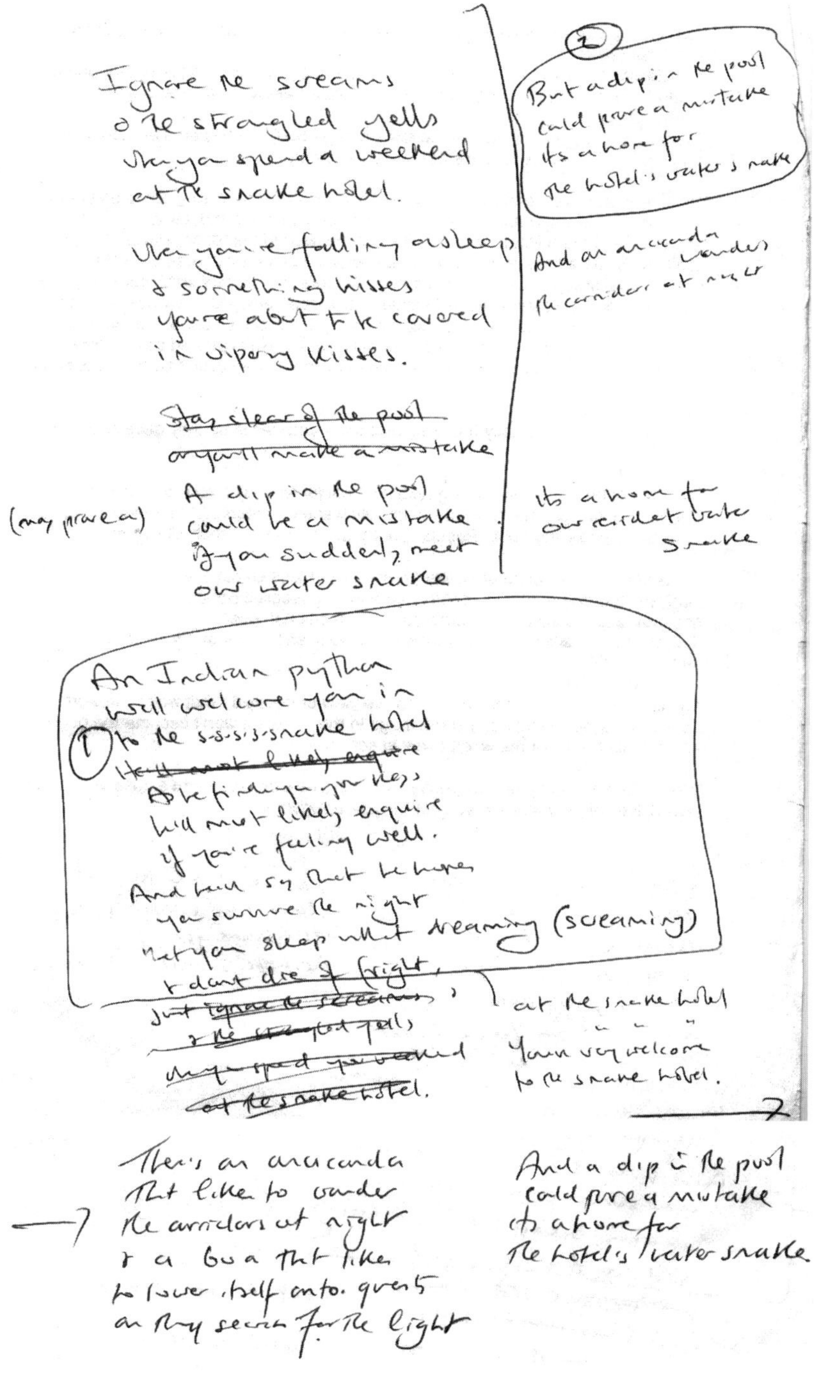

Ignore the screams
o the strangled yells
when you spend a weekend
at the snake hotel.

When you're falling asleep
& something kisses
you're about to be covered
in vipery kisses.

~~Stay clear of the pool~~
~~or you'll make a mistake~~

(may prove a)   A dip in the pool
could be a mistake
if you suddenly meet
our water snake

② But a dip in the pool
could prove a mistake
its a home for
the hotel's water snake

And an anaconda
wanders
the corridors at night

its a home for
our resident snake
snake

An Indian python
will welcome you in
① to the s-s-s-snake hotel
~~He will most likely enquire~~
Before finding you a bed,
will most likely enquire
if you're feeling well.
And will say that he hopes
you survive the night
that you sleep without dreaming (screaming)
& don't die of fright.
~~Just ignore the screams~~
~~& the strangled yells~~
~~unexpected you received~~
~~at the snake hotel.~~

at the snake hotel
" " "
You're very welcome
to the snake hotel.

②

—7   There's an anaconda
that likes to wander
the corridors at night
& a boa that likes
to lower itself onto guests
on any search for the light

And a dip in the pool
could prove a mistake
its a home for
the hotel's water snake

Figure 3.3   *Worksheet 4 for 'Ssssnake Hotel' by Brian Moses*

The Snake Hotel

An Indian python
will welcome you
to the Ssssnake hotel.
As he finds you your keys
he'll ~~most likely~~ enquire *maybe*
if you're feeling well.
And he'll say that he hopes
you survive the night,
that you sleep without screaming
and don't die of fright
at the Ssssnake hotel.

There's an anaconda
that likes to wander
the corridors at night,
and a boa that likes
to lower itself onto guests
as they search for the light.
In the hotel pool
there's a water snake
so taking a dip
could prove a mistake
at the Ssssnake hotel.

When you're ~~dropping~~ *falling*
a ~~off to~~ sleep and ~~nearby~~
something hisses,
~~then you know~~
~~you'll soon be covered~~ *you're about to be covered*
with vipery kisses.
~~And from the room next door~~   *And the room next door*
~~if you hear cracks and groans~~   *with its cracks & groans,*
~~its probably a python~~   *its probably a python*
~~crushing someone's bones~~   *crushing somebody's bones.*
at the Ssssnake hotel

Just ignore the screams
and the strangled yells
when you spend a weekend
at the Ssssnake hotel.

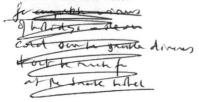

Figure 3.4   *Draft 5 of 'Ssssnake Hotel' by Brian Moses*

Pupils might want to think about if there is a difference in the sounds of these two phrases as well as to consider other ways in which they might order the lines.

By draft 5 (Figure 3.4) the poem has been transferred from notes written in biro on the back of scrap paper to a word-processed page. The main drafting work shown here is on verses three and four, with changes being marked on the printout. Using this, or any other, example of an annotated printout should reinforce the fact that printed material is frequently incomplete. A regular rhyme scheme is now in place and the poet tinkers with the choice of certain words and phrases, mainly in the third verse. It is interesting to see how 'when you're dropping off to sleep' changes to 'falling asleep' before being completely replaced by 'And if, by chance, you lie awake' in the final version. Students could usefully explore the differences between the choice of verbs and structures here as well as their impact when used with the second person.

In the final draft the watersnakes have completely disappeared from the poem. In doing so, they present further questions for young writers to investigate. For example, they could trace how these lines have been used throughout the drafts and exploring potential reasons for their abrupt departure. Were they the weakest link? Could they reappear in another poem? Their ideas could lead to the writing of spin-off poems in the same style or a series of questions from the reader (or the snakes?) to the poet.

The Ssssnake Hotel
An Indian Python will welcome you
to the Ssssnake hotel.
As he finds your keys he'll maybe enquire
if you're feeling well.
And he'll say that he hopes
you survive the night,
that you sleep without screaming
and don't die of fright
at the Sssnake hotel.

There's an anaconda that likes to wander
the corridors at night,
and a boa that will lower itself onto guests
as they search for the light.
And if, by chance, you lie awake
and nearby something hisses,
I warn you now, you're about to be covered
with tiny vipery kisses,
at the Sssnake hotel.   *(continued overleaf)*

And should you hear a chorus of groans
coming from the room next door,
and the python cracking someone's bones,
please don't go out and explore.
Just ignore all the screams
and the strangled yells
when you spend a weekend
at the Ssssnake hotel.

Brian Moses

In contrast, Ian McMillan's poetry seldom reaches so many draft stages, on paper at least. His poem 'The Destiny Girls', included here in its final published form, has been largely drafted in his head and is most suitable for pupils in upper primary and lower secondary classes, although (as with all the poems included in this chapter) adults can enjoy reading it too.

The Destiny Girls

Mum just stood there
At the car boot sale.
Her eyes were watering.
And she was looking upwards

At a vapour trail
Chalking the blue sky.
Dad was holding a flower pot,
One of fifteen,
All different sizes,
For two pounds.

He walked over to mum,
Clutching the flowerpot;
She held something up to him,
It was an old fashioned vinyl single.

I walked over to have a look:
It was called 'He Loves Me'
By The Destiny Girls.

Mum was crying.
Still looking up at the vapour trail
Chalking the blue sky,
And I wanted to ask what was happening.

Dad said to me
'She had a beautiful voice, your grandma,
could have been a star. This was her single,
her band, The Destiny Girls, got to about number
32...'

Dad had never talked about Grandma before.
Mum hadn't either.

She didn't speak now,
Just looked up at the vapour trails
Chalking the blue sky.

'They could have been famous,'
said Dad,
'If they hadn't got on that plane ...'

Mum said
'At least somebody bought it,
even though it's ended up here,
I'll buy it now, put it with the others.'

He Loves Me
By The Destiny Girls.

Overhead the planes hummed.

Ian McMillan

The poet's commentary gives a very clear indication of the stages of this poem's development.

Thoughts on Drafting *The Destiny Girls*
All of my poems start with a bundle of ideas and images; they pop into my head and I let them swim about for a bit before I put any kind of shape to them. This one started with a memory of a car boot sale I'd been to in Cleethorpes: I'd been looking through some old records and I suddenly thought 'What if I come across a copy of the only record I've ever made?' ('Now Then Davos' by The Circus of Poets, Lambs to the Slaughter Label, 1984.) Then I thought about the idea of fame and celebrity, how everybody wants to be famous. Then I went to see the musical 'Buddy', about Buddy Holly the rock and roll singer who was killed in a plane crash.

All those ideas began to mix up in my head. At this stage I'd written nothing down. At the time I was writing a lot of poems for my new book for 8–12 year olds, *The Invisible Villain*, but I didn't want to write just daft rhymey poems for kids, I wanted to write poems that would challenge them, would work for a wider audience.

Then the title came to me: The Destiny Girls. It sounded like the name of an all-girl band from the sixties or seventies. Then I scribbled a few notes, and the poem was still nothing like a poem. I decided at this stage that it wouldn't rhyme.

This was the Summer of 2001: I love looking up into the sky when I'm walking to the bus stop, and I love looking at the vapour trails of jets. I decided that's where the poem would start. I wanted the poem to be a bit mysterious, a bit strange. I also wanted it to be simple, to include no poetic things in it, to be just as simple as a conversation or a memory. I wanted the poem to suggest a story that could maybe carry on in the reader's head after they'd read it.

Only then did I start to write the poem on the computer, and because I'd been thinking about it for so long, I wrote it quickly, keeping it simple as I could. That's what often happens with me: I don't go through many drafts on the page, because I'm drafting it in my head. I realise that's not very useful, and that you need to show your drafts, but all writers are different!

I was quite pleased with the poem, and then September 11th happened. I wasn't sure whether I should put it in the book or not, but the publishers said I should. I don't enjoy looking up in the sky so much these days. History's rewritten the poem for me, somehow, and that's a strange, strange feeling.

Ian McMillan

These comments provide many starting points for discussion about drafting poetry and the way that meanings are made, as well as potential stimuli for writing poetry. Discussion points could include:

- how can a poem be a poem without 'poetic things' in it?
- which lines or parts of the poem might have been scribbled down first?
- what makes the poem carry on in the reader's head?
- why does the writer think history has rewritten his poem?
- did the publishers make the right decision?

Starting points for pupils' own writing could include:

- a 'found' object (from a charity shop, jumble sale or attic);
- reading vapour trails or cloud pictures;
- a family photograph;
- a song title;
- an obituary of a semi-famous person.

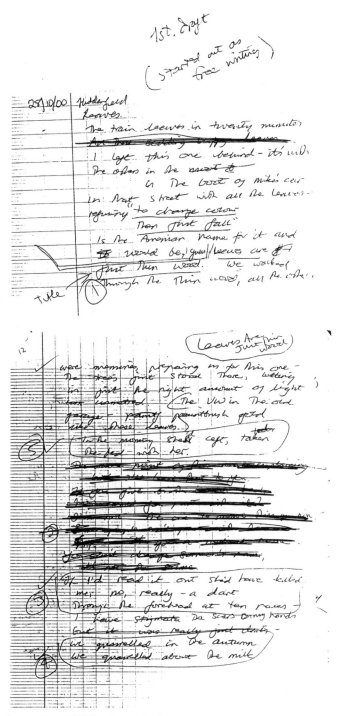

Figure 3.5   *Extract from Cliff Yates's notebook*

Both through his workshops and live performances, Ian McMillan has always been committed to unveiling the mysteries of the writing process to writers of all ages and ensuring that poetry is an enjoyable, even life affirming, experience. In the poetry anthology *Against the Grain* (McMillan, 1989) he includes a section of poets' reflections on drafting of poems which are all entitled 'Against the Grain'. The variety of responses and contrasting ways in which the writers work make this book an excellent resource for use in Year 9 and above.

Cliff Yates's drafts give a good example of how a poem can originate from free writing (for more on free writing please refer to Chapter 2). In this case the free writing stimulus was a single word – 'leaves'. As a lead-in to exploring the drafts, students could be given the same word and activity. In the extracts from his notebook (Figure 3.5) we can see how the poet has created the first draft by: quarrying the free-writing notes for ideas; finding a title; selecting certain lines and removing others; making decisions about the order of lines. In presenting students with draft material you may well want them to identify these actions for themselves.

Draft 1 is then typed up and another poem is brought alongside it which has been drafted at roughly the same time. In commenting on his drafting, Cliff Yates says that he likes to work on two or three poems at one time. Students might want to consider the advantages and disadvantages of drafting several poems at once.

Leaves Are Just Thin Wood

All the other woods are memories
preparing us for this one.

If I'd read it out she's have killed me.
No, really – a dart through the forehead.
Look at my hands – people call it stigmata
but really it's just darts.

We quarrelled in the autumn.
We quarrelled about the milk.
In the morning she'd left, taken the bed with her.

Poem

I'm from Birmingham
Let's go for a walk in the wood. It is raining.

Bring the billiard table.
I have the balls in my trouser pockets.
Can you manage?
Here, let me hold the door.

Yes I agree, the rain. Did I mention
the importance of parks in my writing?
It's not that interesting. Mind
the rosa rugosas, ~~their thorns,~~

and the climber with ~~red~~ orange hips.

Your lips are delicious, by the way.

The 'final' draft, which was first published in *The North*, is a synthesis of the two draft pieces. Many writers would argue that even at this final stage the writing is not complete. W.H. Auden and William Wordsworth revised (some would say disastrously) previously published poems later in life. Brian Moses can only leave a poem alone when it's finally published in a book (Carter, 2001: 15) and some poets who regularly perform their work will update topical references or change lines even while they are performing. It would be interesting to debate with students whether they think writers have the right to do this. Once, while attending an Arvon Foundation poetry writing course, Liz Lochhead, who was tutoring the course, told me I should think about reworking 'Reading Matters', a newly published sequence of poems. She advised me about several words she thought I could lose and ideas I could develop further. Although I did not agree with all her suggestions, many of them struck a chord and the poems were suddenly unfinished again. At the time this seemed cruel, but it was a valuable lesson that a writer can never draw a completely solid line under a 'final' draft.

The practice of combining drafts, or even previously published poems, and reworking them to make a new text is an aspect of drafting which students may not be familiar with. For example T.S. Eliot's poems 'The Hollow Men' and 'Ash Wednesday' were both published in earlier draft forms before becoming part of a sequence (Hall, 1985). When reading Cliff Yates's final draft, students might want to investigate how he has combined the two poems and to think about why he decided to do this. They could track how the free-writing stimulus 'leaves' has been used in the poem. They could also go back to their own drafting books and look at:

- free writing ideas they could now draft into poems;
- potential connections between notes or drafts they have written at different times.

Leaves Are Just Thin Wood

No, I don't read French.
Do you have a translation?
I'm from Birmingham.
Let's go for a walk in the woods. It's raining.

Bring the billiard table.
I have balls in my trouser pockets.
Can you manage?
Here, let me hold the door.

Yes I agree, the rain. Did I mention
the importance of parks in my writing?
It's not that interesting. Mind
the rosa rugosas, their thorns,

and the climber with the orange hips.
Your lips are delicious by the way.

All the other woods are memories
preparing us for this one.

If I told anyone she'd have killed me.
No, really – a dart through the forehead.
Look at my hands – people call it stigmata
but really it's just darts.

We quarrelled in the autumn.
We quarrelled about the milk.
In the morning she left, took the bed with her.

Cliff Yates

Paul Violi's first draft of 'Appeal to the Grammarians' provides a useful demonstration of how a poem can develop from an ending.

The white space surrounding this draft is covered with handwritten annotations added at various stages. These are reproduced overleaf in different fonts (Figure 3.6) to show how the poet is developing his ideas.

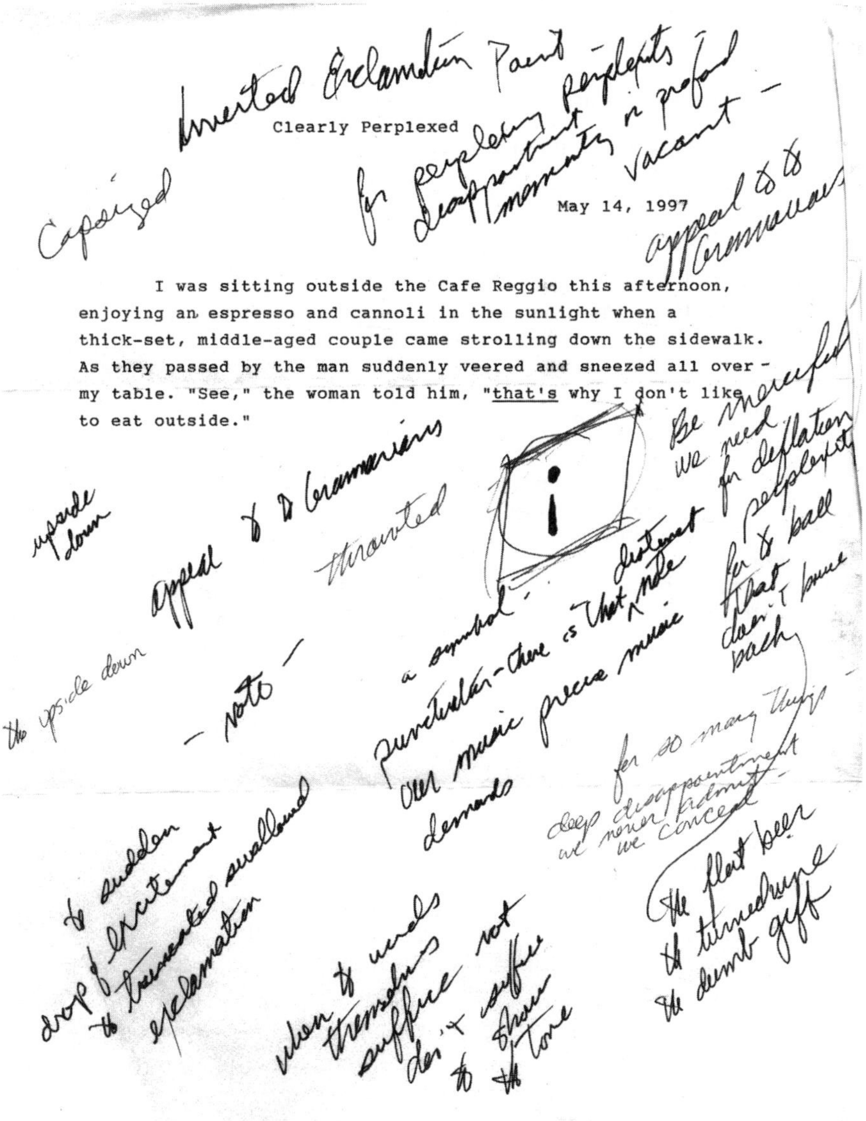

Figure 3.6 *Draft I of* 'Appeal to the Grammarians', *by Paul Violi* (above and overleaf)

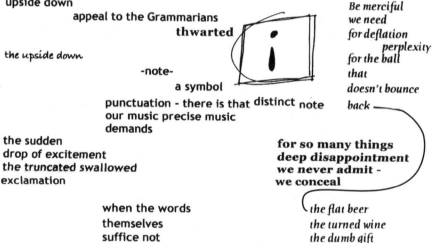

Limited Exclamation Point-
         for perplexing perplexents -
          disappointment
           memory is profound
            vacant -
Capsized   Clearly Perplexed

                                May 14, 1997

                appeal to the Grammarians

      I was sitting outside the Cafe Reggio this afternoon, enjoying an expresso and cannoli in the sunlight when a thick-set, middle-aged couple came strolling down the sidewalk. As they passed by the man suddenly veered and sneezed all over my table. "See," the woman told him, "_that's_ why I don't like to eat outside."

upside down
       appeal to the Grammarians
          thwarted

the upside down

          -note-
           a symbol
       punctuation - there is that distinct **note**
       our music precise music
       demands

the sudden
drop of excitement
the truncated swallowed
exclamation

         when the words
         themselves
         suffice not
         don't suffice
         to show the tone

Be merciful
we need
for deflation
     perplexity
for the ball
that
doesn't bounce
back ——

for so many things
deep disappointment
we never admit -
we conceal

the flat beer
the turned wine
the dumb gift

The inverted exclamation mark (or 'point' as Americans call it) is a central focus in Violi's thinking about this piece. This symbol could be a useful way in to the draft. (What does it seem to signal? How could it provide a key to the rest of the poem?) In the final draft the plea for the new punctuation mark has clearly taken shape:

Appeal to the Grammarians

May 14, 1997

We, the naturally hopeful, need a simple sign
for the myriad ways we're capsized.
We, who love language for its precision,
need a finer way to convey
disappointment and perplexity.
For speechlessness and all its inflections,
we need the inverted exclamation point.
For up-ended expectations,
For every time we are ambushed
by trivial or stupefying irony,
for pure incredulity, we deserve it.
For the dropped smile, the limp handshake,
for whoever has just unwrapped a dumb gift,
or taken the first sip of a flat beer,
or felt love or pond ice give way underfoot.
We need it for the air pocket, the scratch shot,
the child whose ball doesn't bounce back,
the flat tire at journey's outset,
the odyssey that ends up in Weehauken.
But mainly because I need it – here and now
as I sit outside the Cafe Reggio
staring at my expresso and canoli
after this middle-aged couple
came strolling by and he suddenly
veered and sneezed all over my table
and she said to him, 'See, <u>that's</u> why
I don't like to eat outside.'

Paul Violi

In considering how the poem has evolved from its first draft, students could use Paul Violi's annotations as a kind of primer for discussion. They could trace how his original idea has been used to support an argument. The way in which the poet transforms prose into poetry also needs considering. It provides a useful example for discussion of potential differences between poetry, prose and prose poems as well as a model for students' own work. They could go on to experiment with using their own prose notes as starting points for poems. The change of title merits further discussion, as does the introduction of the first person plural into the poem: what are possible reasons for these changes and additions? Before they read the final poem, students might want to use the first draft (in its unannotated form) as a first draft of their own poems and compare their completed poems with Violi's. 'Appeal to the Grammarians' could stimulate students' thinking about the purposes of grammar and experimentation with new punctuation marks of their own. What appeals might they make for their new inventions? This question could provoke lively discussion with a high-ability Year 9 class or even AS/A-level English Language and Literature students.

The example of Moniza Alvi's drafting is from a sequence of poems stemming from the creation myth. She says she was particularly inspired by Kipling's *Just So Stories*. Other titles in the sequence include: 'How the World Split in Two'; 'How the Answers Got Their Questions' and 'How the Animals Tried on Our Clothes'. The influence of reading on writing is important for all writers to acknowledge. Successful poets read and learn from other writers. Both Hull (1988) and Barrs and Cork (2001) highlight the importance of literature-rich environments where pupils can browse,

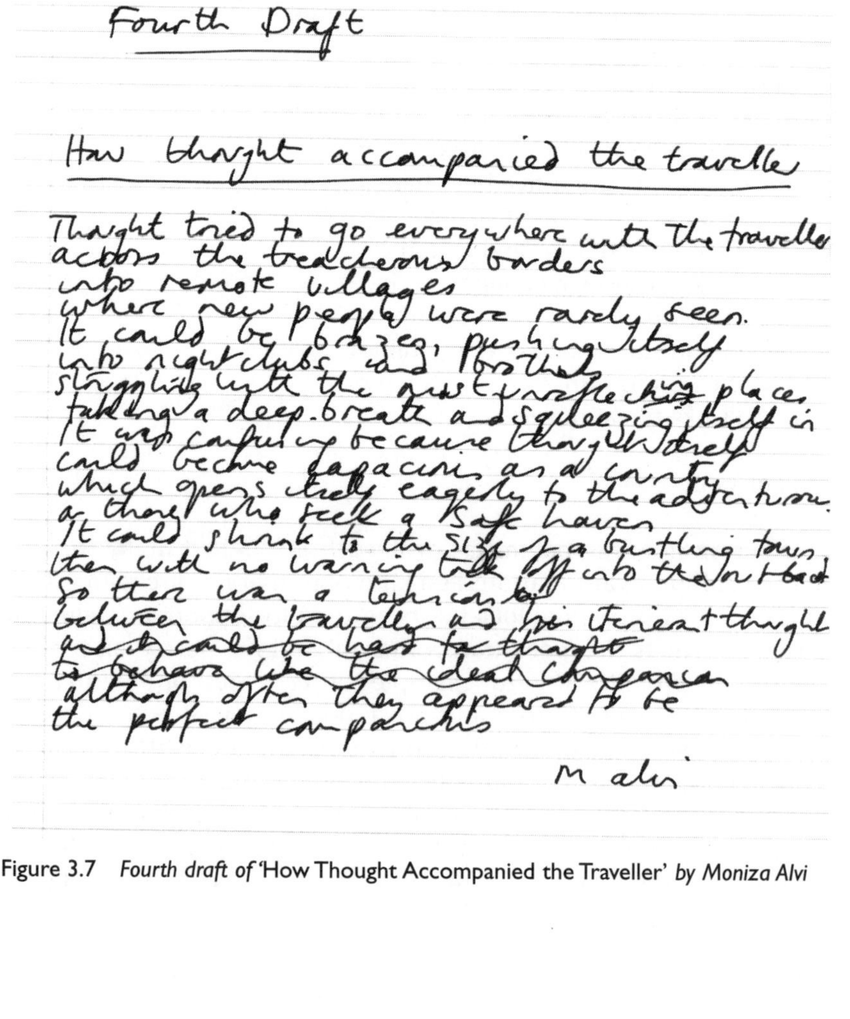

Figure 3.7   *Fourth draft of 'How Thought Accompanied the Traveller' by Moniza Alvi*

read and familiarise themselves with many different types of 'high-quality' texts. However, the reading which informs writing goes far beyond familiarisation with different text types. Poets are magpies who seek inspiration, borrow and adapt ideas from many sources.

Moniza Alvi notes that in this fourth draft (Figure 3.7), which is prior to the first computer draft, her poem has its basic shape but there is still reshaping and some rewording to be completed.

In what might be the final version of the poem (the sequence was still 'work in progress' when Moniza sent it to me) there are some notable adjustments to the form. It has become a 14-line poem consisting of a series of triplets and a closing couplet. Moniza Alvi comments that the poem fell naturally into this form after she had drafted it on the computer. She also notes '14 lines seems a satisfying length for this poem, though it doesn't have any other characteristics of a sonnet'. Although inexperienced writers are less likely to arrive at such a conclusion, they should be encouraged to experiment with arranging their draft lines into different stanza structures when working on screen and to compare the results. The idea that 14 lines is a 'satisfying length' is also an interesting one to explore with students.

How Thought Accompanied the Traveller (final? version)

Thought tried to go everywhere with the traveller,
across the treacherous borders, into remote
villages where strangers were scarcely seen.

It could be brazen, pushing itself into nightclubs
and brothels, struggling with unwelcoming places,
taking a deep breath and squeezing itself in.

And thought could become as capacious
as a country which opens its doors hospitably
to the adventurous, and the destitute.

It could shrink to the size of a quiet town,
then without warning trek off into the outback.
So there was tension between the traveller

and itinerant thought, although often
they appeared to be the perfect companions.

Moniza Alvi

Clive Wilmer's poem 'Bottom's Dream' would provide an excellent starting point for discussion of drafting with older students (especially those studying *A Midsummer Night's Dream* for examinations). The poem, which was originally commissioned by *About the Globe* (the house magazine of the Friends of Shakespeare's Globe), gave the poet the opportunity to realise a long-held idea of fulfilling a wish expressed by Bottom in the play: 'I will get Peter Quince to write me a ballad of this dream. It shall be called "Bottom's Dream", because it hath no bottom' (Act IV, scene i,

BOTTOM'S DREAM

[handwritten draft of the poem]

continued over

ll.212–15). The poem began life in a notebook. Included here are extracts from the first, handwritten draft (Figure 3.8). Clive Wilmer sees these as 'a process of thinking the idea through. On the first two pages, though there are phrases that survive into the poem, I am a long way from the form and approach I then quite suddenly settle on'.

When investigating early notes such as these students could be encouraged to look closely at the thinking processes reflected in them. They might want to:

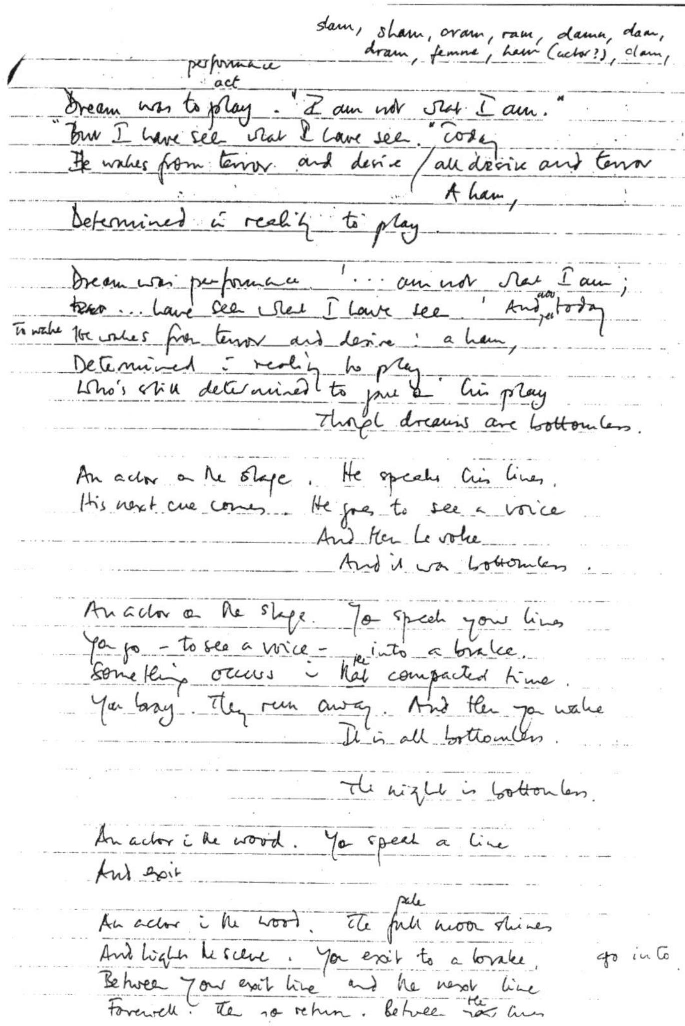
slam, sham, cram, ram, damn, dam,
dram, femme, ham (actor?), clam,
performance
act
Dream was to play. 'I am not what I am.'
'But I have seen what I have seen.' today
He wakes from terror and desire / all desire and terror
A ham,
Determined in reality to play.

Dream was performance '... am not what I am;
... have seen what I have seen' And now yet today
To wake He wakes from terror and desire: a ham,
Determined in reality to play
Who's still determined to pursue his play
Though dreams are bottomless.

An actor on the stage. He speaks his lines.
His next cue comes... He goes to see a voice
And then he woke
And it was bottomless.

An actor on the stage. You speak your lines
You go – to see a voice – into a brake.
Something occurs in that compacted time.
You bray. They run away. And then you wake
It is all bottomless.

The night is bottomless.

An actor in the wood. You speak a line
And exit

An actor in the wood. The pale full moon shines
And lights the scene. You exit to a brake, go into
Between your exit line and the next line
Forever! then so return. Between the lines

Figure 3.8 *Extracts from Clive Wilmer's notebook pages 1 and 2*

~~I trusted in my mastery~~   I trusted I had mastery

~~Of life as lived beneath the moon,~~   Until one night, being left alone,

~~And then I found myself alone~~   /shivering/ I snorted at the

In terror of the mystery   *wandering* moon.

    Which seemed quite bottomless,

It was from here

~~And she spoke out of that, who had~~   And out of that <u>she</u> spoke who had
~~And which she spoke from, she who had~~

No voice, although she stirred my sense,

Who touched me, though she had no hands,

And led me where you cannot lead

    Since it is bottomless.

All this, I thought,
    was mastery   **All this**   I thought of this as mastery
    shook before   I thought all this my mastery
I shivered at the {changing?   Until one night, being left alone,
    {wandering   I shivered, snorting at the moon,
    moon   In terror of the mystery
In terror

    ~~brayed.~~

I tried to speak: ~~I snorted, neighed.~~   after I brayed

I pinched and scratched *my face* ~~myself~~: thick hairs   **rough hairs**

~~Had curled across my cheeks and ears.~~   were curling over cheeks & ears.

And when she drew me in, she made

    The whole world bottomless.

Figure 3.9   *Extract from fifth draft of* 'Bottom's Dream', *by Clive Wilmer*

- identify key ideas which appear to be emerging;
- identify quotations and events from Shakespeare's play and possible reasons for their inclusion;
- explore why certain phrases might be bracketed together;
- discuss the different viewpoints Clive Wilmer appears to be exploring;
- discuss the way he has clustered rhyming words together.

Once he arrived at a form (a five-line stanza with an abbac rhyming structure including a fifth refrain line which plays around with the word 'bottomless') most of the poem quickly took shape. However, there was one aspect of the writing which presented the poet with a real challenge:

> The centre of the poem is Titania's love for Bottom and his transformation into an ass. I wanted to imply many things about the consummation of Titania's love but, because all that is ambiguous in the play, I didn't want to state it crudely or to describe a sexual act. So at first I left it almost unexpressed. Eventually I realised that that wasn't working and that I needed to suggest things through imagery, so I ended up making the poem longer and more deliberately sensuous than I had originally intended. It isn't often that I expand a poem after the first draft. I'm more likely to cut something. But this one grew.

While some might feel it is somewhat salacious to linger over this aspect of the poem, it is important to consider the changes to this section of the poem in draft five (the penultimate draft) in Figure 3.9 and to compare them with the final version. These changes indicate clearly how writers tease away elements of a draft, experimenting with nuances of word order and choice in order to fine-tune a piece so that the desired meaning and tone can be achieved. They also provide a useful lead in to discussion of the effectiveness of Wilmer's portrayal of one young man's realisation of his love for another in the completed poem.

As a result of these revisions, the final published version of the poem, completed some five months later, contains an additional stanza beginning.' I tried to speak: again I brayed.' There are also a number of other small changes which are new: in stanza 6 'rough' becomes 'coarse'; in stanza 8 'Old terror' becomes 'My terror' and in stanza 9 'yes, I' is added. The introduction of 'coarse' gives the phrase a greater immediacy, more of a textural feel, enhanced by the alliteration 'coarse hairs/Were crisping over cheeks and ears'. The other two changes emphasise the narrator's increasing sense of personal discovery.

Bottom's Dream

It shall be called 'Bottom's Dream',
because it hath no bottom ...

I was a weaver, and I wove
The moody fabric of my dream.
By day I laboured at the loom
And glimpsed the image of a love
      I now know bottomless.

We were young men. We played our parts.
We schooled ourselves in the quiet wood.
By night the moon, who draws the flood,
Tugged at the rhythms of our hearts
      And they were bottomless.

I loved a girl who was a boy;
I took my stand and beat my breast.
Yet what was I but fool and beast,
Who did not so much speak as bray
      In bombast bottomless?

I trusted I had mastery
Until one night, being left alone,
I snorted at the wandering moon
In terror of the mystery,
      Which seemed quite bottomless,

And out of that *she* spoke, who had
No voice, although she stirred my sense,
Who touched me, though she had no hands,
And led me where you cannot lead
      Since it is bottomless.

I tried to speak: again I brayed.
I pinched and scratched my face: coarse hairs
Were crisping over cheeks and ears.
And when she drew me in, she made
      The whole world bottomless.

Nothing possessed me. So she said
Do not desire to leave this wood.
Among the mossy clefts I hid
With petals where I laid my head,
      Desire being bottomless.

A most rare vision, such a thing
As who should say what such things be:
My terror turned to ecstasy,
The one much like the other, being
      Both of them bottomless.

And then the change. The sun came up
Brash as a brassy hunting-horn.
I woke and, yes, I was a man.
Was I myself though? Self, like sleep,
      May well be bottomless.

New moon tonight. Another dream
To act. They laugh at our dismay.
Oh but it's nothing. Only play.
Except we just don't feel the same,
      For play is bottomless.

And so the story ends. My eyes
Are sore with weeping, but I laugh
(I who was seen to take my life),
For, having been an ass, I'm wise
      And bottomless. Bottomless.

Clive Wilmer

A Draft: A Winter Morning in Timarpur

The black and white cat snoozes in the shadow
on the tin carport roof, under the ancient mango tree;
tail twitching, it dreams of plump pigeon and tender blue tit.
The scent of a hilsa fish curry floats from the kitchen window;
infiltrates its dream and teases it awake till it yawns and blinks.
A family of sparrows hop in the pomegranate tree:
twittering delight at the young green leaves and orange buds.
Frenzied bees weave among the lemon flowers
and crimson frangipani. High on a branch of the drumstick tree
a tailor-bird's nest swings in the November breeze.
The orange-stemmed white *shefali* flowers make *alpona* patterns
as they fall on the dew-damp grass.
The hibiscus still droops in prayer
to the early morning sun, its double petals
apple-red like crimson-lipsticked lips.
A squirrel mother and child stir in their telephone-box nest
and milkmen balance heavy canisters on bicycle bars.
The roadside *chaiwalla* lights his charcoal fire *biri*
and the newsboy flings, with practised ease,
a rolled *Statesman/Hindustan Times(?)* to the third floor verandah.
Trucks and buses piled with raw produce and day labour
ply from the pastures of Punjab and Haryana;
they thunder down the Grand Trunk Road
and the black and white cat shadow boxes a Tiger Swallowtail
as sleepy Timarpur wakes – and stretches.

Final Version: A Winter's Morning in Timarpur

The black and white cat snoozes in the play of light and shade
on the carport's tin roof, under the crumbling mango tree;
tail twitching, it dreams of plump pigeon and tender blue-tit.
The scent of a hilsa fish curry floats from the kitchen window;
infiltrates its dream and teases it awake till it yawns and blinks.
A family of sparrows hop in the pomegranate tree:
twittering delight at the young green of its leaves,
playing among the orange of its buds.
Frenzied bees weave among white lemon flowers
and crimson frangipani fragrance the air.
High on a branch of the drumstick tree a tailor-bird's nest swings
in the November breeze, fresh with a hint of henna coolness.
The coral-stemmed white *shefali* flowers make *alpona* patterns
as they fall on the dew-damp grass.
The hibiscus still droops in prayer
to the early morning sun, its double petals
luscious red like much-kissed bridal lips.
A squirrel mother and child stir in their telephone-box nest
and milkmen balance heavy canisters on bicycle bars.
The roadside *chaiwalla* lights his charcoal fire *biri*
and the newsboy flings, with practised ease,
a rolled *Hindustan Times* to the third floor verandah.
Trucks and buses piled with raw produce and day labour
thunder imperially down the Grand Trunk Road
from the conquered pastures of Punjab and Haryana.
The black and white cat shadow-boxes a Tiger Swallowtail
as a sleepy corner of Old Delhi wakes – and stretches.

Debjani Chatterjee

A Winter's Morning in Timarpur: a commentary on the final draft by Debjani Chatterjee

The final title is slightly changed. It's hard to explain why, but I like the sound of 'winter's' which adds to the 's' of 'snoozes' in the first line.

At the end of the poem when I brought back the cat and had it shadow-boxing (to pick up on the shadow in line 1), it seemed a good idea to return to line 1 and insert the quality of playfulness that is inherent in the cat's shadow-boxing a butterfly – even though the cat itself is asleep and the playfulness then has to be transferred to the 'light and shade'. (Playfulness was also something that I wanted to pick up in my description of the sparrows, hence the changed lines in the final version.) I think a cat is like a little tiger and so the association with the Tiger Swallowtail came to mind. There seems something ridiculously endearing about a cat boxing a 'tiger' or a butterfly. I also like the incongruity of something so tiny and fragile as a butterfly having a name that incorporates 'tiger'.

The 'ancient' mango tree became 'crumbling' because the latter is more descriptive and also original when used to describe a mango tree.

The poem's richness is partly due to a piling on effect achieved by listing the plants, animals, birds and insects in the garden. By adding the 'hint of henna coolness', the suggestion is that the garden also contains the henna plant, and the effect of the henna juice on the palms is not only a decorative orange pattern (picked up in the poem also by the *alpona* pattern'), but also a cooling effect that is valued in a hot climate. The 'coolness' reminds that November in Delhi has a hint of coolness in the morning. *Alpona* patterns are traditionally made with rice paste and are drawn on the floor outside a house to welcome visitors. My poem also tries to make good use of colours, with the warm colours of orange and red, which are considered auspicious by Hindus, very much in evidence. The *shefali* flower has tiny white petals but an orange stem, but by describing the colour as 'coral' I try to add to its 'value', coral being precious and decorative. 'Lemon flowers' suggests the colour yellow, but by adding 'white' before it, I continue my strategy of a piling-on effect. Lemon flowers are in fact white and the whole plant has a lemony fragrance. The poem's richness is also heightened by alliteration in the final draft ('hint of henna' and 'frangipani fragrances').

Normally my later drafts tend to be shorter than the earlier ones, as I try to delete superfluous words. But in the case of this poem, more lines and longer lines seem to convey the sleepy hazy effect of the day and so the final version is longer. The description of the double petals of the hibiscus as 'lips' in both versions is made more romantic in the final version. The reference to 'bridal' lips reminds the reader that red is the colour of a bride's clothes in India.

In the final version I kept *'Hindustan Times'*, not only because it is longer and more sonorous than *'Statesman'*, but also because it sounds more Indian (Hindustan or the 'Land of the Indus' is a North Indian name for India).

Although I liked the alliteration in 'ply from the pastures of Punjab' – and therefore found it hard to let go, I felt that in the end it was enough to just have 'pastures of Punjab'. (But I am still not altogether sure that this was the right choice!) But the Grand Trunk Road is associated with India's colonial past (it's an exotic road that Kipling describes in *Kim*, for instance) and so I decided to underline this by adding 'imperially' to my description of the trucks and buses, and 'conquered' to my description of the pastures.

In my final line I changed Timarpur to Old Delhi, partly to help locate the place better for many readers who won't know where Timarpur is. It also seemed better to say that a 'corner of Old Delhi wakes' rather than the whole neighbourhood of Timarpur wakes because it contributes to the effect of the garden being a special enclosed world in itself. The garden, like the cat, stretches and wakes.

© Debjani Chatterjee, 2001

Using draft manuscripts of canonical and other well-known poems

It is not always easy, but it can be very enlightening to access drafts of well-known poems which students might be using as models for their own writing or studying for examination purposes. Drafts of Wilfred Owen's works, including 'Anthem for Doomed Youth', are now accessible on the World Wide Web (for further details refer to Chapter 4). They are accompanied by a plethora of supporting photographic and interview material which should inform students' readings of the drafts. I found it a very moving experience to encounter them for the first time and print-off pages from his notebooks, including his unfulfilled publishing plans for 1919. While students may not understand the emotional reactions of their English teachers, or the strange juxtaposition of printing out drafts written in fountain pen, I agree with Andrew Goodwyn (2000) that it is appropriate for students to appreciate how manuscripts can be revered.

He argues that the Owen site can be used to initiate discussion of the changing nature of textual creation within the electronic age. He suggests a number of ways in which students can use the resource, including:

- working backwards through the drafts and reconstructing the original from memory and the first draft;
- choosing the most powerful draft and revising or representing it;
- creating parallel versions on a split screen;
- tracing Owen's response to advice offered by Siegfried Sassoon on his work (Goodwyn, 2000).

The draft manuscripts of other canonical poets can be found in facsimile editions in major public and university libraries. While it is interesting to see works written in a poet's own hand, they can be difficult to read and are often supported by academic treatise on their origins, which make them of limited use in the classroom. There are some exceptions to this however. A facsimile of *The Waste Land* by T.S. Eliot (published by Faber and Faber in 1971 and edited by his wife Valerie Eliot) contains a transcript of the original drafts with Eliot's revisions and annotations by Vivien Eliot and Ezra Pound. (Pound's annotations are helpfully reproduced in red ink to distinguish them.) Investigation of just one section of this draft by A-level students would bring them much closer to understanding how this poem eventually took shape. For example, they could consider reasons for cancelling the first page of 'The Burial of The Dead' and compare its potential impact with that of the published 'April is the cruellest month' opening. The original section heading 'He do the Police in Different Voices' is also worth exploring.

Another poet frequently studied for examination purposes is John Keats. His odes, transcribed by Robert Gittings (Keats, 1970), are published in a volume with an introduction and notes on each ode which should be accessible to young readers. Gittings provides a clear account of how Keats drew on both Shakespearean and Petrarchan sonnet forms to devise a poetic structure which suited his purpose as a vehicle for 'a poem of substance and yet of unity' (Keats, 1970: 15). He believes that the sight of Keats's hand in the act of creation can enable a reader to share in the spiritual triumph of the odes.

Edward Thomas's poem 'Adlestrop' is another text read by pupils of a wide age range. This manuscript, along with others from the British Library (BL) collection, is often exhibited. (A class visit to the BL's permanent collection could be a day well spent at the beginning of a literature course.) The 'Adlestrop' manuscript (Figure 3.10) reveals that the first stanza of the poem was the most intensely worked on (with four versions) while the rest of the poem needed very few alterations before it was printed.

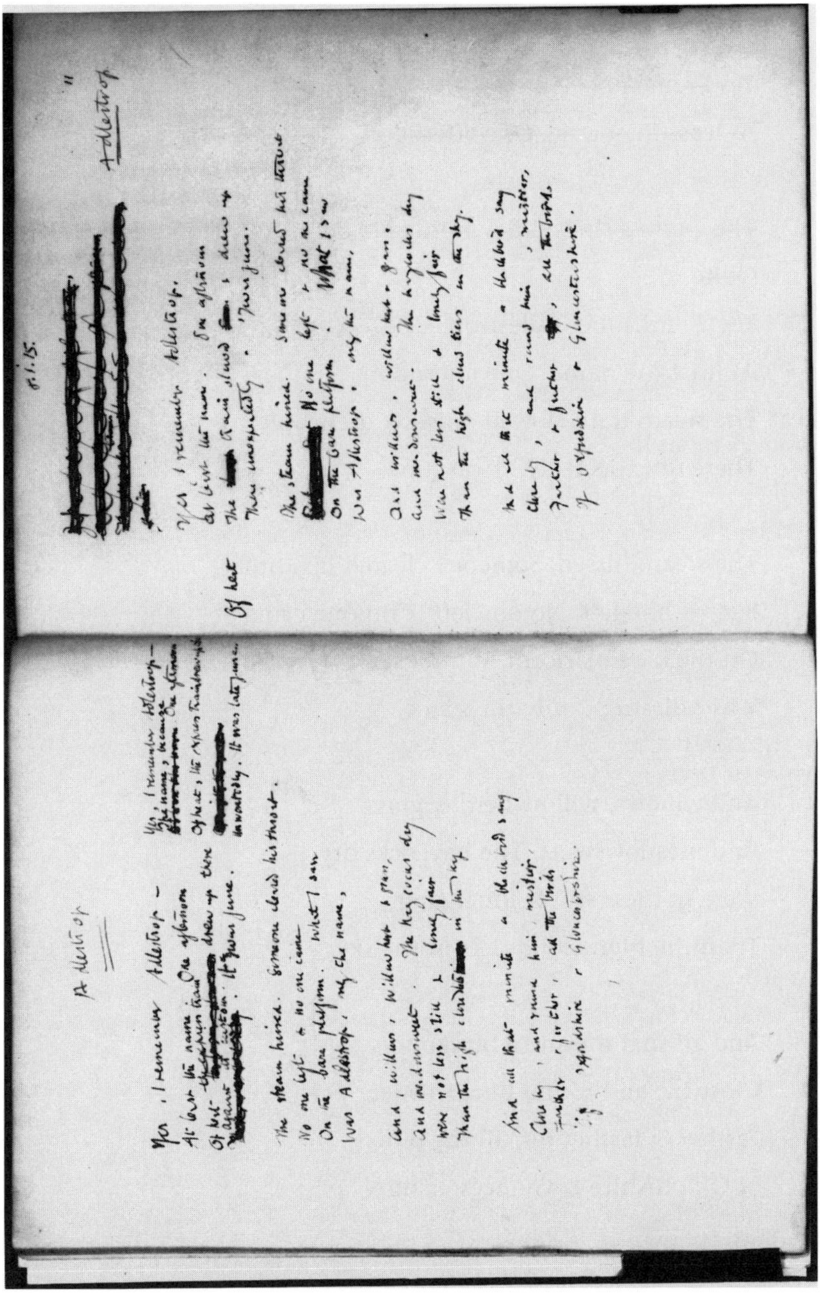

Figure 3.10 Drafts of 'Adlestrop' by Edward Thomas, ADD 44990 f10v–11r, by permission of the British Library

First Draft

8. 1. 15

Yes ~~I remember Adlestrop~~,

~~At least the name. One afternoon~~

            ~~— train~~

~~The express slowed down there & drew up~~   Adlestrop

~~Quite~~

Yes, I remember Adlestrop,

At least the name. One afternoon

Of heat The ~~steam~~ train slowed ~~down~~ & drew up

There unexpectedly. 'Twas June.

The steam hissed. Someone cleared his throat.

~~But no one left~~. No one left & no one came

On the bare platform. What I saw

Was Adlestrop, only the name,

And willows, willow herb & grass,

And meadowsweet. The haycocks dry

Were not less still & lonely fair

Than the high cloud tiers in the sky.

And all that minute a blackbird sang

Close by, and round him, mistier,

Farther & farther ~~off~~, all the birds

of Oxfordshire & Gloucestershire.

Second Draft

Yes, I remember Adlestrop –	Yes, I remember Adlestrop –
At least the name. One afternoon	The name, because
the express train	~~At least the name~~. One afternoon
Of heat ~~the train slowed &~~ drew up there	Of heat, the express
	train drew up there
Against its custom.	~~Against the custom~~
~~There unexpectedly~~. It 'Twas June.	Unwontedly. It was late June.

The steam hissed. Someone cleared his throat.

No one left & no one came

On the bare platform. What I saw

Was Adlestrop, only the name,

And, willows, willow herb & grass,

And meadowsweet. The haycocks dry

Were not less still & lonely fair

Than the high cloudlets ~~tiers~~ in the sky.

And all that minute a blackbird sang

Close by, and around him, mistier,

Farther & farther, all the birds

Of Oxfordshire & Gloucestershire.

There are some variations in punctuation which are worth exploring with students. In *Adlestrop Revisited*, her study of the poem, Anne Harvey (1999) explains that a full stop was added after the opening 'Yes', replacing the original comma. Nevertheless some anthologised versions of the poem have kept with the comma because their editors prefer it. She notes that, although this might appear to some to be 'a minor detail ... The comma seems to allow a moment's reflection; the full stop is more positive. The punctuation particularly affects the speaking aloud of the poem' (Harvey, 1999: 20).

In considering the difference between the drafts it is necessary to allow time for detailed comparison and discussion. Pupils must be given the opportunity to read the different versions of the poem aloud and to experiment with the impact of the differences in punctuation in their readings. An example of an investigative approach which could be used with pupils in Year 8 or 9 is included below:

'Adlestrop' by Edward Thomas

What happens to the phrases?	*Within draft 1?*	*Within draft 2?*
'At least the name.'		
'train' (and phrases using 'train')		
'unexpectedly'		
'against its custom'		
''Twas June'		
'high cloud tiers'		
'slowed down there'		
'Yes I remember Adlestrop,'		
Other lines of your choice		

What to do

(a) Copy out the chart and in pencil write in all the different versions you can find of the lines listed. Some of them have already been added to guide you.

(b) Now decide on your own what has happened to each line and give each change a code. Is the change connected with:
   - punctuation @
   - word order *
   - vocabulary = (one word directly replaced with another of a similar meaning)
   - word or phrase deletion – –
   - word or phrase addition +

You may find yourself using more than one code in some cases.

(c) Now explain to a partner exactly what changes you think have taken place in the poem. Try to use grammatical terms wherever you can. For example, you might say Thomas uses an apostrophe and a contracted phrase "'Twas' in the first draft but in the second draft he drops the punctuation, changing the phrase to 'It was'. Make a list of any grammatical terms you use.

(d) Now think about what might be the reasons for the changes Thomas makes and the effect they have. Share your ideas again. Reasons for changes in poems can be to do with:

- sound;
- shape;
- atmosphere or tone;
- sense;
- flow or link between lines or verses;
- introduction of a new idea.

To start you off, think about the change from *'Twas* to *It was*. What difference does that change make?

(e) Now decide which draft of the poem you prefer and why. You might find that you like sections from each draft instead. Share and compare your versions. Then look at a final published version.

f) Now read this second poem about a train journey. How does it compare with 'Adlestrop'?

Coast Train

Pigeons fly east with us:
an ever-flexing boomerang
across the fading blue.

Sometimes they race ahead
or swerve out of sight,
eyes on the warm loft at journey's end.

Across the aisle a woman writes letters home.
Her words are inky insects
scurrying across the ivory paper.

Opposite an old man sleeps,
arms gripped round his chest,
dreaming of daughters far away.

A baby's cry is lost over the empty fields
and everything seems to turn back
except us,

our heads buzzing with excitement,
as we speed towards the start of summer
and the afternoon sea.

Sue Dymoke

(g) Can you find any other poems about train journeys or places which complement or contrast with the two poems you have read so far? Use the poetry book box, the poetry section in the library and the *Poetry Plus* CD-ROM to help you.
(h) Think about different journeys you have been on. Is there a significant journey (or even an unexpected break in the journey) which you might want to draft a poem about? Look back in your notebook for ideas.

If you are able to obtain a copy of *Adlestrop Revisited* students could go on to consider annotations in Thomas's Field Note Book dated 24 June 1914. Students could discuss how Thomas used this notebook entry, which describes a train journey, when writing his poem in the following January. They could identify which words and phrases from it appear in the final published version of 'Adlestrop' and speculate on why he has not mentioned the song thrush or other places (such as Oxford, Campden and Colwall) which are referred to in the notebook entries. The period of time which elapsed between the journey and the drafts is also worth drawing attention to (together with the principle of dating drafts in general) because it further demonstrates how ideas may need time to develop, or even go cold on a writer, before they can be transformed into poetry.

Further draft manuscript resources

Michael and Peter Benton (1990) *Examining Poetry*, London, Hodder and Stoughton – contains a chapter entitled 'Writers' and Readers' Drafts'. Although intended primarily for GCSE students, the section on drafts of Phoebe Hesketh's poem 'Paint Box' is particularly useful for pupils in Year 8 or 9.

Mike Ferguson (1999) *Poems in your Pocket: Imaginative Aproaches to GCSE Poetry (Teacher's Guide)*, Harlow, Pearson Education. This photocopiable resource contains a wide variety of poetry writing workshop activities as well as two pages of sound advice on drafting poetry by Rupert Loydell (managing editor of Stride Publications) which is directly addressed to students.

Chris Fletcher (ed.) (2000) *Chapter and Verse: 1000 Years of English Literature,* London, British Library – published on the occasion of the Chapter and Verse exhibition at The British Library, this short book contains examples from the BL's magnificent manuscripts collection. It includes images from: the tenth-century manuscript of *Beowulf* and the draft of Seamus Heaney's modern translation; sonnet XCII from *Sonnets from the Portuguese* from Elizabeth Barrett Browning's notebook and an extract from 'Kubla Khan' by Samuel Taylor Coleridge. An inexpensive resource to share with students of all ages.

Sue Hackman and Barbara Marshall (1995) *Into Literature*, London, Hodder and Stoughton – aimed at examination classes this includes a unit on 'The Writing Process' featuring an activity in which students look closely at six versions of Carol Rumens's poem 'Moment of Faith' and an accompanying commentary written by the poet.

Michael Harrison and Christopher Stuart-Clark (1992) *Writing Poems Plus*, Oxford, Oxford University Press – designed for use with older students, this includes some brief drafting activities on 'Ozymandias' by Percy Bysshe Shelley and 'Stopping by Woods on a Snowy Evening' by Robert Frost as well as drafts used for illustrative purposes by Gerda Mayer and U.A. Fanthorpe.

Anne Harvey (ed.) (1999) *Adlestrop Revisited*, Stroud, Sutton Publishing – a fascinating in-depth account which traces the origins, drafting and impact of the poem 'Adlestrop'. A useful resource for teachers.

C.B. McCully (ed.) (1994) *The Poet's Voice and Craft*, Manchester, Carcanet – contains informal essays by 13 poets (including Fleur Adcock, Douglas Dunn, Edwin Morgan and Anne Stevenson) who describe their techniques for writing poetry, how they structure poems, their choices of words, sounds and metrics as well as some details about how ideas are generated and revised. A good teacher resource, especially to support AS/A-level examination study.

Morag Styles and Helen Cook (eds) (1990) *Inkslinger: Poems about Putting Words on Paper*, London, A & C Black – a poetry anthology with a variety of accessible poems about writing poetry. This would be a good addition to a poetry book box or school library. Poems could also be used to introduce different aspects of the writing process.

This chapter has demonstrated a variety of ways in which poets' drafts can be used with students to enable them to develop a keener understanding of how writers select and manipulate elements of language in the act of composition. In turn this understanding should inform students' own poetry writing and provide a context for the developing dialogue about drafting within the poetry classroom.

4

Poetry and ICT

Information and communication technology in its many forms can be a very powerful tool in poetry teaching. For a number of the poets featured in the previous chapter, the word processor is a vital tool in the drafting process. This chapter will consider the different ways in which ICT can support the teaching of poetry writing. These include: drafting on screen; using e-mail and conferencing; using CD-ROM packages and other software; strategies for teaching the fast developing subgenre of text message poetry; accessing websites; using OHTs as well as audio and video materials. Details of recommended classroom resources and websites are provided.

Drafting on screen

The word-processing functions of school computers are probably those most extensively used by English teachers. With the pressure on access, it is still common to see pupils dutifully typing up and presenting final drafts of classwork rather than using computers for the whole composing process. Poetry, which can be short and word-processed in lesson-sized bites, can be a particular victim of this approach. Overemphasis on the presentational aspects (the fancy font in different sizes, underlinings, centred text and so on) can distract pupils from the real value of the word processor as a drafting tool which enables writers to make and unmake decisions about structure, line length, word choice and word order in an instant. The opportunity to print work immediately can also prove too much of a temptation for pupils. This may sound like a negative introduction to drafting 'on screen'. However, it is important to be aware of these potential pitfalls in order to establish good practice.

In order for pupils to see the potential for using the computer in making meaning, rather than just as a presentational tool, it is important that they can make connections between reading and writing processes and are aware of the particular opportunities which the computer offers for interpretation and composition. Both Louise Rosenblatt in *The Reader, the Text, the Poem* (1978) and Dias and Hayhoe in *Developing Response to Poetry* (1988) have insightfully explored the ways in which readers of poetry can make new meanings on their response journeys. For Rosenblatt the poem itself is created in the space between what the writer provides and what the reader brings with them to the poem. In this way each reading of a poem is a kind of rewriting. This blurring of the boundaries between reader and writer can occur naturally and instantly when using a word processor.

On screen, words do not immediately have to be fixed in ink but can remain in a temporary state without closure. Poets have the facility to save as many different drafts as they wish, to replace and undo changes along the way to the final draft. Researchers (including Chandler [1987] and Vincent [2001]) comment on how the process of drafting on a word processor is much more continuous, with the distinction between first and later draft stages being lost. Sometimes it is a good idea to ask students to save all their drafts for one specific poem under different file names. In this way they can then reflect on the changes they have made and the development of their poem. This activity is particularly valuable for coursework assignments (as outlined in Chapter 2). Once the poem is complete each draft can be annotated in a different colour or font and printed out. (If the printer has the facility to print a draft watermark this would add to the effect.)

Alternatively, students' poems might remain unfinished for ever. In drafting my own poetry on the computer I recognise that the technology can make me pick away at the words in a poem much more than when I used a typewriter. I am sucked into the revising process almost without thinking. The number of drafts sometimes runs into the twenties as the opportunity to experiment with tiny shifts or changes is so much easier than it once was. Poems can become overwritten as a result of this process. Overwritten and left on file in limbo, their words are like earth which has been sieved to a fine dust. Knowing when to stop drafting as well as how to start can be a real challenge for writers of all ages.

The vexed question of whether writers improve their writing through using the word processor has been explored by many researchers. At one stage Bereiter and Scardamalia argued there was 'no indication that using a word processor causes students to adopt more sophisticated composing strategies' (Bereiter and Scardamalia, 1987: 358). However Scardamalia and other researchers in her team have more recently acknowledged the dramatic impact of computer-assisted learning on the enhancement of pupils' cognitive skills (Scardamalia, 1994, cited in Smith and Elley, 1998).

It is certain that word-processing packages, voice recognition software and scanners can make the writing process much less of a physical chore for writers who may be impeded by their own handwriting skills and feel frustrated by the need to constantly revise, recopy out sections and rewrite their drafts. Dauite (1983) (as cited in Snyder, 1993) claims that the word processor allows such students to keep up with their thoughts as they write. The immediate opportunities to experiment with new word combinations or to reorganise texts can make the idea of drafting much less of a daunting prospect for young writers. Although by no means fool-proof, spell-checker programs can also make life easier at the proofreading stage. However the jury is still out on evidence of an improvement in quality. Cochrane-Smith (1991) argues that, although more revisions may take place when work is word processed and the work may be more attractive to read, the changes made can often be minor or trivial. Bangert-Drowns (1993) (as cited in Snyder, 1993) is more convinced by the improvement in quality and quantity of the writing when using a computer. Interestingly, however, he does not observe a more positive attitude towards writing on the part of his students. Snyder concludes that 'students tend to write longer texts with word processors than with traditional tools. Students tend to revise more but at a surface level rather than a meaning level' (Snyder, 1993: 63). In her research overview of 57 studies on writing with word processors, Snyder indicates that writers bring with them to the computer the writing strategies and abilities they had previously acquired: experienced writers show greater inclination to use cut and paste functions and to make notable insertions and deletions in their drafts, whereas students have a tendency to use overtype and simple delete and insert functions. Now students are gaining more regular access to computers much earlier in their development as writers, it is no longer possible to make such a clear-cut distinction between the two groups.

Snyder is equivocal about the extent to which word processors can improve the quality of writing, acknowledging that their use is influenced by the whole writing context. To address the issue of quality, and to ensure pupils are using their computers as something much more than glorified typewriters, I think there *is* a need for teachers to make explicit use of certain keyboard functions with pupils. *Twenty Things to Do with a Word Processor*, an eminently practical book by Trevor Millum and Chris Warren (2001) provides a number of starting points, which can easily be adapted for use in the primary or secondary classroom, to ensure that real engagement and learning take place. Based on the Microsoft Word program, these activities include: marking and reorganising to structure thinking about text; using insert and underline to transform text from one genre to another; using find and replace to create found poetry. Once pupils become fully familiar with these functions they should begin to use them more instinctively when drafting their own work.

There can be little doubt that the word processor presents pupils with opportunities to redraft their own poetry as well as to read and respond to that of others on screen. A number of DARTs can now be readily transferred to the individual computer screen, data projector or the class interactive whiteboard and used to inform pupils' own work.

Sequencing

Sequencing is a strategy which is ideally suited to the study of poetry. It draws pupils' attentions to forms, structures and sounds within the poems while reinforcing the flexible nature of language and the way meanings can change through new juxtapositions of words. Readers are invited to construct texts for themselves by reordering words, lines, phrases and even whole verses. For this ICT activity, rather than cutting up class sets of poems into endless (and easily lost) slips of paper, the poetry text(s) – preferably reasonably short poems – need to be entered on screen. The text should be divided up into a bundle of randomly arranged lines, words and phrases. The title could be included within this bundle or provided separately as an additional clue. More able students can be challenged with a jumble of several poems on the same subject with contrasting styles. Students should read the lines aloud and use the cut and paste facility to experiment with reorganising them. They could change the colour or font of individual lines once they are happy with the choices they have made.

Sequencing works best if completed as a pair or small group. Pupils should be encouraged to read lines aloud, to tap out rhythms and to apply the approaches they have used while sequencing when redrafting their own work. They must be able to give reasons for the choices they make. (This could be in the form of bullet points underneath their completed sequence or as a tabbed list alongside particular lines.) When pupils are redrafting any poem the computer room should not be a silent space: there is much more to redrafting on screen than the muffled tapping of keys. Once pupils have become familiar with this activity, they could experiment with sequencing each others' drafts and providing responses in the same way.

Cloze

Cloze is another strategy which will be familiar to many teachers and is also referred to in Chapter 2. With this DART (which can be used with prose texts too) words, phrases or even whole lines are blanked out of a text. Pairs of pupils are asked to use contextual clues such as the surrounding words or grammar of the text, the tone, form, rhyme and rhythm of the piece to help them fill the gaps. Sometimes words are provided in a bank below. While one could argue that this level of support may be necessary for some learners, I think it emphasises the idea of a poem being too much like a puzzle into which right answers can be slotted. By transferring the cloze activity from paper to screen pupils can be encouraged to experiment more with potential word choices and a closer focus on the writer's craft. Pupils can view their completed cloze poems as 'drafts' for the original poem. A whole set of different drafts can be saved and further opportunities for comparison easily generated.

Developing Tray was one of the first computer programs to encourage pupils to use their own knowledge of language in their reading of a text (Tweddle, 1993). In my experience it worked most successfully with poetry. The program drew on some of the principles of cloze. The teacher set up a text on screen which had some clues in place such as punctuation, some capital letters (which would reveal names), initial letters of some words and dashes to indicate undeveloped letters. Pupils worked collabo-ratively to gradually develop the poem on the tray/screen. Like many DARTs, the real value in this activity was in discussion of the emerging text and the pupils' excitement about this process. Sally Tweddle's sugges-tion of using scratchpads as an assessment tool to provide pupils with 'a metaphorical as well as a literal place for reflection' (ibid.: 103) was an excellent refinement of this program. Although Developing Tray is no longer widely used, its principles can easily be adapted for use with cur-rent word processing packages. (For example, Millum and Warren's [2001: 7] 'Code Breaking' idea, in which text is coded using a symbol font, has similarities with this activity.)

Desktop publishing (DTP)

Publications of students' poems, including class anthologies and maga-zines to showcase work produced during writers' residencies, are another welcome offshoot of the ICT revolution. Programs like Microsoft Publisher can easily be used in the classroom by many pupils (at least by Year 9). For Goodwyn 'Conceptually … DTP still belongs to the domain of the pub-lisher' (Goodwyn, 2000: 122). When publishing class texts it is essential that pupils are involved in all the different stages of the production process (not just designing their page and typing in the poems). This should include making group decisions about overall design and editorial content. A class publication could provide good opportunities to compare features of collections the pupils like and to consider how single and anthology collections are arranged and titled.

Using e-mail, conferencing and hypertext

Like slate and chalk, pencil and paper and all the other writing technologies which have preceded it, a word processor is designed for solitary use. Tweddle et al. (1997: 26) acknowledge: 'If, therefore, we want to generate deliberate collaborative work both in writing and in talking on which writing will be based, we need to plan and teach in such a way as to achieve this end. The technology will not, in itself, change or determine the culture of the classroom.' DARTs, such as those outlined above, represent one way in which this can be achieved. Another approach, which can promote informal and flexible collaboration, is through the use of the World Wide Web and e-mail. Many schools are now publishing children's work on their school websites (as can be seen in the list towards the end of this chapter). Some of these are well worth reading. However the potential for using the web in interactive ways is even more exciting.

The concept of drafting or response partners, described in Chapter 2, can take on another dimension if those partners are reading and writing in another classroom somewhere else in the country or the world. The network of schools using the World Wide Web is forever expanding and it is now extremely easy for pupils and teachers to link up with other institutions (for guidance consult the National Grid for Learning website: www.ngfl.gov.uk). When the web was still in its infancy in schools, some of my A-level students were already beginning to subscribe to lists and 'talk' to students in Canada and elsewhere about texts they were studying in order to develop awareness of a range of interpretations. Barrell and Hammett argue that computer technology can provide a 'disrupting influence' to the narrow ways in which students have previously been positioned in their reading of texts. Hypertext and other forms of technology 'foster textual resistance' (Barrell and Hammett, 1999: 23) by releasing and enabling students to rewrite text, publish alternative opinions and challenge traditional readings.

Sharing drafts electronically is one way of encouraging students to respond to texts. This approach can further develop pupils' understandings of how poems are being drafted and enable them to participate in the writing of a number of texts. It can be carried out individually through pupils' school e-mail addresses, via conferencing or hypertext links to particular words or phrases within a draft on a web page. Whichever method is used teachers must put safeguards in place to ensure pupils are corresponding in a secure interface/environment. It is important to recognise the very public nature of the computer screen in the classroom: pupils should also be given opportunities to write poetry in more private contexts (Chandler, 1987).

Universities and other institutions now use conferencing extensively for their distance learning courses. Messages are stored up and individual members of the group can read them at their convenience and contribute to the discussion on screen rather than face to face. This type of learning may be convenient and cost-effective but many e-mail lists and conference groups are littered with silent readers rather than talkative reader-writers. The method does rely on individual students taking an active role in developing the 'text' or discussion as well as attentive tutors who can steer the group when necessary. Connections with multiple authors and texts, over which the individual has no control, do present their own set of difficulties. For example, once created, the poem can be redrafted at speed by another site user or the planned anthology project can take off in a very different direction from that which the originator intended. Nevertheless, if tight deadlines and parameters are established at the onset and the site is carefully monitored, a conference *is* potentially an ideal location for negotiating joint anthology projects, redrafting poetry, sharing responses to alternative versions and forging links between hyperpoems.

Hypertext

Increasingly more user-friendly web-writing software such as *Dreamweaver* has made it much easier for those unfamiliar with the complexities of Hypertext Mark-up Language (HTML) to write their own hypertexts. The hypertext brings with it a raft of possibilities for writing and reading poetry, some of which have already been explored. Once the reader of a web page has clicked on a word or phrase in a poem marked up in hypertext she could be transported to: a dictionary definition of that term; a range of critical interpretations; a live performance; an image; another poem on the same subject; a news article; a film clip; a historical footnote; an advert and so on. The list is endless and forever changing and with it the notion of what constitutes a text. On one level hypertext offers the reader a series of concealed footnotes, accessed according to need and at the moment the reader desires (rather than by flicking to the end of the chapter or to the bottom of the page). On another level it can offer access to a series of unexpected links which could send the reader in many different directions as they make their own route through the text. Smith and Elley (1998) suggest that, in the light of such changes, our linear approach to reading and writing may no longer be appropriate. Bolter (1991, cited in Smith and Elley, 1998) argues that we may be returning to a writing and layout style reminiscent of the Middle Ages where texts contained marginal annotations as well as many illustrations.

Hyperpoems

A number of the school websites listed in this chapter include examples of
hypertext links. These are fairly rudimentary at present (in that they tend
to lead to other poems on the same site which also include the marked up
word), however, there is real potential for innovation, as demonstrated by
Richard Bain's work. Richard Bain, when a teacher at Norham Community
College in North Tyneside, experimented with using hypertext as a means
of taking students beyond what he sees as the 'superficial skimming,'
which can result from Internet surfing, towards a deeper understanding of
a text. In an article, first published in the *Secondary English Magazine*, he
describes three projects he designed to introduce his students to a range of
web skills. One of these is concerned with 'hyperpoems' and includes
opportunities for collaborative work involving critical reading, drafting
and response.

The aim of this project was to use the structure of hypertext to explore a
poem in detail.

I typed William Blake's poem 'The Garden of Love' into a 'Word' document
and then I created ten further pages, each with a bookmark. I selected ten
'key' words from the poem and linked each of them to the one of the extra
pages. I also placed a link on each page to take the user back to the original
poem. This meant that when the file was opened, the poem was displayed
with certain words highlighted in blue. A click on any of the highlighted
words would bring up a blank page with a link back to the poem.

I began work with a Year 7 mixed ability class by reading and discussing the
poem with pupils, focusing particularly on the imagery. I then put the pupils
in pairs, giving each pair ten slips of paper and asking them to write each of
my ten 'key' words at the top of a separate slip. Finally they were to write
four words or feelings or ideas connected with ach of the key words on the
appropriate slip.

The next stage was to divide the class in to ten groups and to give each
group all the slips of paper for one of the key words. Their task was then to
prepare a single page in Microsoft Word to explore and develop the ideas on
all their slips. Their page might include:

- the pupils' own descriptive writing about the key word;
- the pupils' own poem about the key word;
- a list of words/feelings/ideas connected with the key word;
- the pupils' own comments or questions about the key word.

When all the pages were complete I slotted them into my original document,
which I then made available to the whole class to read. Having read each

others' pages, each group was given the opportunity to revise their own page before the whole document was placed on the school intranet.

I was very pleased with the way that this 'hyperpoem' process enabled pupils to share ideas, discuss and explore the poem in detail, and create their own text which led others to reflect more closely on the poem. I have also written an alternative version of the exercise and this will allow pupils to type in their own poem, select their own key words and create appropriate hyperlinks. (Bain, 1999: 20–24)

Shape, sound and movement on screen

Along with hypertext, a range of computer programs are making it easier to write poems which are less print-bound and may never appear in a printed form. Concrete poetry (otherwise known as shape or kinetic poetry) is made for the screen. Although pupils may have been introduced to the form in their primary schools, I think its potential can be under-valued in the secondary classroom. It can be revisited in a more sophisticated way. Concrete poetry can provoke lively debate about the nature of poetry as well as leading pupils to experiment with customising fonts and blurring those artificial boundaries between poetry and other art forms for themselves. It is ideal for exploring connections between form and meaning. Widely anthologised poems such 'A Weekend in the Country' and 'Easy Diver' by Robert Froman, 'Cup Final' by Roger McGough or 'The Honey Pot' by Alan Ridell are appropriate models to use with Key Stage 3 pupils to demonstrate what can be created using simple word-processing and drawing programs. Stanley Cook's work is another point of reference here. He wonderfully blurs the distinctions between visual art and literature in poems such as 'Kinetic Poem' and 'People'. In 'The Computer's First Christmas Card', and elsewhere, Edwin Morgan experiments with typography, language and form, often creating seem-ingly random but highly crafted juxtapositions of letters and words. This poem could be used as stimuli for investigating the computer's impact on the creative process.

Programs like Aldus Type Twister and Word Art can provide opportuni-ties for creating words and phrases in different shapes, fonts and colours. Another approach, is to provide pupils with a number of shapes into which they can type their poems. Shapes such as hearts, skulls and bottles are very popular and can also be downloaded for use in other types of writ-ing. For this approach to work effectively (and for the form to be more than a presentational device) pupils need to choose their shapes at the ini-tial drafting stage so that they can structure their poems appropriately.

Found poetry is another form which readily lends itself to ICT approaches. With Found poetry, texts from other genres, including newspaper reports, brochures and adverts, are manipulated with few, if any, changes into poems. Such material can easily be imported and manipulated on screen. Students can also create montage or collage poems, in the vein of those produced by the Surrealists, by scanning in and/or manipulating images and combining them with fragments of their own or found texts.

Innovative software, such as Flash and Shockwave, can facilitate production of animated poetry texts (as exemplified on a number of the websites listed in this chapter). RealPlayer, MediaPlayer, Apple's iMovie and Quick Time Pro are enabling pupils to 'bring learning to life' (Baugh, 2002: 52). Students can create their own poems using digital video and accompany them with sound effects, music, moving images and pictures. Writing is just one element in this multilayered process. Other multimedia and authoring software, such as that produced by Immersive Education, aims to bring drama and poetry texts off the page by using games technology. Pupils can choose three-dimensional characters, backgrounds, props and effects, add sound and spoken lines from texts as well as their own thought bubbles to reinterpret texts for themselves.

Texting

With access to such technology, the nature of text as well as the processes of reading and writing are being redefined. In discussing use of DTP in schools, Goodwyn argues that pupils who are passive readers and writers need to move towards an 'active and profoundly different role of *manufacturing* text' (his italics) (Goodwyn, 2000: 122). It is interesting to note how, in some instances, the word 'writing' is being replaced with terms such as 'making' and 'producing'. For example the Ambleside Primary School website (www.ambleside.schoolzone.co.uk) includes poems which were 'made' by class 6 during the literacy hour.

Text message poetry

With the widespread use of mobile phones, the term 'texting' has rapidly become common parlance for sending messages via mobile phone message. In the spring of 2001 the Online section of the *Guardian* newspaper ran its first text message poetry competition. The staggering number of entries it received (7500 – many texted by people who claimed never to have written a poem before) underlines how new technology can revitalise writing in an age-old genre. In introducing the poetry competition, Online editor Victor Keegan (2001) commented: 'This is a new medium. There are no rules about how text poems should be constructed. They can be written in ordinary English, in text abbreviation, in the regional texting dialects that are starting to emerge (like "wid u" in the North) or in any combination of all three.'

Although students' text messages can occupy too much time in a classroom for all the wrong reasons, it is well worth making them legitimate for once: the art of texting is an immediate example of how the English language is constantly evolving. Writing text message poetry can make students think about being economical with language. Use of rhyme and rhythm in the poems are also notable features as can be seen in the following examples:

OUT OF REACH
Y DON'T U CALL?
R U OK?
I MISS U LOTS
200 MILES AWAY
U MET SUM 1 ELSE
U LIKE MORE THAN ME?
OR IS THERE NO SIGNAL
LANDLINE 555 613
I LV U SO MCH
PLZ GIVE ME A SHOUT
OR I'LL GET ON A TRAIN
SPELL IT OUT

2 the quick
txtin is keepin
yr i on the lttrs
txtin is keepin
yr i on the nmbrs
txtin is keepin
yr i on the screen
txtin is shavin
yr words 2 the bne
txtin is cuttin

Alison Creaghan

Guidelines for text message poetry

- Students can only have a maximum of 160 characters in their poems. Therefore stress the importance of economic use of words. (They could also explore how this is different from the restrictions imposed by such forms as cinquains or sonnets.)
- They should avoid trying to tell a complicated story.
- Text poems can be jokey but they do not have to be. 'A text poem has to find one truthful moment and describe it.' (Wilson, 2001) If students are familiar with haiku poetry, and the way it captures a tiny event or moment, this would be a useful point of comparison.
- Mobile phones all have different layouts so it is difficult to predict how someone will receive/read the poem. This means students should focus on how their word and punctuation choices can drive the rhythm and pace of their poems.

- Experiment with internal rhymes. (U.A. Fanthorpe, one of competition's judges, commented that many entries seemed to experiment with rhyme as a substitute for imagery.)
- Make use of abbreviations where appropriate but be aware of their impact on the reader and the tone of the poem. (For those unfamiliar with texting abbreviations,the basic abbreviations can be found at: www.cellular.coza/sms_shortcuts.htm or, better still, consult the students!)
- Ask students to experiment with writing straight onto screen and drafting on paper, and talk about the differences. How is the process of texting a poem different from writing one with pen and paper or a word processor? (One immediate difference is that a text counter tells you how many characters are left.)
- For more examples of text poems refer to: http://books.guardian.co.uk/departments/poetry/story/ (adapted from advice offered to competition entrants by text message poet Andrew Wilson [2001]).

Websites

Teachers and students can tap into a wide range of poetry materials on the Internet. These include: examples of manuscripts; audio recordings of interviews and performances; on-line writing activities; anthologies of students' work; lesson plans and downloadable writing frames. The number of sites on offer can seem overwhelming. Some undoubtedly are much more useful than others. I have only reviewed a small selection of the most useful sites here. For ease of reference they have been coded in the following ways:

AP = Sites which present poems using Flash and/or other animation software.

B/C = Sites containing biographical and/or critical material about poets.

D = Sites containing examples of poets' drafts.

I = Sites containing interviews with poets.

PP = Sites containing examples of pupils' poetry.

R = Sites containing poetry reviews.

RP = Sites containing readings of poems.

T = Sites providing tips on poetic terms, forms and/or writing processes.

TM = Sites providing poetry teaching materials.

WP = Sites where pupils can write poetry.

www.poetryclass.net

This site should be your first port of call. It contains a wealth of information to support the teaching of poetry at across the 11–18 age range, including: writing workshop materials provided by poets in the poetry-class team; links with kids' poetry sites; interviews with poets; information on assessment, training and resources together with a report on the Exeter project carried out by poet Ann Sansom with PGCE students. **TM, PP, AP, I.**

www.poetrysociety.org.uk

The Poetry Society's site is well worth bookmarking. It features information on poetry events, readings, new publications, poetry competitions, educational services and National Poetry Day. It also has useful links to other sites **I, TM, R.**

www.poetryzone.ndirect.co.uk

Another essential site which publishes children's poetry and contains: recommended reading lists; poetry book reviews written by children; advice from poet Brian Moses about inviting poets into schools and a teaching zone aimed at primary teachers. This offers a range of teaching materials including worksheets. Some of the frameworks for poetry writing appear overly formulaic, however, they can be easily adapted to suit individual pupils' needs. The teaching zone also includes advice on improvising free verse to music and tips for young writers by James Carter. **TM, PP, I, R.**

http://www.edleston.cheshire.sch.uk/projects/projectshtm

A lively site created by Edleston Primary school which demonstrates the staff's commitment to exploring the potential of ICT and the Internet to encourage children to write. Contains samples of on-line projects which use Macromedia Flash 4 player plug ins. Some poems are animated and include group readings. **PP, AP.**

www.ambleside.schoolzone.co.uk

An inspiring site which makes one wonder if teachers at this primary school ever go home at night! It gives a real insight into the possibilities for poetry on the web. The site manager has taken considerable care to provide information about programs used and other practical information. Includes many examples of pupils' poetry such as an interactive haiku poem-maker page, 'Dr Who and the Daleks' (using Flash 4), a raindrop's eye view of the world and the long poem 'Troutbeck', written in a Year 6 guided writing session, which cleverly uses colour to imbed the changing shape of the water into the poem. **PP, AP.**

http://kotn.ntu.ac.uk

Kids on the net includes collections of young writers' work (such as selections of kennings sent in by different schools), examples of hypertext poetry and information on ezines. Kids on the net is one strand of trAce – the on-line writing centre based at Nottingham Trent University. trAce regularly runs competitions, workshops and on-line projects (such as the ambitious noon quilt which stitches together 'patches' of text submitted by writers from all around the world to form a quilt of noon-time impressions). It would be well worth exploring the rest of the site for an indication of the potential for using hypertexts and collaborative writing on-line for writers of all ages. **WP, PP, AP.**

www.theworksplus.net

An extensive on-line poetry resource designed for primary pupils, teachers and librarians. Includes contemporary and classic poems matched to the NLS, teaching resources, poetry games and a poetry corner for biographical information and on-line chat with poets. **I, B/C, T, TM.**

www.bbc.co.uk/educationlistenandwrite

An entertaining and imaginative site which supports Literacy Hour work in the primary classroom and is linked with the BBC Education Schools programme of the same name. The site provides both 'standard' and 'hi-tech' versions of activities based on rap poetry, word choices and using similes. (To make the best use of this site you will need to ensure you have downloaded RealPlayer.) Pupils (and teachers) can listen to recordings of poems, take part in quizzes, write and submit poems, using either a range of starter ideas to inspire their own work or the supplied structured frameworks. Be warned that, when completing a framework, the stanza structure of some of the poems can change slightly. Child-friendly writing tips are integrated into each page and writers are encouraged to use the back button to revise their work before submission to a poetry showcase. **TM, T, WP, PP, AP.**

www.shunsley.eril.net/armoore/default.htm

Andrew Moore, an English teacher at South Hunsley School, created this extensive site to support English teachers. Primarily geared to preparing students for GCSE and GCE examinations (including poetry set texts), it also includes useful advice for teachers on making full use of the word processor with their pupils when responding to and writing texts. **TM**.

www.englishl.org.uk/poetry.htm

This site, created by the irrepressible Harry Dodds, is an indispensable resource which provides links to a huge number of poetry sites, especially those linked with named authors. Probably most useful for GCSE/Standard grade, NQ and A-level teachers. **T, I, D, RP, B/C**.

www.bbc.co.uk/radio3/sonnets/index.shtml

A sonnets site suitable for Key Stage 3 pupils and teachers onwards. Includes: a grid of sonnets which can be listened to; a brief history of the sonnet by Ruth Padel; a sonnet writing game. **WP, RP, B/C**.

www.bbc.co.uk/arts/poetry/rca

A very interactive site, parts of which will keep teachers and pupils occupied for hours. It includes a do-it-yourself poetry tool kit. This works on the same principle as the Magnetic Poetry Kits™ and enables visitors to 'write' poems by grabbing words and backgrounds either with a romantic, gothic, sci-fi or natural theme. (You will need to download a free Shockwave player to use this.) Poems can then be e-mailed directly to the BBC gallery or to a friend. Other site features include an animated poem by John Hegley and students from the Royal College of Art, poetry readings and interviews with a range of well known poets (these require a RealPlayer). **WP, AP, I, B/C, RP**.

www.poeticbyway.com/glossary.html

Most suited to teachers and older students, this site provides a comprehensive glossary of poetic terms which is carefully cross-referenced, easy to access and includes literary quotations. **T**.

www.hcu.ox.ac.uk/jtap/

If you only have time to access one site from this list then this should be the one. The Wilfred Owen Archive provided here includes manuscripts from the British Library and the Oxford University English Faculty. The poems 'Mental Cases', 'The Send Off', 'Strange Meeting' and 'Dulce et Decorum Est' (along with many others) can be accessed in a number of draft stages and are linked with copies of the poems in their final published form. The site also features photographs, interviews with veterans, Owen's letters and 'workings' such as lists of words from his notebooks. This is a fabulous resource which can be used by teachers and students at many levels. For example, a word list might provide a good starting point for exploring Owen's diction or as stimulus for students' own poetry. Close reading of poems at different draft stages should inform students' developing understanding of Owen's work and would be particularly useful for those studying literature of the First World War for their A-level synoptic paper. **B/C, D, RP.**

www.teachit.co.uk

Includes examples of pupils' poetry which you can scroll through. **PP.**

www.teachit.co.uk/teachit/KS5

The KS5 section includes teaching ideas and activities for responding to poetry at A-level. Includes pages on Carol Ann Duffy's *Mean Time* collection. **TM, B/C.**

www.proquestlearning.co.uk/literature

This ProQuest subscription site offers a huge range of poetry texts and critical materials together with audio recordings and video clips of over 70 poets performing their work. An invaluable resource for those studying poetry for examinations. **B/C, I, RP.**

CD-ROM

Many of the CD-ROM materials currently available to support students' poetry writing seem to be rather limited in their scope in that they fail to exploit the potential of using ICT. Perhaps inevitably they concentrate on introducing the forms of poetry through a series of writing frames. Such CDs do provide opportunities for teachers to modify materials and/or for students to work independently. However, unless adapted and used very skilfully, I think these materials can reduce writing poetry to a worksheet based activity which does not allow for children to experiment with drafting original work. Clearly there are exceptions to this rule. For example *The Making of Poetry* (Published by AVP), suitable for pupils aged 11–16, includes manuscripts of poems by Wordsworth, Keats, Hopkins and Owen, and explores the way in which their drafts were altered. The CD accompanying James Carter's *Rap It Up* (2000) includes rap backing tracks which students can use for writing and recording their own rap poetry. Other CDs which feature audio readings of poets include *Sharing Poems: Teaching Poetry at Key Stage 2* (Bibby and Priest, 2000), *Silver Hooks and Golden Sands* (published by Headstrong, 2000) and *Poetry Plus* (published by Chadwyck Healey, 1995). The last two titles are largely intended for reading or researching poetry and the latter is particularly useful for students compiling their own poetry anthologies.

Video

Using a video camera with pupils to record their poetry videos and performances is another way to bring ICT in to your poetry classroom. There are also a number of high-quality pre-recorded videos which offer insights into the writing process. These include: *Roots and Water* (Jones/BBC, 1999) and videos produced by Studia (2002) both featuring poets in AQA's GCSE (Spec. A) poetry anthology; *The Key Stage 3 Poetry Video* – a 90-minute video, produced by the English and Media Centre, which contains poetry writing ideas together with the poet Sophie Hannah's reflections on drafting as she drafts a poem to camera; *Tony Harrison: Six Poems* (English and Media Centre) which contains an absorbing interview with Harrison who comments on his craft and the role of poetry in society; *A Poet's Life,* a resource for lower secondary students (published by teamvideo) which features readings, activities and interviews with two poets – Jackie Kay and Matthew Sweeney – and *Why Poetry?* (also from teamvideo) which contains interviews and readings, of their own work and poets they admire, by Joolz, Roger McGough, Benjamin Zephaniah, John Hegley, Grace Nichols, Ian McMillan and Martin Wiley.

Overhead projector

In comparison with some of the other resources discussed in this chapter the overhead projector may seem like technology from the Dark Ages. However, as English teachers are increasingly discovering, this piece of equipment is an invaluable tool which can make the drafting of a text much more of a shared experience. When preparing OHTs on computer aim to use a large font size (at least 18) and avoid cramming too much text onto one transparency. Using different coloured pens or fonts to mark the draft stages can be very helpful. Try experimenting with a series of OHT overlays to show particular changes in the draft. Drafts can be annotated and changed very quickly on an OHT as the teacher, pupil or visiting poet talks through the choices they are making. A useful record of the writing process remains on OHT and can be reused during the plenary or the introductory stage of another lesson. Another advantage of transparencies is that students can instantly 'publish' their completed poems for all to see. (One group of Year 6 children I worked with during a summer school workshop responded extremely positively to the immediacy of this method of publication.)

This chapter has demonstrated how ICT can both support and enliven drafting poetry in the classroom by providing closer access and insight in to the dynamic nature of the process. Use of a word processor alone can transform students' approaches to writing poetry. By using ICT in its various forms, the relationship between the reading and writing of poetry is brought ever closer. Furthermore students can be given opportunities to experiment with poetic language in many, increasingly multi-layered, collaborative ways.

5

The Visiting Poet and Poetry Workshops

Bringing a poet into the classroom is the ultimate way of breathing life into the process of writing poetry. If the visit is to be a success and to have a long-lasting impact on students' perceptions of poetry, then it must be properly planned. This chapter explores good practice for working with visiting professional writers to create a productive writing workshop environment in classes across the secondary age range. Contact details are given for those wishing to plan poetry visits in and out of the classroom. I will also consider how teachers can build on the workshop experience to develop the poetry curriculum further by referring to the development of a scheme of work on writing ghazal poetry.

During the last 20 years there has been a burgeoning of poetry residencies (these include placements in schools and more unusual venues such as London Zoo, Marks and Spencers and Barnsley Football Club) as well as other poetry promotions such as W.H. Smith's Writers in Schools, The Poetry Places scheme, National Poetry Day and Poetryclass. Poetryclass is a DfES funded initiative spearheaded by the Poet Laureate, Andrew Motion, to encourage teachers use poetry in the classroom 'to develop creative writing and extend children's literary experience at all Key Stages' (Blunkett, 2000: 3). By enabling students and teachers to meet and work alongside published poets, these events have had an influence on the teaching of poetry (Arts Council of England, 1998; PN Review, 1999; Wilson, 1998) although how widespread and how long lasting this will be is difficult to judge. Experience of arranging and participating in such placements leads me to believe that their impact can be felt in the buzz about poetry, which can be created in a school. During a residency given by Jackie Kay, a student commented to me: 'after that workshop the five of us talked about writing for over an hour – something we have never really done before,' (Dymoke, 1994: 86). If any visits can stimulate this kind of discussion about writing they must be worthwhile.

I was lucky enough to begin my teaching career in an English department which understood the value of bringing poets, playwrights and prose writers into the classroom and ensured that as many staff and pupils as possible had contact with them. It still surprises me how rare this experience is. With an increased squeeze on curriculum time, many colleagues mourn the loss of opportunity to arrange visits, either in or out of the classroom. Too often visits are viewed by senior managers in schools as something 'extra' or a special treat which will have a disrupting effect on other curriculum areas. However, if they are to be successful, and to reap meaningful rewards in the long term, they need to be an integral part of English department schemes of work and should contribute to the spiritual/aesthetic development of the school as a whole.

People can have very strange ideas about what poets are like. When Ian McMillan first visited with his donkey jacket and canvas bag, a number of my Year 11 students thought he was the plumber! Visits from writers can break down all kinds of preconceptions and encourage discussion about poetry in the most unlikely quarters of the school canteen. They should further the conversations about poetry which teachers have with their pupils.

Planning a visit

When planning a visit there are a number of points to consider. Probably the most important concern is who to choose and what type of visit would be most beneficial for the pupils. There are three main types of visit (as well as endless variations on these):

1 A 'one-off' one-day visit.
2 A series of half day or day regular visits over a number of weeks.
3 A residency (lasting a week, fortnight or longer depending on the budget).

The 'one-off' option is probably the route taken by most schools. The writer might visit during a school's book week or on National Poetry Day. The format of such a day might consist of two writing workshop sessions with different groups and a performance/question and answer session, perhaps with a larger group. If other departments are accommodating, the school's timetable for that day could be changed to allow, for example, all pupils in a particular year group to participate. However, these arrangements can be difficult to negotiate.

Such day visits can be very useful for raising the profile of poetry in a school, giving some pupils an insight into a poet's work, and initiating some drafting of poetry. The main disadvantage of them, however, is that their impact can be very short-lived and only impinge on a small section of the school community. Unless the day is carefully followed up after-wards, incomplete drafts can disappear into a vacuum. The poet Sandy Brownjohn is critical of the one-day workshop approach and prefers to read and answer questions instead if on a short visit. In an interview with Anthony Wilson she states that poets tend to follow a set pattern or frame-work which they know will work. Nevertheless, because of time pressures, they 'cannot really begin to explore creative thinking in any real depth. So what happens is the children fit their ideas into this pattern or framework, they write a little better than they have before, and everyone is chuffed. But the poet goes away and then what happens?' (Wilson, 1998: 126).

By far the more preferable (and usually more expensive) routes are options 2 and 3. Option 2, the series of visits, allows the writer to build a much more sustained relationship with pupils and teachers in several classes. A workshop activity can be developed over a number of weeks. Rather than just providing the initial stimulus for writing, the poet is able to support pupils with their drafting, and provide greater insights into the process as a whole. This type of visit is invaluable for those pupils who are lacking in confidence. It can take time before they are ready to trust visitors and get the best out of such an input. With a residency, perhaps extending over a week or longer, the poet can become more established as a part of the school community. It then might be easier to create flexible arrangements such as working with small groups of pupils or even indi-viduals during lunchtimes or at an after-school writing club. Time could also be set aside for staff and parents and carers to attend a writing workshop or an evening performance.

Choosing the writer

Choosing the right person to work with pupils can be difficult. Sometimes availability can be the deciding factor, while cost is always a major con-sideration. However, it is important to think about what pupils could gain from the experience and to do some research before rushing to book someone. Ask the following questions:

- Do I want to invite a famous national figure or someone with a local reputation?
- Does the visit need to link in with a specific scheme of work?
- Do I want pupils to work with someone whose work they are studying for an examination?
- Do I want the emphasis to be on the poet's writing and performance or on the pupils'?
- Do I want to use the visit to support a new curriculum initiative? (For more on this refer to the section on ghazal poetry later in this chapter.)

It is not necessary to hire a big name (even if the budget is available): it is more important to book someone who is positive about working with young people and will engage them. Ask the literature development officer at your regional arts board (RAB) or the Education department at the Poetry Society for recommendations. Consult the writers' database on the National Association of Writers in Education (NAWE) website. (For contact details of all these and other organisations please refer to the list at the end of this chapter.) Find out about other schools' experiences – who has been a success with their students and how have they organised their visits? Is there a possibility that two schools could share a writer? Before booking make sure you have read some of the poet's work yourself. If at all possible, try to see the poet in performance: some writers are not as successful at bringing their own work off the page as others.

Dos and don'ts

Who should participate?

Involve other members of staff in making this decision. Enable pupils of all abilities to participate and try to spread the allocation of groups fairly among members of staff. Don't restrict access to top groups or the best behaved class. Ask the writer about suitable group sizes. Some prefer to work with a maximum of 20 pupils for a writing workshop but are happier to talk and perform to much larger groups. If you are planning to record their performances, seek consent beforehand.

When should the visit take place?

Think about the preparation time needed beforehand as well as time afterwards for productive follow up. Where possible avoid having a visit during the last week of term or on a Friday afternoon.

How should the visit be structured?

Before making any firm arrangements consult with the poet about what seems reasonable. Make sure that the visitor is not expected to work during every lesson and at breaktimes. Allow time for at least one break of a decent length. Other members of staff may like the chance to meet the visitor informally but only plan for a full day if the poet offers this. English lessons can last between 40 and 75 minutes. You may want to negotiate reorganising part of the English timetable to create some lengthier sessions. Check carefully on travelling times before slotting in sessions at the beginning and end of the day.

How should each session be structured?

Make sure the writer is happy with the agreed lengths of sessions and then discuss an outline structure. Some poets coming into the classroom may be very aware of the Framework four part lesson format (and may even follow it loosely) but this should not be expected. Be flexible and suspend this structure during the visit. Allow visitors sufficient time to generate excitement about poetry, to take risks with language and to give pupils genuine opportunities to extend their writing skills.

What role should teaching staff have during workshop sessions?

Some writers complain that a minority of schools treat them like supply teachers when they are running a workshop. Although the visiting poet may have had considerable classroom experience they are not being employed as a teacher and should not be expected to undertake crowd control. More importantly, they are not insured to do so. At least one member of staff, preferably someone who knows the pupils, should always be in the room during the sessions. This advice is not only for health, safety and discipline reasons, but also because the teachers should want to be involved so that they can share the experience with their pupils and follow up effectively afterwards. Sometimes writers will ask a teacher to act as a scribe (for example, to collate suggestions made by the group on a flip chart). Wherever possible teachers should participate in the writing activities. This will make it so much easier to share drafts and to discuss responses at a later stage. Writers tend to feel very insulted by staff marking books at the back of their sessions. Make sure all support staff involved are introduced to the writer and that they know what they will be expected to do during the sessions.

How should you prepare for a visit?

Ideally the writer's visit will not be the only opportunity for pupils to read and write poetry during the term (although I have visited one school where I was told that my workshops constituted the class's poetry lessons for the whole year!). The visit should not be a complete surprise to pupils. If they are going to get the most out of the visit, the classes should be well prepared. At the very least it would be a good idea to ensure that the pupils have had a chance to draft poems and read some of the poet's work in the week before the visit. Remind them of other poetry work they have completed previously. It may be appropriate to complete other kinds of preparation such as research, word collection or drafting questions. In the rush to organise the visit and the specific classes involved, do not neglect to publicise the visit to everyone else. Some pupils could make poetry posters, featuring examples of the poet's work. Make sure that multiple copies of the writer's publications are available in the library. It may be worth contacting the local media but check that the writer is happy to be interviewed/photographed before doing so. Be warned that the photographer always seems to arrive at the most inconvenient moment during a workshop.

Provide the writer with very clear details confirming all the arrangements for the planned visit at least a week in advance. Do not leave this until the last minute: remember that the poet may frequently be working away from home. Some writers will send you a contract, which acknowledges the arrangements, as soon as a booking is confirmed. If this is not the case, ensure that they acknowledge receipt of your letter.

Details should include:

- home and school contact details of the organiser;
- the exact timings and locations of sessions;
- the number of pupils involved in each session (plus any essential information about them);
- resources needed for each session;
- writer's travel arrangements;
- where she/he will be staying;
- directions;
- dietary and other needs;
- confirmation of payment arrangements (both fees and other expenses).

Resources and rooms

Ensure that photocopying and any other materials needed are discussed with the writer beforehand and collected in advance of the visit. Schools are often very overcrowded places but try to arrange for workshop and performance sessions to take place in spaces which will not be disturbed by other classes. It can be a real strain to be 'on show' all the time: if a writer is going to be working in school for longer than a day try to provide them with a private workspace and access to a computer.

Payment

Contrary to popular belief, most writers in the UK earn less than the average wage. Workshops and performances can provide them with a considerable slice of their annual income. Therefore, it is essential that they are paid promptly. If it is a single visit, many will insist that they are paid on the day. Make sure you clarify this is in advance to avoid any embarrassment. The Poetry Society has a recommended minimum fee for a day's work. Expenses will need to be budgeted for in addition to this. If the school needs to raise funding for the visit try approaching the literature development officer in your region for advice. He or she may know of local grants or sources of funding. This person could also help to reduce your costs by combining the visit with a public reading or arranging for you to share the poet with another school. Parent–teacher associations can be another valuable source of financial support, especially if it can be shown how the visit would benefit the school as a whole.

Follow-up

The follow-up to a visit should be just as important as the visit itself. If the visit involved writing workshops, time should at least be set aside for completion of draft work and, preferably for further poetry writing. Writers seldom get to see what has been written after they have gone; try to send them a few examples of completed poems and a thank you note. Performances during assemblies, evening readings or displays are always good ways of drawing attention to the outcomes. Publication is another valuable spin-off, particularly if pupils are involved in the associated editorial, design, production and marketing processes. If your poet has written new work during the visit or residency they may be willing to let you publish it. When Jackie Kay did a week's residency at West Bridgford School, she generously dedicated 'Amber and Chocolate', first drafted in a Year 9 poetry workshop, to the school. This gave us all a real thrill and certainly helped sales of the anthology we produced. The poem was later published in *Three's Gone* (Kay, 1994).

There should, however, be an opportunity, beyond such published outcomes, for students to reflect on what they have experienced in ways which might inform their developing definitions of poetry. Pupils could be asked to jot down thoughts informally in their drafting book or in a learning log. They could reread poems by the writer and choose one for themselves as a model for their own work. They could investigate or compare other poems or poets which the writer has referred to as influences. All of these activities should be flexible and negotiated with individuals.

Using visits to support a new curriculum initiative

Visiting writers can inform, and even contribute to, the curriculum development work of the school or English department. One example of this, which I was involved in, centred on an introduction to teaching the ghazal and is described below. This work originated as part of a NATE International/Multicultural Literature project funded by the Arts Council of England. Two publications resulting from this project are *Opening New*

Worlds (Goody, 1995) and *Multicultural Literature in the Classroom* (Goody, with Thomas, 2000). Both contain examples of poetry initiatives which provide useful models for teachers. They include accounts of: poetry writing in Years 5 and 6 from Aborigine and other perspectives; introducing modern European poetry; developing a coherent approach in Key Stage 3 to reading poetry from a range of multicultural perspectives; approaching international literature of struggle with International Baccalaureate EAL students.

Ways into teaching the ghazal: a multicultural literature project

West Bridgford School is a large 11–18 comprehensive in a suburb of Nottingham which serves quite a diverse catchment area. A minority of the pupils are Urdu, Hindi, Pujabi-Sikh and Cantonese speakers, while at least 10 other languages are also spoken along with English. At the time of the project the English team were committed to giving pupils opportunities to: read a wide variety of literature from different cultures; develop personal responses to texts and work with visiting writers. The project's aim was to develop pupils' understanding of the distinctive voices and forms used by Asian poets, their perspectives and selection of subject matter.

A small part of the funding was used to carry out research and to purchase suitable resources. While it was relatively easy to access websites it was much harder to locate in-print resources which would be appropriate for use with younger students (aged 11–13) especially. The form of the ghazal proved to be the key to the project. It was clear that this would be a useful addition to the range of forms within the poetry curriculum and might enable pupils to build on their knowledge of the haiku, which many of them had already encountered at primary school, and develop a further understanding of syllabic forms. For information about the ghazal see Appendix 1.

After latching on to the form as a way in, and sharing this with other staff, we needed to seek advice from writers of ghazals who could bring it alive for both students and teachers. A group of poets called Mini-Mushaira (Debjani Chatterjee, Simon Fletcher and Basir Sultan Kazmi) were approached and two of the group, Debjani and Simon, came into school. Their writing workshops involved Year 8 (see Figure 5.1) and Year 12 classes, a small lunchtime writers' group, five English teachers and two learning support staff. With Year 8 the emphasis was on familiarising pupils with the form, performance techniques and the experience of the mushaira. With the A-level students the poets aimed to provide literary and historical background, coupled with a brief writing activity.

A Midsummer Night's Dream

Opening night of the new play,
I'm so nervous, got butterflies.

Time to put on my costume,
Can't help it, still got butterflies.

I can hear the audience out there,
Can't get rid of these butterflies.

Finish makeup, quick look at my lines.
Forgotten them, ooh, butterflies.

Ruth comes in, gives us some pointers.
I've never had butterflies.

Into place, ready to start,
Disappearing butterflies.

Curtains open, I walk onto stage,
Audience loves us, bye butterflies.

A Midsummer Night's Dream – Will Shakespeare,
I am Flute -Thisbe, with no butterflies!

Carly

Leave me Alone

You can beg and plead and moan and groan,
But I don't want your reasons – just leave me alone.

If you call me up I'll slam down the phone.
I don't need you, just leave me alone.

You can stand in the rain till you're chilled to the bone.
But I don't want you – just leave me alone.

'Slow down Karen, let me walk you home.'
'Get lost Jerry, JUST LEAVE ME ALONE!'

Caroline

continued over

Going to Bed

I was walking on the landing
and I heard something banging. Oh Mum!

I was walking through the door
and I heard some more. Oh Mum!

I heard a noise in bed.
It sounded like the dead. Oh Mum!

I was turning off the light
and I got a fright. Oh Mum!

Eekekeekek goes the door.
Creak, creak goes the floor. Oh Mum!

Twit Twoooo. Oh boo!
Ian is that you? Oh Mum!

Charles

Friends

She used to live near me, now
she lives far away. It's just not the same.

She used to be my friend, now she's
my enemy. It's just not the same.

We would ring each other up and be on
the phone for hours. It's just not the same.

Once a week we would go shopping
around the big centres. It's just not the same.

We rode our bikes till dark in the summer,
just around and around. It's just not the same.

We both wore friendship rings but hers
seems to have disappeared. It's just not the same.

Come on Jenny! Let's just be friends.
Otherwise it's just not the same.

Chelsea

Figure 5.1   *Examples of ghazals written by Year 8 pupils*

Through working with visiting writers in this way, pupils directly involved could begin to appreciate the richness of a literary tradition which was different from many of their own cultural experiences. With the help of the two poets, the department was able to develop a new scheme of work which would have more of a lasting impact on the poetry experience of all pupils in the Year group.

Main features of the ghazals unit

The main features of this unit are described below. Some elements have been adapted from Mini-Mushaira's workshops. A number of these activities could be used as starter activities within the four-part Framework structure whereas others are more appropriate for extended work.

1   Introductory exploratory and recap activities to consider range of poetic forms pupils are familiar with and possible reasons for use of different forms. (These might include haiku, limerick, ballad, shape poem, acrostic, nursery rhyme, renga and cinquain.)
2   Identifying rhyming patterns by using a selection of poems with different rhyme schemes (either on an OHT or a worksheet). Consolidation of poetic terms such as couplets, quatrains, stanza lengths.
3   Close focus on how couplets can be used as riddles or witty, terse summaries of people or situations (using a poster or worksheet of examples). A pupil investigation of how Shakespeare uses couplets in his plays is a good development from this activity.
4   Pupils should draft two single couplets summing up their favourite and their most despised character from television, film or literature. Others in the class should try to guess who is being described.
5   Provide examples of ghazals for pupils to read and discuss in pairs. What common features can they find? They should be able to comment on some of the following: the form; the distinctive rhyme scheme; the syllabics; the use of repetition; how the name or pen name of the writer or the subject of the poem is included in the final couplet and, possibly, the tone and range of subject matter. (*A Little Bridge* by D. Chatterjee, S. Fletcher and B. Sultan Kazmi published by Pennine Pens [1997] has some examples of ghazals.)
6   Investigation into the origins of the ghazal, famous ghazal writers and the languages in which ghazals are written using the internet and drawing on the knowledge of group members and local community. You may also want to play some ghazals. (The CD *Ghazal Lost Songs from the Silk Road* [1997, Shanachie 64096] is recommended.)

7   Pupils to devise a radif (refrain) for their own ghazal. This will form the second line of the couplet. Share ideas for refrains and offer ideas if pupils find this difficult. Suggestions for radifs:

... always changing

... blazing like diamonds

... onwards forever

... I'm going far

... and none came to help me

8   Once pupils have a workable refrain line they can begin drafting their ghazal. The poems can be any length (at least four couplets proved a useful guideline) and should include as many of the other features as appropriate. Encourage writers to use a consistent syllabic count throughout the poem and to tap out the syllables as they draft. (They may well be familiar with this approach from writing haikus.)

9   Work with drafting partners to redraft and polish as necessary. Encourage pupils to read out drafts and to follow principles described in Chapter 2.

10   A class or public performance. Explain the term mushaira. Encourage close listening and audience participation. (Mini-Mushaira asked pupils to cry out Wah! Wah! or Bravo! Bravo! for lines to be repeated but pupils could decide on their own terms of appreciation!)

Visiting the poet

Attending a poet's public performance is another way of bringing a poet off the page. Some of the big name poets who feature in examination syllabi regularly take part in conferences for students in which they give readings of their own, and sometimes other poets' work. These performances usually last about half an hour and are followed by questions. Held in huge venues, the scale and content of these conferences can be overwhelming. The poet is often sandwiched between prose writers and sessions on examination technique. Although the best of these conferences can be good value for money, your students can have closer contact (and perhaps a more realistic chance of asking questions) by attending a public reading at a local library or bookshop. Libraries will occasionally organise afternoon readings or workshops just for local schools, before the main evening event.

Writing out of the classroom

Educational visits of all kinds can provide excellent opportunities for poetry writing. Students will have the chance to write from real experience and respond to a range of stimuli seldom available in the conventional classroom context. Liaison with art, history, geography and modern languages departments can be very fruitful in this respect for developing cross-curricular literacy work. The list of potential venues is endless. Art galleries, museums, National Trust and English Heritage sites are particularly good locations. Two specific recommendations are Magna and Beth Shalom. Magna, the award-winning museum of earth, air, fire and water is in Rotherham, South Yorkshire. Based in a old steel works it is a remarkable place for writing. Its fire tornados, crackling light shows and gale simulators cannot fail to inspire. On the surface Beth Shalom Holocaust Memorial Centre is a calmer location but anyone who has visited will know what a thought-provoking experience a visit can be. The centre provides educational facilities and resources on the Holocaust and the Jewish tradition, including an extremely powerful exhibition. Students can meet with Holocaust survivors and refugees. Teachers of English examination classes should consider using a visit to stimulate poetry for original writing coursework. (For contact details please refer to the list at the end of this chapter.)

Other venues such as churchyards, marinas, airports and canals are also worth considering. You could either lead the writing activities at a venue yourself or book a writer to work with pupils in residence at a specific location. The Poetry Places scheme (which ran from 1998 to 2000) has highlighted the diversity of locations which can stimulate new writing, including hospitals, law courts, football clubs, supermarkets and commuter trains. Details about the poetry produced during this scheme are available on the Poetry Society website.

The Arvon Foundation

The Arvon Foundation has four houses in beautiful country locations where teachers can take small school groups for tailor-made residential courses to work with professional writers. Some bursaries are available for individual participants and whole groups. Alongside its annual programme of writing courses for adults, Arvon also runs courses specifically designed for teachers. The Arvon experience is highly recommended.

The Windows Project

Based in Liverpool, the Windows Project has been working for over 20 years with schools and school groups from nursery age to post-16 to provide readings and workshops to suit specific needs. The team of writers are very experienced and the project will be able to offer advice about how to get the best out of the visits as well as potential sources of subsidy.

Poetryclass

If you are unsure about teaching poetry or planning a poetry visit, try contacting the Poetry Society about Poetryclass which offers practical
tailor-made in-service training for teachers across the age ranges. Courses
are all run by poets who are very experienced workshop providers. They
will equip you with fresh ideas and methods for exploring poetry in the
classroom, as well as with information about resources and support.

Poetry libraries

In the UK there are three poetry libraries run by knowledgeable and
extremely helpful staff. They have a wealth of information about poetry
events, publications, recordings of performances, extensive databases and
provide education services. The Voice Box at the Poetry Library in London
promotes a regular programme of performances.

Contact information

The Arvon Foundation
Website: www.arvonfoundation.org.uk

The Arvon Foundation at Lumb Bank
Hebden Bridge
West Yorkshire
HX7 6DF
Tel: +44 (0) 1442 843714

The Arvon Foundation at Totleigh Barton
Sheepwash
Beaworthy
Devon EX21 5NS
Tel: +44 (0) 1409 231338

The Arvon Foundation at Moniack Mhor
Teavarren
Kiltarlity
Beauly
Invernessshire IV4 7HT
Tel: +44 (0) 1463 741675

The Arvon Foundation at The Hurst (a new centre in Shropshire to be
opened in autumn 2002).

For details contact one of the other Arvon centres above.

Beth Shalom Holocaust Memorial Centre
Website: www.holocaustcentre.net
Beth Shalom
Laxton
Newark, Notts
NG22 0PA
Tel: + 44 (0) 1623 836627

Magna
Website: www.magnatrust.org.uk
Sheffield Road
Templeborough
Rotherham
South Yorkshire
S60 1DX
Tel: +44 (0) 1709 720002

National Association of Writers in Education (NAWE)
Website: www.nawe.co.uk
NAWE
PO Box 1
Sheriff Hutton
York YO60 7YU
Tel: +44 (0) 1653 618429

Poetry Ireland
Website: www.poetryireland.ie
Bermingham Tower
Upper Yard
Dublin Castle
Dublin 2
Republic of Ireland
Tel: + 003531 (01) 671 4632

The Northern Poetry Library
County Library
The Willows
Morpeth
Northumberland NE61 1TA
Tel: +44 (0) 1670 5345324/534514

The Poetry Library
Website: www.poetrylibrary.org.uk
Level 5
Royal Festival Hall
London SE1 8XX
Tel: +44 (0) 20 7921 0943

The Poetry Society (and Poetryclass)
Websites: www.poetrysociety.org.uk
          www.poetryclass.net
22 Betterton Street
London
WC2H 9BX
Tel: +44 (0) 20 7420 9894

Regional Arts Boards (RABs)
Website: www.arts.org.uk
5 City Road
Winchester
Hants
S023 8SD
Tel: +44 (0) 1962 851063

The Scottish Poetry Library
Website: www.spl.org.uk
5 Crichton's Close
Canongate
Edinburgh EH8 8DT
Tel: +44 (0) 131 557 2876

Young Book Trust and Bookstart
Website: www.booktrust.org.uk
Book House
45 East Hill
London
SW18 2QZ
Tel: +44 (0) 20 8516 2977

The Windows Project
Website: www.windowsproject.demon.co.uk
Windows
Liver House
96 Bold Street
Liverpool L1 4HY
Tel: +44 (0) 151 709 3688

6

Assessing Poetry

Poetry is deemed by many teachers to be 'notoriously hard to assess' (Andrews, 1991: 75) but if teachers (who are not generally novelists or newspaper reporters) are able to mark responses written in prose, chosen from a range of genres such as letter, diary or narrative, then should they not be able to assess poems too? This chapter investigates the reasons for perceived difficulties with poetry assessment, while offering practical advice about approaches. If practitioners lack confidence in teaching the writing of poetry, it is inevitable that that they will remain uncertain about its assessment. Teachers' attitudes to assessing poetry and the assessment frameworks of both the National Curriculum for English and the UK public examinations system are considered, together with views about what constitutes progression in poetry writing. The chapter draws on the critical perspectives of Carter, Benton, Driver and D'Arcy and alternative models for the assessment of writing. It argues for regular poetry assessment in the hope that this outcome might remove the mystique surrounding the genre and establish it on an equal footing with prose text types.

Teachers' attitudes to assessing students' poetry

In researching the poetry teaching repertoires of a small sample group of secondary English teachers working in 11–18 state schools, I found at least three types of attitude to assessing poetry. The first type included such responses as: 'Poetry can't be wrong but it can be commented on and pupils rewarded for their efforts' and 'if poetry is creative and individual who am I to assess it? … Because it's so personal it seems almost intrusive to be over critical'. The teachers' views corresponded with a belief in the personal, emotional and experiential nature of poetry, which prevents a teacher-assessor from passing final judgement. These teachers, like all those interviewed, were comfortable with intervening and supporting pupils during the drafting process but they were particularly anxious not to be intrusive. The fact that both of these speakers did feel able to award marks for effort endorses the focus on the individual. Such comments arguably have their roots in the Creative Writing or Progressive Movement (Abbs, 1982). As is explored more fully in the contextual overview of poetry teaching in Chapter 7, its followers, including Marjorie Hourd, believed that teachers should accept all their pupils' written outpourings, rather than make them: 'Strain ... to produce something to satisfy the teacher's demands instead of yielding up generously what they themselves have to give' (Hourd, 1949: 96).

This concentration on experience has its limitations. It will tend to focus on the intensity with which the experience has been conveyed and opportunities for comparisons with the work of other writers will be restricted (Shayer, 1972). However, like Driver, I am convinced that creative writing (including poetry) should take heed of assessment measures if it is 'not to be simply (and rather wetly) self expression' (Driver, 1977: 6). For Driver, whose set of values I will explore later in this chapter, a poem should be assessed 'in relation to the writer, not simply in relation to success measured against a model' (Driver, 1977: 6). The need for consideration of contexts as well as the cognitive and affective processes used by the developing writer are well-rehearsed arguments in critical debates about the assessment of writing (D'Arcy, 1989; Hill, 2000; Protherough, 1995).

The second set of comments made by teachers interviewed included: 'the National Curriculum offers no help with the assessment of poetry', 'I would like something that would give me phrases and terminology for assessing poetry' and '[With A-level creative writing modules] students will choose to write in prose rather than poetry because of the anxiety of teachers at not being able to say how good it is ... and the students' anxiety at not being able to assess for themselves how good it is'. These comments show that the teachers concerned wanted to assess poetry. Their comments have been echoed by many other teachers I have since spoken to, all of whom have been seeking guidance. One of the sample teachers wanted to place herself in a position where she could apply the same strategies for assessment which she used when marking work written in other generic forms. She was determined that pupils should be able to make progress with poetry in assessment terms. She felt on safest ground if she could mark for technical features that a poetry unit may have highlighted (such as use of particular forms or types of image) but stated that she lacked confidence in her own abilities as a poet to make overall judgements about a piece.

The lack of familiarity with the poetry writing process does present a challenge to teachers at all levels. In the past many critics have endorsed the need for practitioners to attempt to write poetry in the classroom in order to contribute meaningfully to the writing dialogue (Dunn, Styles and Warburton, 1987; Nicholls, 1990; Powell, 1968; Yates, 1999). Stibbs describes the need for this approach most vividly: 'teachers encourage ... writing poetry by writing it themselves: unless teachers do that they are tailor's dummies in a nudist colony – very bad manners' (Stibbs, 1981: 49). In spite of such encouragement, and the increased emphasis on shared writing within the National Literacy Strategy and the KS3 Strategy, it seems that the majority of teachers are still likely to feel more confident about modelling the writing of prose to their classes. As has been stated in Chapter 1, this is evident in the *Grammar for Writing* materials which focus on using sentence level work to 'improve writing' (DfEE, 2000: 19) and include teacher demonstrations of writing different prose forms.

Some of the teachers I interviewed attempted to use National Curriculum level descriptors for writing (DfE, 1995: 28) but they were frustrated by the lack of direct guidance, in the form of specific words or phrases, that they could use. Two of the sample referred to the now defunct Associated Examining Board 660 AS/A-level English Literature assessment grid as a potentially useful model. The third comment, concerning A-level creative writing modules, is particularly interesting for what it reveals both about levels of teacher confidence with poetry and the factors that could influence a student's own choice of genre for his or her writing. When discussing indicators of pupil progress in poetry writing, a number of the teachers identify a pupil's ability to make an independent choice of genre as a key element of progression. However, if pupils are being undermined in making this choice by lack of teacher confidence, then one must question the extent to which potential high-level performance in writing poetry might be affected.

The final comment cluster had some links with the previous set. It included such views as: 'A high level of achievement for children with all abilities is possible with poetry' and 'A pupil who is not particularly able might suddenly produce a little jewel of a phrase which might be difficult to compare with something which was workmanlike but not inspired'. Both of these comments seem to be of what one might call the 'you can assess it but ...' school. These respondents, like those in Peter Benton's survey (Benton, 1999 and 2000, see Chapter 1), recognise poetry writing as a skill that students of a wide range of ability can demonstrate. One of the teachers interviewed above had considerable experience as a GCSE English coursework moderator and a head of faculty. He frequently encouraged poetry writing in his classroom and department, believing this activity made language accessible: it enabled pupils to write 'with a kind of honesty and ... economy' that was not necessarily found in other language forms. However he considered that the potential for otherwise low-achieving pupils to write a 'jewel of a phrase' meant poetry was 'not a good discriminator' in assessment terms. For him, use of poetry for final written examination or coursework assessment raised questions of comparability and consistency which were difficult to reconcile. Very few schools submit students' own poetry for final GCSE coursework assessment. A chief examiner has told me that the limited number of poetry assignments he has seen have tended to be of a very high quality, submitted by a few centres who 'know what they are doing in this area'. It is debatable whether other centres are disenfranchising their students by not actively promoting poetry writing as a viable coursework option or whether they are simply being pragmatic about the parameters for GCSE assessment.

In analysing the work of teachers it soon became clear that, with one notable exception, poetry writing had become an activity which was largely confined to their Years 7 and 8 classes – a finding which echoes that of Peter Benton's survey across one local education authority (Benton, 1999). The sample's Key Stage 3 schemes of work reflected what Fleming identifies as a shift of emphasis from experiencing to studying poetry (Fleming, 1996) resulting in an increased focus on reading and responding to published work. While the majority of teachers were hoping to find the time to reinstate poetry writing for assessed GCSE original writing coursework eventually, they all felt under severe pressure to prepare pupils for end of Key Stage 3 tests and GCSE examinations in which the demands of prose writing dominate. One only has to look at the level descriptions within the National Curriculum for English to recognise that assessment of prose takes priority over other genres. The single direct reference to poetry in any of the three attainment targets occurs in En2: Reading level 7. Those pupils attaining Level 7 will: 'articulate personal and critical responses to poems, plays and novels, showing awareness of their thematic and linguistic features.' (DfEE and QCA, 1999: 57).

Where Writing (En3) is concerned, narrative and non-fiction are the only text types specifically mentioned – notably in the descriptions for the high-achieving Levels 7, 8 and Exceptional performance. All other text types are referred to by the blanket terms 'different forms' or 'a range of forms'. For Dennis Carter the omission of any direct reference to poetry assessment is unacceptable and at odds with the commitment to poetry shown in the National Curriculum programmes of study and the National Literacy Strategy (Carter, 1998). Confident poetry teachers will look for opportunities regularly to include poetry in their planning. However, without such references, it can be very difficult to convince teachers, who may be reluctant or uncertain about poetry writing, to risk its inclusion in their schemes of work for pupils in Year 9 and above.

The problem of teachers' uncertainty about poetry assessment is further exacerbated by the limited number of examples of assessed poetry provided by curriculum authorities. Without more exemplars prose will understandably be viewed as a safer assessment route. The *Grammar for Writing* materials do include three paragraphs of Key Stage 2 pupils' reflections on the process of writing poetry (DfEE, 2000: 166). While these are commendable, it is unfortunate they are not accompanied by further examples of pupils' drafting and final assessed pieces. Instead, the support materials provide an example of a Year 6 pupil's personification list drafted into a poem entitled 'Autumn'. The beautifully handwritten final draft does contain some promising attempts at using personification and alliteration. However, it remains a list of separate sentences rather than a poem. The teacher awarded the writer a star and the comment: 'Very good personification and quite a lot of effective alliteration' (DfEE, 2000: 173). The poet should definitely be praised but how will this comment enable the pupil to move beyond sentence-level work and develop an overall shape or movement in the poem? How will this example help teachers using these materials for training purposes? Two further examples of Year 4 and 5 drafts, based on observations of an autumn leaf and road repairs, indicate, thankfully, that drafting can be a messy business. However, the final draft is simply accompanied by a tick. While I am sure that the class teacher will have commented, either orally or in writing, on the finished piece, the fact that the teacher's response is not included represents a missed opportunity to demonstrate formative assessment in action.

For some years poetry writing has been marginalised within the assessment framework at GCSE. Although critical responses to poetry texts are a substantial feature of English and English Literature GCSE written examinations (in the form of questions on unseen poems or a prescribed anthology), there are no requirements for students to write their own poetry either in the examination or for coursework. The chief examiner for NEAB English has gone so far as to express surprise that some candidates chose to write poems – in response to an examination question which invited students to write descriptions of a given place 'in such a way that it can be easily imagined by your reader' (Paper Two, Section B, English for Higher tier candidates; NEAB, 1998b: 4). Although the students were not directly penalised for writing poems, the chief examiner's report noted: 'by adopting a form not generally suited to an examination of this kind, some candidates clearly limited their own personal achievement' (NEAB, 1998b: 5). It is striking that the author of the report neither considers why the students limited their achievements nor indicates where such a poetic response could have been more appropriately located. Peter Thomas (Thomas, 2000) and other examiners frequently advise that both teachers and candidates need to understand how assessment objectives underpin GCSE question setting. However, when the Paper Two Section B invites students to 'inform, describe and explain' and this particular cohort of candidates had already been asked to write analytically about descriptions of place in poetry for a previous question, one would hope that the creative application of their understanding might have been commended. The poet Tom Leonard, one of the few to pass comment on poetry assessment, supports the idea that poetry writing has no place in an examination (Leonard, 1988). However the validity of such a stance is questionable: why is students' poetry writing considered an inappropriate activity in this examination context and why is it only an optional element of coursework?

With the arrival of new GCSE specifications for 2004 (for England and Wales), the neglect of poetry writing could continue. Within the 2004 specifications only one examination board, the Welsh Joint Education Committee (WJEC) explicitly mentions the idea of submitting poetry for one element of written coursework assessment. Even then the specification advises: 'problems of comparability may arise in the case of shorter writing forms such as poetry and letters. In these cases it will be advisable to give evidence of ability to sustain these skills: e.g. as selection of poems, a pair of formal letters' (WJEC, 2002: 15). Other boards make it more difficult to find a place for poetry coursework. For example the Oxford, Cambridge and RSA (OCR) board's English syllabus states that all its written coursework tasks 'require answers in continuous prose' (OCR, 2002: 27). The Assessment and Qualifications Alliance (AQA) specification A – developed from the NEAB syllabus previously described and widely considered to be the syllabus most likely to attract the largest number of candidates – carries a warning that teachers should closely consider the assessment objectives when selecting appropriate original writing coursework tasks which 'explore, imagine or entertain'. In a proposed timetable, included in training materials for centres, the board suggests that original writing could be attempted in the first term of the course, a year before it suggests the candidates begin studying sections of their poetry anthology. The specification advises that 'the emphasis should be on *crafting* writing of different types' and warns against what it calls a 'portfolio approach'. Its list of 'appropriate examples' includes narrative, empathetic response to text, autobiographical writing and travelogue. (AQA, 2002: 34–5). All this seems like sensible advice, but at a closer glance at the assessment objective for writing (AO3 which is common to all boards) reveals that rather a narrow interpretation of it is being favoured:

GCSE AO3 Writing (En3)
candidates will be required to demonstrate their ability to:

(i) communicate clearly and imaginatively, using and adapting forms for different readers and purposes;
(ii) organise ideas into sentences, paragraphs and whole texts using a variety of linguistic and structural features;
(iii) use a range of sentence structures effectively with accurate punctuation and spelling. (QCA, 2002)

Although examination boards defend themselves by stating that they have devised their specifications to comply with rules and assessment objectives stipulated by the QCA, no aspect of the writing objective above actually appears to preclude poetry. It would seem that poetry writing is being marginalised for no real reason, both through setting extra conditions for its inclusion and the omission of references to it in lists of exemplar tasks. This pattern of omission is also prevalent in the guidelines for original or experimental writing coursework within A-Level Language/Language and Literature specifications. The examination boards have not made it easy for candidates or teachers to develop the explicit links between prior reading and writing which may have been a familiar feature of many of their primary and lower secondary poetry lessons. As a result poetry writing remains a risky option.

Building on the achievements of Key Stage 2: progression and difficulty

As already stated, secondary level poetry teaching needs to build systematically on the poetic challenges which pupils will have already faced at primary school. If they have experienced the Literacy Hour, these challenges will have included introductions to haiku, shape poetry, poetic sequences, experiments with imagery and alliterative writing: aspects of the genre that secondary English departments would at one time have considered uncharted territory for primary pupils. The Framework for implementing the KS3 National Strategy in secondary schools inevitably contains less specific references to forms and styles of poetry (see Chapter 1) but this should not be a reason to ignore poetry. Providing frequent opportunities for pupils to revisit poems, experiment with words and established forms (as well as to devise new ones of their own), and to engage critically a range of poems which offer different types of difficulty should all be essential if they are to make further progress with their own writing.

Fleming considered that difficulty in poetry becomes more problematic as pupils move from experiencing poetry at primary school to studying it at secondary (Fleming, 1996). His application of Steiner's taxonomy of

difficulty in poetry (Steiner, 1978) to classroom practice is worth exploring in this context. Steiner identified four different types of difficulty:
'contingent' where archaic or unusual words or phrases need to be looked
up by a reader; 'modal' where a reader fails to 'fully grasp what the poem
is about at a deeper feeling and aesthetic level' (Fleming, 1996: 39); 'tactical' which arises when poets deliberately use original or unusual forms to
'recharge language which has become worn or clichéd' (ibid.); 'ontological' where difficulties are concerned with challenging previous definitions
of poetry and the ways in which meanings can be arrived at. In applying
Steiner's four different types of difficulty to poems selected for classroom
use, Fleming concluded that: different types of poems needed handling
differently; a student's diet of poems could be a meagre one if the chosen
poems, predominantly selected for their thematic links or predictable subject matter, merely contained a few 'contingent' difficulties (Fleming,
1996). It would be a useful exercise for other practitioners to review their
own choices of poems (particularly poems used as models for writing)
with reference to Steiner's categories. Steiner's essay could also form part
of an introductory unit on the nature of poetry for A-level English
Language and Literature students.

In researching the poem choices of secondary English teachers over one
academic year, I found that teachers *were* anxious to select appropriate
approaches for individual poems. Their choices of texts included some
poems from all four types of difficulty. These choices were influenced by
three main factors: teachers' assessments of their students' abilities and
previous experiences; their own views about the functions of poetry; and
their professional judgements about how the difficulties of chosen poems
would extend their students' understanding of the genre. One teacher,
who had developed a distinctive nurturing environment for poetry with
her classes, insisted poems did not 'belong to a particular year group'. She
would revisit poems for different purposes, believing that, with support,
pupils would overcome issues of difficulty as they gained further experience as readers and writers. For her this was a key indication of their
progress. Other indicators which teachers identified as demonstrating
pupils' progress included:

- developing a greater awareness of the writer's craft (including use of
  structures and techniques to inform and inspire their own writing;
- learning to draft (and, in some instances, to work with a drafting
  partner);
- learning to look critically at one's own work and to accept constructive
  criticism from others;
- developing figurative writing and imaginative selection/use of
  vocabulary;

- moving away from constant use of rhyme or 'rhyme for rhyme's sake';
- extending understanding of what could be potential source material or subject matter for poetry;
- moving away from over reliance on the pattern or form of a model;
- making an independent, deliberate choice to write a poem (rather than an alternative generic form) (Dymoke, 2000b: 28).

Writers of poetry need to be readers too. The framework includes an objective for text level writing in Year 7 which states that pupils should 'make links between their reading of fiction, plays and poetry and the choices they make as writers' (DfEE, 2001a: 24). If pupils are to sustain their progress in writing they should continue making connections between what they read and how they write throughout Key Stage 3 (and beyond), both in and out of the classroom. Suggestions for poetry texts which could offer new challenges to lower secondary readers are provided in Appendix 2.

Models of poetry-writing assessment

Assessment models or schemes which map progression in poetry writing are extremely few in number. While some nuggets of advice can be gleaned from close reading, even these are rare. Participants in the National Writing Project observed that: 'Faced with a child's poem too many teachers tend to determine the strengths and weaknesses of the piece and identify useful changes which might be made. In effect they take over the writing' (National Writing Project, 1990a: 65). A heavy interventionist approach to assessment should be avoided. However pupils should be given the kind of guidance which will help them to become critical readers of their own drafts. Once on a marking treadmill, it can be all too easy to make swift judgements and for markers to focus on how they would redraft a piece if it were theirs.

In an ideal classroom situation all teachers would have sufficient time to talk through final drafts of poems face to face with their writers. They would maintain an ongoing dialogue which would inform each pupil's development. In this way the resulting assessments would never be 'a surprise' (Graves, 1983: 93) and would be discussed in the context of the student's prior achievement in the genre. Indeed, the recommendation that sincere constructive comment is more useful for a student's writing development than marking errors (Dunn, Styles and Warburton, 1987) is one which many English teachers endorse. With this method of assessment the final comments are an extension of the preceding interventions on drafts and the teacher does not award a level or a grade. Formative assessment is crucial (not just for assessing students' poetry but for all the text types they have experimented with). Nevertheless the thorny question of how poetry can be placed on an equal footing with narrative, within a school system which ultimately measures a pupil's success in summative grades and levels at the end of a Key Stage, still remains. If a regular formative assessment dialogue occurs, arguably it should make summative judgements (for example, for teacher assessment levels at the end of Key Stage 3) less onerous and perhaps less significant in the overall context of a student's development.

Driver, a Head of English writing before the development of the National Curriculum, devised a set of criteria to be considered when marking pupils' poetry. These 'values' included:

1. verbal skills
2. the particular not the general
3. imagery
4. sensory perceptions
5. rhythm
6. humanity
7. speech in their own voices
8. honesty
and possibly
9. *pace* Orwell ... ignore all these if something new and exciting turns up. (Driver, 1977: 5–6)

Arguably many, if not all of these values could equally be applied to different types of prose or dramatic writing. Although Driver neither perceived them as a mark scheme nor wanted assessment to control the poetry writing process, he did feel the need to contribute to the assessment debate in the belief that pupils skilled in poetry writing can be disenfranchised by the lack of assessment opportunity. He also offered the reader a vision of a future English curriculum in which teachers and their students might be forced to abandon writing poems in favour of examination-style compositions. It is disconcerting to recognise how familiar this vision has become.

Dennis Carter aimed to provide a Key Stage 2 framework for assessment in his 'Poetry-making descriptions'. Designed to supplement National Curriculum Level descriptions for writing attainment at Levels 1–6, they chart progression from a Level 1 poetry writer who has begun to use their imagination and some traces of poetic feature to an accomplished Level 6 writer who is producing original, effective poems (see Figure 6.1).

Level 1: Able to use imagination.
          Some trace of poetic feature: rhythm, rhyme, alliteration, colour in use of
          vocabulary, figurative language, metaphor and simile.
Level 2: Increasing use of imagination.
          Clearly discernible poetic features.
Level 3: Confident use of imagination and some originality.
          Poetic phrases and lines are created.
Level 4: Shows some originality in creating poetic ideas.
          Well structured verses, passages or short forms created.
Level 5: Shows flair in creating poetic ideas.
          Increasing control over poetic form.
Level 6: Summons poetic ideas quickly and uses them effectively.
          Creates well-structured, original and effective whole poems.
                                                          (Carter, 1998: 39)

Figure 6.1   *Poetry-making descriptions devised by Dennis Carter*

Carter's assessment framework foregrounds the importance of the children's imagination and the quality of their ideas as integral elements of the writing process, together with the developing use of poetic form and increasing independence in writing. Carter applied his model to six examples of children's writing, emphasising the need for assessors to be able to compromise and express 'honest judgement according to … experience' (Carter, 1998: 39) when using the descriptions. With one exception, his selected examples are free verse poems. Some have a strong sense of rhythm while many contain striking observational details and imagery. An example assessed at Level 6 is commented on as 'this very nearly perfect child poem' (ibid.: 42). It is interesting that a child can be deemed close to attaining perfection without being accredited with an 'exceptional performance level' (that is, beyond the final Level of 8). In reading these descriptions Level 6 seemed something of an arbitrary stopping point and caused me to question if it might be possible to surpass this level of poetic achievement. I began experimenting with further descriptions to encompass the whole Key Stage 3 ability range:

Level 7:

   Confident choice of poetic form and techniques. Ideas and voice are developed. Stanza structures and punctuation make ideas and events clear to the reader.

Level 8:

   Is able to use specific poetic techniques, words or phrases to convey particular moods or tones to the reader. Coherent and controlled use of language in the development of ideas. Writer shows firm grasp of punctuation and stanza structures.

Exceptional Performance:
> Poetry has distinctive shape and creates an impact on the reader. Ability to evoke a particular mood through sensitive and imaginative use of language and structure. (Dymoke, 2001)

The three additional descriptions were originally intended for use as best-fit models for assessment of a pupil's collection of poetry or a sequence of poems. However, in beginning to trial them with secondary English teachers, they have provided a springboard for colleagues to discuss specific features of student's poetry and to consider their own poetry assessment practices. Many teachers have acknowledged that such opportunities are rare. One frequent discussion point has been whether certain poetic forms restrict the level of attainment which can be achieved. Concrete and haiku poetry were regularly referred to in this respect. One wonders where such restrictions would leave the distinguished literary careers of poets like George Herbert or Basho if they were pupils today. The need to revisit forms is vital. (Suggestions about how to develop work on concrete poetry using ICT are provided in Chapter 5.)

In her critique, *Two Contrasting Paradigms for the Teaching and Assessment of Writing,* Pat D'Arcy argues that there is neither a place for the role of the reader nor recognition (*pace* Vygotsky) that 'thinking generates language' within the 'narrowly linguistic paradigm' (D'Arcy, 2000: 49) that dominates the National Curriculum orders for English. She offers guidelines for 'responding interpretively' (ibid.: 48) to a pupil's story suggesting a two-step response, which focuses primarily on engagement before moving on to appreciate the writer's achievements. Her persuasive argument for the amalgamation of both the linguistic and process-based paradigms complements Carter's model.

In contrast to the writing levels within the National Curriculum Orders for England and Wales with their linguistic focus and narrative prose bias, the New Zealand Curriculum's 'written language achievement objectives' distinguish between three different writing functions – expressive, poetic and transactional. The poetic strand offers a broad interpretation of the writing process in which a growing awareness of the reader and the development of creative thinking skills are integral. Students should make progress in their poetic writing from being able to 'write on a variety of topics, beginning to shape ideas (at level 1) … write on a variety of topics, shaping ideas in a number of genres, such as letters, poems, and narrative, and making choices in language and form (at level 2)', to: 'write on a variety of topics, in a wide range of genres, shaping, editing and reworking texts and demonstrating depth of thought, imaginative awareness, and secure use of language, including accurate and discriminating use of the conventions of writing, and integrating techniques with purpose' (at level

8). At level 8 there are no distinctions between different poetic forms – all text types are on an equal footing.

Like most assessment models for writing, all these descriptions raise issues concerning the intentionality of the writer and the objectivity of the assessor. In her discussion of GCSE coursework assessment, Marshall (with reference to Wiliam, 1998) notes 'it is the interpretation of evidence that is crucial rather than the criterion descriptors themselves' (Marshall, 2000: 162). What the assessor brings to the piece and how they use this as a filter for their judgements are important to reflect on. The making/event of the poem (*pace* Rosenblatt) and its assessment will be informed in part by: the reader's own previous attitudes to poetry; their knowledge and relationship with the writer and the subject of the poem; and the nature of the writing task. No matter how scrupulous the assessor, subjectivity is undeniably a feature of English assessment but is it more so with poetry than other genres? I have found no reason for it to be so.

Another assessment model which addresses the issue of subjectivity has been developed by Atkinson, Cashdan, Michael and Pople for the assessment of creative writing portfolios in higher education (see Figure 6.2). In devising their five criteria of language, observation, structure, voice and commentary/analysis, for potential use on undergraduate courses, they were careful to choose terminology which made the criteria equally applicable to drama, poetry and prose. For example, characterisation, normally the preserve of novel writers, was subsumed under the term 'voice' (Atkinson et al., 2001: 27). The commentary/analysis column provides a focus on a student's consideration of the redrafting and editing processes he or she has undertaken. Such a column would be a useful addition to assessment criteria for public examinations. Their observation category is perhaps the most unfamiliar and contentious. The writers define it as 'the discerning of details which render situations vivid to the reader; the principle of "showing not telling"' (ibid.: 28). They view this as encompassing observation from the writer's standpoint while enabling an assessor to step back from the work and focus on a student's technical manipulation of content. Such a category could provide a way in to assessment for those who are reluctant to mark poetry: it places a distance between the assessor and the content and enables him or her to concentrate primarily on the poem's construction.

Advice on poetry assessment

The following advice is closely allied to suggestions on teacher and pupil roles during drafting, made in Chapter 2. It builds on the firm beliefs that written poetry assessment needs to be more fully integrated into the curriculum to inform planning and that assessment at secondary school level needs to build systematically on the poetic challenges which pupils

An overall class is given based on an assessment of the portfolio in terms of the five criteria outlined below.

	Language	Observation	Structure	Voice	Commentary/Analysis
Defini-tions	Control of the language — especially adjectives, adverbs and cliché	The discerning of details which render situations vivid to the reader; the principle of 'showing-not-telling'.	The organisation of text with the needs of genre, reader, content and economy in mind.	Control of narrative voice, dialogue, register and tone; may well be 'achieved' as against 'innate' and, thus, is linked to observation.	The student's own exploration of their writing portfolio which engages with the four other assessment criteria.
1st	Language fully controlled: fully particularised use of language that shows complete control of selectivity, originality and editing of language at all stages of the text.	Full control and use of observed detail.	Fully explores creative possibilities and economies of structure.	Full control of narrative voice and dialogue; complete awareness of demands of tone and register; effective use of idiom where necessary.	A full exploration of the redrafting and editing processes; showing this in thorough analysis of those processes Completely engages with the other criteria of assessment.
2:1	Overall control of language: language is particularised at most stages of the portfolio. There is considerable evidence of selectivity and editing of language in most parts of the text.	Overall use of observed detail.	Overall use of creative possibilities and economies of structure.	Overall control of narrative voice; awareness of demands of tone and register; shows control of idiom where necessary.	An overall exploration of the redrafting and editing processes. There is engagement with the other criteria of assessment although the analyses may not be thorough.
2:2	Partial control of language: there is some evidence of originality and particularisation of language. However, there may be some reliance on cliché. There is some evidence of selectivity and editing of the language of the text.	Partial use of observed detail: observation can be competent but inconsistent.	Control of structure is partial and/or inconsistent.	Partial control of narrative voice and dialogue; shows occasional awareness of tone and register, and some limited control over idiom.	A partial exploration of the redrafting and editing processes. Commentary may be limited to a description of the portfolio contents. Engagement with the other assessment criteria is also partial.
3rd	Limited control of language: substantial dependence on clichéd language. Low levels of selectivity and little evidence of editing of language. Some technical errors, i.e. mistakes in spelling, grammar and punctuation.	Observation is limited and inconsistent.	Limited control of structure.	Limited control of narrative voice. Dialogue is inappropriate to the stylistic context, i.e. naturalistic, stylised, absurd etc.; awareness of tone, register and idiom is very limited.	A limited exploration of the processes of writing. Often limits commentary to a description of the contents of the portfolio.
F	No control of language: total dependence on cliché and/or archaisms and generalities. Technical errors and generalities. Technical errors may inhibit communication.	No evidence of observation.	No evidence of controlling the structure.	No evidence of control of voice or dialogue.	No evidence of exploration of the processes of redrafting and editing: wholly inadequate in terms of length and engagement with the contents of portfolio. No engagement with the other assessment criteria.

Figure 6.2   *Creative writing in higher education: criteria for assessment of portfolios of writing (Atkinson et al, 2001: 26–8)*

will have already faced within their primary English curriculum. Poetry has been variously described as: hard to pin down (Andrews, 1991); containing different types of difficulty (Steiner, 1978); demanding 'a new effort of attention' (Lawrence, 1929: 255, as cited in Benton, 1990) from its readership. Given these definitions and the changing, often uncertain, place of poetry within the English curriculum (as outlined in Chapters 1 and 7) it is axiomatic that, historically, the genre has presented great difficulty for its interpreters in assessment terms. However this difficulty should not serve as an excuse for present neglect.

Regular assessment dialogue

A regular assessment dialogue (both written and spoken) should take place with pupils. Formative assessment should offer guidance about the ways in which pupils might progress in learning, linked to a clear conception of the curriculum and its learning goals' (Black, 1998: 26). Wherever possible the dialogue about reading and writing poetry which has developed throughout the drafting process should continue during the final assessment stages. There is a fine balance between advice and heavy-handed intervention: assessment comments could be open-ended and include questions, examples, references back to previous work as well as to potential new poetry projects. For example:

- You have really started something here! This poem has great potential to develop into a sequence. If you like that idea we can talk about how you might do this.
- Well done! You have tried hard to choose verbs which convey the slow clumsy movement of the animal in your poem. How do you think you could structure the lines to emphasise this slow movement even more?
- You are using visual images very well. How easy do you think it is for a reader to experience the <u>sounds</u> you describe in your poem?
- Splendid! You have really developed your use of this form since the autumn term. Have you thought about writing a companion poem with the same structure which gives a contrasting point of view?
- Some striking ideas which sometimes remain a bit too hidden. You might want to think about your use of line breaks here so that all your words can really work for you. Why not try reading your work aloud again. How does it sound with the breaks as they are? With the breaks in different places?
- This is a very lively original piece. Now you have clearly established your view it might a good idea to look at how other poets have tackled this subject. You would find poets such as ... interesting. Why not have a look in the poetry book box or on the internet?

Assessment should not be based on the 'once a term poem'

Such assessment is unfair to the writer and can give an unrealistic picture of his or her progress. Begin by basing assessments on a small group of poems written during a poetry unit. Once more confident, you may feel able to consider individual pieces. When taking this approach try to ensure assessment occurs regularly so that pupils can build on their achievements.

Be selective in assessments

If pupils are writing poetry regularly and using draft books they should, to some extent, be able to negotiate which poems will be formally marked. Do not try to assess every poem.

Use self and peer assessment

In order to develop real shared writing practices then all writers should be encouraged to reflect critically on each other's work.

Use commentaries

As has been outlined in Chapter 2, commentaries can help to make the writing journey explicit by enabling students to reflect on the drafting process. A thoughtfully written commentary can actually rescue a flawed creative piece if the writer can demonstrate an understanding of how they have used language and whether their choices have had their intended impact. This is not to say that every poem should be accompanied by a commentary, but judicious use of this approach will inform future drafts. In *Original Writing*, Peter Simpson advises A-level English Language students that it can sometimes be helpful to write 'a pre-commentary, in which you set out what you hope to achieve and how you hope to achieve it' (Simpson, 1999: 73). This pre-commentary then becomes a starting point (at the end of the writing process) for reviewing whether writing intentions have been fulfilled and how the drafting and/or research processes have initiated changes.

Ensure there is an appropriate match between the task(s) and the desired outcomes?

It is important to ask if the task is a viable one for poetry assessment: are the pupils actually being assessed for their progress in writing poetry or is the assessment really concerned with whether they have demonstrated an understanding of abstract nouns or alliteration? (If the latter is the case, the assessment might need a rethink: poems should be judged as poems.)

Ensure that the purpose of assessment and the chosen assessment objectives are clearly explained to pupils

It is accepted good practice to share these with pupils at the beginning of a unit of work and to ensure that they are expressed in terms which the pupils will understand. Use objectives sparingly. As Myhill warns, do not 'obscure the learner behind a morass of things to be taught' (Myhill, 2001: 18). Pupils can also be involved in negotiating and devising assessment criteria.

Using the 'model' poem as an assessment tool

It is common for pupils to write poetry based on a model. When using this approach it is important to establish with students:

(a) how they might use the model in their own writing (these alternative ideas should be starting points not a definitive list);
(b) how the influence of the model will be considered when their work is assessed.

It may be appropriate to identify some specific features which an assessor will look for but the key word here is flexibility. An assessor should not be looking for a slavish copy of the original but evidence that a writer has used the poem to inform their own original work in some way and been able to make their own language choices. (Of course, this could include complete rejection of the model!) When selecting models and planning how to teach them, try to ensure that the end results will not involve marking 30 almost identical poems. While it might be easier to compare the poems for assessment purposes it will not help pupils to develop as independent original writers and the marking will be very tedious. Allow time for exploration of ideas and layers of meaning of the poem as a whole rather than a quick 10 minutes to soak up a template. If a writing frame, based on a model, is being used ensure that pupils do not have to adhere rigidly to suggested formats. Encourage them to break out of the frame. Writing frames are being used increasingly in secondary schools. Although these may be time saving and provide valuable support for students, too often they are unnecessary props which can stifle originality. If the class has a wide ability range it might be more appropriate to introduce several poems which present different levels of challenge and are thematically or stylistically linked. When using one model for the whole ability range, ask more able students to include a brief commentary which demonstrates how they have used the poem as a starting point for their own work.

One of the most frequently used poems as a model for writing with younger pupils is 'The Magic Box' by Kit Wright. A copy of this poem, together with Vasko Popa's thought-provoking 'The Little Box', can be found in *Jumpstart* (Yates, 1999). As a visiting poet I used 'The Magic Box' as one of a number of models with mixed ability classes of Year 7 pupils involved in a school sculpture garden project at The Minster School in Southwell. The poem was chosen for its striking use of colour, sound, image and juxtapositions of words (such as 'three violet wishes'). The structure and rhythm of the poem provided useful hooks for less confident writers. All pupils were actively encouraged to experiment with their own structures. Magazine pictures of gardens and wildlife and a range of library resources were provided. Pupils could also listen to music as they drafted (a common practice at the school) and to consult both me and their regular class teacher as they worked. Work on the poems was completed in the week after my visit. Some of their final drafts are included here to illustrate the variety of ways in which pupils might respond to a model. I have also demonstrated how three of these poems could be assessed (with reference to the poetry-making descriptions outlined earlier in this chapter/the National Curriculum descriptions for writing) and what advice for further development could be offered.

The magical garden

Ice
melting under hot lava
Secret doors leading somewhere else.
    Misty webs
Upright statues
a rope ladder leading
to a big tree den

Jack

Response   Jack was very proud of his poem and it was also considered to be a significant achievement for this pupil by his class teacher. It provides a good example of how students of all abilities can rise to the challenge of poetry. The short but visual piece takes the reader in several different directions through the garden and creates a quite mysterious atmosphere. The contrasts of ice and hot lava and the secretive feel of the poem provide some discernible link with 'The Magic Box' although it is clearly an original response.

Assessment   It would appear to fit the Level 3 criteria as it shows some originality and imagination as well as an attempt to use poetic lines and phrases.

Development   Praise for achievement coupled with encouragement to develop the references to the 'misty webs' and the 'upright statues' more fully – perhaps with an additional line for each. (For example, could the reader know more about where these objects are in the garden or what

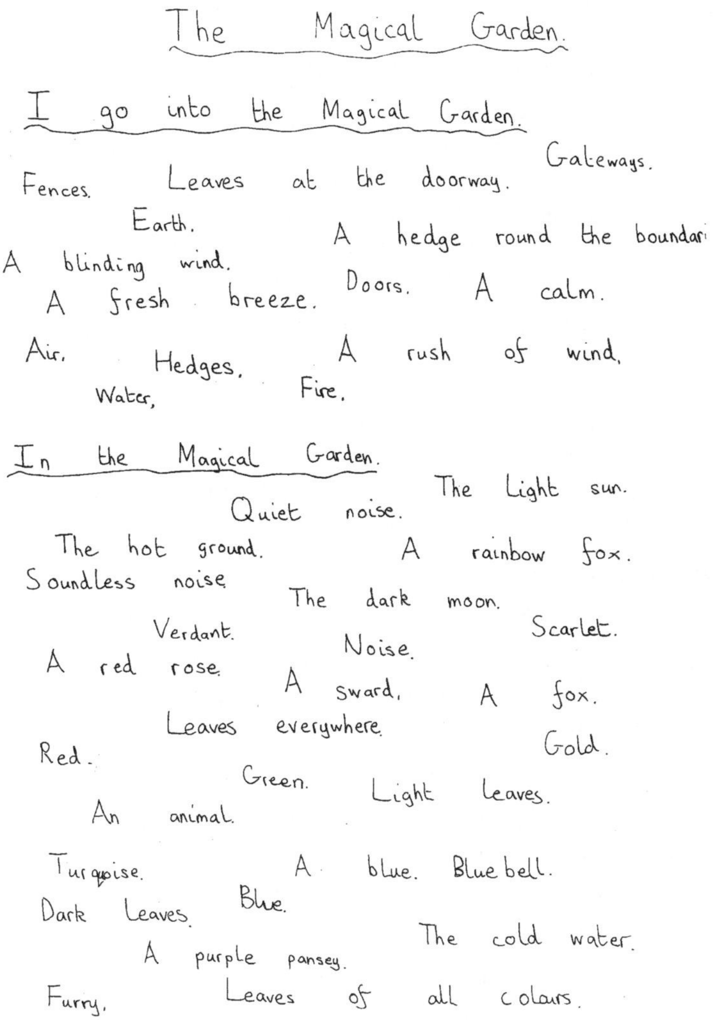

The Magical Garden.

I go into the Magical Garden.

Fences. Leaves at the doorway. Gateways.

Earth. A hedge round the boundari

A blinding wind.

A fresh breeze. Doors. A calm.

Air. Hedges. A rush of wind,

Water, Fire.

In the Magical Garden.

Quiet noise. The Light sun.

The hot ground. A rainbow fox.

Soundless noise

The dark moon.

Verdant. Noise. Scarlet.

A red rose. A sward, A fox.

Leaves everywhere. Gold.

Red.

Green. Light Leaves.

An animal.

Turqoise. A blue. Bluebell.

Dark Leaves. Blue.

The cold water.

A purple pansey.

Furry. Leaves of all colours.

Figure 6.3 'The Magical Garden'

happens when someone approaches them?) Another follow-up (which might lead to a further poem) could involve research on the sounds ice makes when it melts.

Sean wrote the poem 'Magical Garden' (see Figure 6.3).

Response Sean chose to break the mould with his poem and some readers might be tempted to argue that it is not a poem. While he decided on his structure very quickly, he selected his words with some care. He takes the reader on a journey which has different stages and is threaded with layers of colour and sound. The writer plays with language and form, trying out different combinations of words, including repetitions and juxtapositions. Phrases such as 'a blinding wind', 'soundless noise', 'a rainbow fox', 'a blue Bluebell', and the rather archaic 'a sward' are all striking.

Assessment   One could argue that this piece is distinctive enough to attain exceptional performance. Although it is not perfect in any conventional sense, it is an ambitious poem which takes the reader by surprise. However, some of the word choices are much weaker than others and the poem seems to be missing the clinching original detail. For these reasons I would assess it as being at the top of Level 5.

Development   Praise for being so adventurous and encouragement for further experimentation. I would ask him to think about some of his more general word choices (such as 'noise', 'green' and 'furry') to give the poem a more vivid, striking feel and to consider the impact on the reader of the final phrase 'Leaves of all colours'. I would encourage him to investigate the concrete poetry of Ian Hamilton Finlay and Edwin Morgan and to experiment further with other new structures.

The Magical Garden

In the garden there will be,

the swish of the wind running through the trees,
the sound of birds chirping and squawking,
the humming of the bees searching among flowers.

In the garden there will be,

the happiness of an old man reaching 100 years old,
the khaki colour of leaves on bushes,
the rosy-red of roses.

In the garden there will be,

the roundness of a tree trunk,
the smoothness of the leaves and petals,
a glazed effect of the holly.

My garden will have all plants in the world
and they will never die,
they will mix and make more new flowers,
my garden would be the world.

Ian

Response: Of all the poems included here, Ian's most closely adheres to the form and rhythm of the model. He uses a refrain line to introduce the three-lined stanzas which describe items found in the garden and a concluding stanza which gives an overview of the garden and its contents. He describes textures, visual images and sounds, borrowing the word 'swish' from the original poem. The 'happiness of the old man', 'the rosy-red of roses', the description of the holly and the final stanza are the most striking features which recreate something of the magic of the original.

Assessment This is a competent effort which falls within the Level 4 descriptions. It is has some flashes of originality and is generally well structured.

Development First congratulate the writer on the way the structure of the model has been used. He would perhaps benefit from another look at 'The Magic Box' to compare the punctuation used. With further support and reading aloud he might focus on unnecessary words included (such as 'old' and 'colour') which arguably dull the impact of some of the lines. Consideration of the tenses and modals used would also be beneficial. Ian's image of the garden of the world has potential. Is there another poem to be written about the magical plants which never die?

Two poems from the same Year 7 class demonstrate other ways in which the model has been used:

My garden

The tall waving grass,
The sound of no noise,
The flash of a brilliant fish,
The splash of a dry fountain,
The crunch of a foot on frosted grass.

The creak of ancient trees,
The buzz of a thousand bees,
The rustle of last year's leaves in the wind,
The smell of a colour,
The heat of a blazing sun.

Henry

Tim's poem also was titled 'My Garden' (see Figure 6.4).

GCSE assessment

The poems and the accompanying commentaries featured in Chapter 2 are examples of work assessed for GCSE. (It would be worth referring back to these when considering the following assessments.) They were all included in the students' final coursework assessment folders. My written assessment comments appeared at the end of each piece. Additional comments were written next to specific lines in the poems and/or points made in the commentaries. The written assessments were supported by: individual discussions with each student about their assignments;

MY GARDEN

By Timothy Shaw

My garden has chocolate ponds
Surrounded by toffee plant pots
With story trees in them.

My garden has a Twix maze
With grass of money
And a purple red sky.

My garden has the sound of birds.
It is peaceful and tranquil
With a wall to do your homework.

My garden has corners
Which are full of sports,
Sorrow, secrets and joy.

My garden has a wafer wall
With Smarty stepping stones
And a patio of pillows.

My garden has a wall of shame,
A time-out bench and table.
My beautiful garden has a syrup waterfall.

My garden has ideas in thought.
The whisper of the wind spells out my words.
My garden opens out onto a wavy field.

My garden has had its last words
But now I've destroyed it
For I've eaten all my dream.

Figure 6.4   *My Garden*

target-setting; peer discussion and sharing of assessed work. The GCSE Original Writing assessment criteria, used specifically for assessing this assignment, are included below for reference, together with the General Criteria which apply to all pieces assessed for writing. These were taken from page 39 of the NEAB 2000 English GCSE syllabus. All the criteria for writing assessment remain unchanged in the 2004 AQA A GCSE specification.

Tom's poem 'The Tornado' and commentary were assessed at Grade B for GCSE.

- *Written assessment comments:* Poem – You have worked hard on the shape of this poem. It has a real compactness – like the shape of a tornado perhaps? I am pleased you have persevered with poetry. Your punctuation is somewhat erratic! The first verse has one full stop but then you neglect punctuation altogether after that. Think about this. Commentary – A good effort, Tom, in describing the decisions you have made in drafting. I would have liked a bit more detail about actual words you chose to use too.
- *Grade B Original Writing criteria*: Candidates 'enhance meaning and effect by the successful use of appropriate structural and stylistic devices'. They 'give powerful accounts of real or imagined experience'.
- *Grade B General criteria*: 'Candidates' writing is coherent and controlled, demonstrating an assured match of style and form to audience and purpose. Candidates follow syntactical conventions with paragraphing aiding meaning, and spell most complex words correctly. Punctuation is used effectively. Work is presented attractively, with occasional lapses not inhibiting readers' enjoyment.'

Ekaterina's poem 'The Torrent Raged' and commentary were assessed at Grade A for GCSE.

- *Written assessment comments*: Poem – 'This poem has got some wonderful touches to it. I really like the way you show the contrast between the river and the "reckless" torrent, particularly in the treatment of nature. I am interested in your choice of gender for the river and the torrent.' Commentary – 'Your piece has clearly gone through a number of drafts and you explore thoughtfully your difficulties in the writing process. You should, I think, be *very* pleased with your poem.'
- *Grade A Original Writing criteria*: Candidates 'use structure and vocabulary to achieve a range of original effects'. They 'produce specific, sustained and committed writing in appropriate forms'.
- *Grade A General criteria*: 'Candidates' writing has shape and assured control of a range of styles. A wide range of grammatical constructions is used accurately; paragraphs are well constructed and linked to clarify the organisation of the writing as a whole. Vocabulary and punctuation are often ambitious and usually accurate.'

Tom's poem 'Bird Flight' and commentary were assessed at Grade A* for GCSE.

- *Written assessment comments*: Poem – 'Stunning. You should be absolutely delighted with this.'
- Commentary – 'It certainly filled the brief! You are already writing extremely confidently about language at work here in your very thoughtful exploration of the drafting process. I could not ask for more at this stage. Splendid comments – good writing does contain a lot of the writer.'
- *Grade A* Original Writing criteria*: Candidates 'consciously shape and craft language and structure to achieve sophisticated effects'. They 'use standard and non-standard forms convincingly and effectively'.
- *Grade A* General criteria*: 'Candidates' writing is elaborate or concise, vigorous or restrained, according to purpose and audience. It employs a wide vocabulary and a precise, fluent style in which syntax, spelling and punctuation are almost faultless.'

With its focus on sentence and paragraph structures, the General criteria continues to follow the lead from the prose-biased National Curriculum assessment levels. However, in applying both sets of criteria for AQA A, it is clear that the phraseology does not actually preclude assessment of students' poetry. Developing GCSE Writing criteria which is evidently poetry-inclusive, and thus encourage more teachers and students to submit poetry coursework, represents the next challenge in this field.

In order for poetry assessment to be both viable and of value for the young writer pupils should be: writing poetry on a regular basis; developing poetry portfolios; experimenting with models; making their own choices and reflecting on their work and that of others. The major constraints on curriculum time are all too evident in many classrooms and poetry is becoming increasingly, even deadeningly, linked with critical responses on terminal examination papers. Nevertheless it is important to restate notions of best creative practice. Creativity does not need to be separate from assessment but assessment procedures do need to embrace the many different forms of written expression beyond the prose narrative. As someone who was fortunate enough to be taught by English teachers who were not afraid to intervene in drafts or to assess my poems, I am convinced that a further productive dialogue about assessment approaches can prevent poetry from remaining neglected on a pedestal, dusted down like the best china for a special visitor when the serious work of prose writing is completed.

7

The Context: Forty Years of Poetry Teaching

To provide a context for the poetry classroom of the twenty-first century we need to look back some 40 years, to the beginning of the 1960s. In that decade a number of the poets, teachers and educationists were gaining recognition for their work which would help to shape the kind of poetry teaching familiar in UK classrooms today. Their influence can be seen both on practical approaches to poetry teaching and on the place of the genre within the English curriculum. This chapter concentrates primarily on the key figures and movements that contributed to debates about the teaching of writing poetry. However, it also acknowledges the inevitable and fertile links between writing, reading, performing and listening to poetry.

The Newsom report

In the early 1960s in UK primary and secondary schools English (and by implication poetry) was still regarded as a subject which could be taught by non-specialists. This view appeared to inhibit the credibility and progress of the subject (Ball, 1985). The writers of the Newsom Report, published in 1963, recognised the major role of poetry within the English curriculum whilst admitting that some teachers were reluctant to accept its centrality: 'It is of course within poetry and drama that the use of language goes deepest. Nobody should have to teach poetry against his will but without it English will never be complete; poetry is not a minor amenity but a major channel of experience' (Newsom Committee 1963: 156). Newsom supported the development of writing skills through practised writing from experience. Although the report acknowledged that the resulting 'free outpourings are shapeless often and lack control over words, grammar, spelling and punctuation' (ibid.: 157), Newsom valued those teachers who were seen to encourage their students in this raw creativity rather than shackling them to correctness. In a number of schools what are described as 'very ordinary' (ibid.: 156) children were observed writing for pleasure. However, the shortage of subject specialists prevented this approach becoming more widespread. Members of the committee voiced a concern over the many weaker students who never reached 'the real point where English begins' (ibid.: 152) and were fed a diet of comprehension and grammar exercises often by unqualified staff. Indeed, the report referred to a potential situation where a Head of English in a secondary school could be driven to dividing up the English lessons of one class, allocating poetry to one and composition to another member of the department to teach.

The spirit and tone of the Newsom Report's comments on poetry teaching were echoed in sentiments expressed by David Holbrook. Holbrook emphasised the need for enjoyment of poetry by students of all abilities, and their teachers. He saw poetry teaching as being located at the heart of a teacher's practice – a view which I strongly endorse: 'If we know what we are doing when we teach poetry then we shall be secure; the rest of our work in English will follow by implication' (Holbrook, 1961b: 63). Holbrook detailed 12 potential classroom poetry activities along with recommendations for texts and sound recordings. He was keen to revitalise the role of folk song as a means of securing a link with the 'oral verse culture' of students' ancestors. He was particularly concerned with the provision of materials for less able students as exemplified in his two collections of verse, *Iron, Honey, Gold* (Holbrook, 1961a), and *English for the Rejected* (Holbrook, 1964). Shayer argued that Holbrook initiated the 'major battle' in the 'campaign' (Shayer, 1972: 148) to provide a real and meaningful education for all secondary school children. Although the actual title, *English for the Rejected*, is perhaps now considered an inappropriate one, Holbrook's intentions should still be applauded. Pupils of all abilities should be given access to poetry in its infinite variety, and many teachers (including those whose responses are detailed in Chapter 6) recognise what can be achieved by less able pupils through their reading, performance, discussion and writing of poetry. Throughout this book are poems written by young people of a wide range of ability together with teaching strategies, which, I hope, demonstrate how poetry can open windows onto language that might otherwise remain firmly closed behind the impenetrable shutters of prose.

The Cambridge School of English

Holbrook was one of the 'acolytes' (Ball, 1985: 63) of F.R. Leavis whose leadership of the Cambridge School of English caused it to have considerable influence on the way English was taught at Secondary School level (predominantly in post-Second World War UK grammar schools). The school's practice developed from the work of George Sampson at school level and the leadership of F.R. Leavis within the university. *Culture and*

Environment provided the major statement of the school's philosophy in its recommendation that students should be trained in 'critical awareness of the environment' (Leavis and Thompson, 1933: 5). As a teacher, Leavis inspired many students who were to become key players at all levels in English teaching and more broadly in education as a whole. Ball charted the patterns of influence and points of contact of this group which included such figures as David Holbrook, Douglas Barnes, Fred Inglis, Denys Thompson and Frank Whitehead (Ball, 1985: 66).

The Progressive movement

Just as the Cambridge School influenced secondary practice, the 'Progressive movement' (Abbs, 1982: 10), which had previously been a major influence on practice in elementary schools, contributed most significantly to the philosophy of primary education in the 1960s and the teaching of creative writing especially. (Elementary was the name historically given to schools for pupils of 5–13 in the UK and is now obsolete.) The Progressive movement's concerns were with processes of creative writing and stirring the imagination rather than with end products. Key figures in the 'Progressive movement' (otherwise labelled as the Creative Writing movement) were Percy Nunn, Greening Lamborn, Edmund Holmes, W.S. Tomkinson and Caldwell Cook, followed slightly later by Herbert Read and Marjorie Hourd (Ball, 1985). Hourd's influential *Education of the Poetic Spirit* included collections of students' own compositions, drawn from her work in a girls' public day school. She strongly emphasised the need to nourish the unconscious in order to develop imaginative self expression, including poetry writing skills. For Hourd a text was to be used 'as a kind of filter through which she might obtain the finer essences of her own personality and reach her own level of attainment' (Hourd, 1949: 94). Hourd argued the results of such indirect imitations had to be accepted by teachers, even if the results might not be considered satisfactory by adult standards. Students should not be 'straining to produce something to satisfy the teacher's demands instead of yielding up generously what they themselves have to give' (ibid.: 96). This view continues to influence some teachers' attitudes to the assessment of poetry, as can be seen in Chapter 6.

The Romantic approach to the development of the child's poetic spirit focused on the intensity of the writing experience. Shayer questioned whether it was realistic to have such Romantic faith in a child, arguing that students would have no engagement with poetic form or points of comparison in their work beyond the levels of intensity they achieved. This could lead the young writers to become 'more confined and restricted than before' (Shayer, 1972: 163). Shayer also suggested that considerable teacher input would actually be required to enable students to release their original thoughts: 'every experienced teacher knows that for every hour of "giving out" the pupil needs something like three hours of "putting in" – of reading, discussing, listening and observing' (ibid.: 161)

Other publications by members of the movement, such as Baldwin (1959), Langdon (1961) and Marshall (1963), also promoted the belief that natural growth of the young writer and continuous enjoyment were key elements in the development of expression and in the teaching of poetry. The authors described their classroom methods in similarly enthusiastic tones to those of Hourd. Marshall's class, inspired by Beethoven's Pastoral Symphony and walks in the Cambridgeshire countryside, produced poems which were 'outpourings of sheer jubilation, controlled and deepened by sympathy for and understanding of the rural past' (Marshall, 1963: 196).

Baldwin described himself as a teacher who had been 'educated to worship a muse who wore corsets' (Baldwin, 1959: 140). He wanted to move away from the traditional confinements of poetry in the classroom to adopt a celebratory, relaxed approach where his students would be sufficiently at their ease to create and would develop a lifelong pleasure in poetry. Baldwin did not approve of poetry's prostitution to serve other functions such as training memory and teaching grammar. It is interesting to reconsider his concerns about the fate of poetic texts with reference to the National Literacy Strategy. Unless they adopt a coherent approach to using poetry, teachers could be guilty of using single poems and extracts to launch a thousand lesson starters without allowing the poems (or their readers and writers) to complete their journey of discovery.

Another seminal text of this time, Clegg's *The Excitement of Writing,* explored the 'revolution' (Clegg, 1964: 3) which was perceived to be taking place in English teaching, in some schools at least. Teachers were said to be moving away from writing exercises. They were encouraging their students to develop both confidence and pride in their work and to respond intensely to their environment and individual experiences. Clegg's collection of examples of students' poetry had an experimental feel which had not been present in the more formal, conservative pieces previously collected by Marjorie Hourd (Andrews, 1991).

LATE and NATE

Although the influences of both the Progressive movement and the Cambridge School were felt far and wide in the 1960s, during this decade another group emerged in opposition to the 'classical grammatical paradigm of English teaching' (Ball, 1985: 67). This group was based at the London Day Training College (later to become the University of London Institute of Education). Percival Gurrey and his student James Britton were the founder members of the London Association of Teachers of English (LATE) in 1947. This organisation was closely linked with the spread of comprehensive education. LATE became a part of the National Association of Teachers of English (NATE) in 1963.

The National Association of Teachers of English had been established by followers of Leavis – Boris Ford, Denys Thompson and Frank Whitehead. At this time its concerns within English were largely focused on language rather than literature. In consuming LATE, 'NATE had incorporated within itself a militant dissenting incubus' (Ball, 1985: 69) as many of the key LATE figures such as Douglas Barnes, Harold Rosen, Nancy Martin and James Britton would take on leading roles in the organisation in the 1960s and 1970s and move NATE away from the influence of the Cambridge English School.

The Dartmouth Conference

The Dartmouth Conference of 1966, at which the most widely accepted models of English teaching from Britain and the USA were debated, was a turning point in English teaching. Jon Dixon's account of the conference described these models succinctly:

> The first centred on *skills*: it fitted an era when initial literacy was the prime demand. The second stressed the *cultural heritage*, the need for a civilising and socially unifying content. The third (and current) model focuses on *personal growth*: the need to re-examine the learning processes and the meaning to the individual of what he [sic] is doing in English lessons. Looking back over the history of our subject, we see the limitations in the earlier models and thus the need to reinterpret our conception of 'skills' and 'heritage'. (Dixon, 1967: 1–2)

The models and the tensions between them would underpin debates about the development of the National Curriculum 20 years later. Shayer indicated that the American delegates at Dartmouth perceived British attitudes towards English teaching as being 'determined ... by a sense of release from, or rebellion against, a long-established authoritarian regime only now showing signs of relaxation' (Shayer, 1972: 185). Dixon observed the Americans' unhappiness with 'the chaotic nature of the British child centred curriculum in which the major concern was social adjustment and not a child's growth in intellectual, imaginative and linguistic power' (Dixon, 1967: 72). The Americans saw the limited and sometimes vague definitions of growth inherent in this model and sensed teachers needed more structure. In reflecting on the discussion about different ways poetry could be used in the classroom, Dixon arguably exemplified the Americans' concerns with his observation that 'Poems, for instance, need not always come out of the blue' (Dixon, 1967: 64). In spite of the Americans' dissension, the personal growth model predominated.

Frank Whitehead

In the same year as Dartmouth, Frank Whitehead feared for the future of poetry which he saw as being taught without redress to its context. He commented on the paucity of adults who read poetry and hoped to swell their ranks. Whitehead understood that poetry could be perceived as remote and 'the product of a self-conscious and sophisticated culture' (Whitehead, 1966: 107) but he mourned its relegation to the periphery, recalling a time when both spoken and sung poetry had formed part of every child's background. He argued that teachers should concentrate on making poetry both accessible and enjoyable to all those in their classrooms, urging them to relinquish the feeling that 'poetry because of its difficulty calls for a devious, gingerly approach' (Whitehead, 1966: 100).

Like Holbrook (1961b), Whitehead suggested teachers should make more use of poetry and music from the English folk tradition, especially with 'less gifted' pupils (Whitehead, 1966: 107). However, Whitehead did not appreciate the inclusion of pupils' stories and poems in collections alongside works by mature adult authors.

Fred Inglis

Whitehead's concern with the lack of context for poetry in the classroom was subsequently taken up by Fred Inglis who presented a bleak view of students encountering poetry:

> the product of our schools, the individuals of our society, do not know what to do when they are faced with a poem, and consequently they have no way either of describing or even of perceiving the significance of poems or poetry. I do not mean... that they dislike poetry unconditionally. Some do. What matters is that nobody has begun to provide an adequate language in which they can discuss a poem. They, and their teachers perhaps, do not see the poet as an image-maker, an iconographer nor do they know what images, of nobility, fineness, ceremony, courtesy, they lack. (Inglis, 1969: 89)

Peter Benton considered that this paragraph was at the heart of Inglis's whole argument about poetry and was underpinned by a 'moral judgement upon the spiritual barrenness of the age' (Benton, 1986: 5) which echoed both Leavis and Arnold. Inglis's *The Englishness of English Teaching* (1969) originated from research carried out by a group at Southampton University on curriculum reform, examinations and assessment. The text featured Inglis's highly idiosyncratic account of the findings. A survey of secondary school students' reading behaviours (which formed the second section of an investigation of English) and the growth of their values, included questions which were pertinent to consideration of poetry's place in the curriculum. Pupils in the sample (taken from grammar schools and the top two streams in secondary moderns where literature was taught as a separate subject) were asked to select from a bank of statements a description which best matched their attitude to poetry. They were also asked to describe and, if possible, quote from the poem they could remember most clearly. Inglis interpreted the children's selections of attitude statements as indicating 'there is not the powerful antipathy to poetry which all children are presumed to feel nowadays' (Inglis, 1969: 170). He was puzzled by the very narrow range of works they mentioned in response to the second question, on best remembered poems. Two hundred and twenty six poems were referred to by the 482 respondents. Their choices were largely nineteenth-century poems. Inglis concluded that students must have chosen poems at random from those recently discussed in class, although this view is not supported with evidence.

In spite of Inglis's and Whitehead's observations on the lack of context for or familiarity with poetry in the classroom, during the late 1960s and 1970s a number of 'poetry method books' (Shayer, 1972: 160) appeared. These offered complementary approaches to poetry. They encouraged teachers and students to encounter poetry at close hand through writing. In Hughes (1967), Powell (1968) and Mole (1973) writing is portrayed as a serious process to be worked at with commitment and concentration. When suggesting classroom activities, the writers make extensive use of models and underline the importance of the teacher's role in the writing processes.

Ted Hughes

In his capacity as a 'practising writer of verse' (Hughes, 1967: 11), Ted Hughes produced *Poetry in the Making* – a text directly aimed at children which was designed to 'spur my audience – aged between ten and fourteen – to more purposeful efforts in their own writing' (Hughes, 1967: 11). His refreshing and enriching book was based on a series of BBC radio programmes with some additional points of advice for teachers. Hughes used a range of poems, including a number of his own, as models for writing but advised teachers against using models which were 'beyond the sympathy of children' (ibid.: 12). He recognised that if they encouraged students to write imaginatively (about characters, weather or landscape), teachers would be fighting against tradition. For Hughes, teachers were enablers in the writing process. They opened up the potential for poetry by providing opportunities for concentrated writing activities and then assisted students in gradually narrowing down the focus of their drafts.

Over 30 years on, both this text and Hughes's own poetry still have a key place in English classrooms and in the poetry workshop approaches used by visiting writers. In the light of the poet's death in 1998, it is poignant to note his own comment about the immediacy and longevity of the images which can be achieved through writing poetry: 'I suppose that long after I am gone, as long as a copy of the poem exists, every time anyone reads it the fox will get up somewhere out in the darkness and come walking towards him' (ibid.: 20).

Poetry and spirituality

Hughes endorsed a belief that an English teacher's words 'should be not "How to write" but "How to try to say what you really mean" – which is part of the search for self knowledge and perhaps, in one form or another, grace' (Hughes, 1967: 12). Previously, the Newbolt Report had described literature as a 'means of grace' and expressed concern about the rejection of its 'great spiritual influence' (Newbolt, 1921: 253). Peter Benton remarked on the significance of 'grace' as an example of the 'amalgam of analysis and religion' which was often found in the vocabulary of the Creative Writing movement (Benton, 1986: 2). John Mole (whose work in schools is described below) saw writing poetry as 'a kind of going to Church on Sundays for those who have got out of the habit of praying.' (Mole, 1973: 202) while Holbrook, observed that 'poets write to put their souls in order' (Holbrook, 1961b: xxii).

The potentially spiritual nature of poetry within our own predominantly secular age is interesting to explore. Both Muir (1962) and Heaney perceive poetry as a vital element within their cultures: 'divination, as a restoration of the culture to itself' (Heaney, 1980: 60). It has, for example, become increasingly popular to recite poetry on significant personal/public occasions such as at weddings and funerals. (The main public library in Nottingham keeps two folders of 'Most Requested Poems For Funerals and Services' for members of the public to consult.) This trend was perhaps rekindled by the recitation of W.H. Auden's poem 'Stop all the clocks' at a funeral in the 1994 film *Four Weddings and a Funeral*. It is interesting to note how schools are able to promote pupils' spiritual, moral, social and cultural development through their teaching of literature, and poetry in particular.

(In my last school this was even commented on in an Ofsted report.) Has poetry, therefore, become a more socially acceptable alternative to scripture? Conversely, could poetry's association with spirituality also cause some teachers to shy away from fully engaging with the genre? Are they suspicious of poetry's potential for religiosity and the challenge it offers to their atheism? Are they wary of a genre on the edge of language, functioning, as Heaney describes it 'as the rim of the silence out of which consciousness arrives and into which it must descend' (Heaney, 1989: 11)?

Teacher-poets: Brian Powell, John Mole and Kenneth Koch

Writing primarily for a teaching audience, Brian Powell, in his *English through Poetry Writing* (1968) devised a detailed programme for poetry writing. His idyllic presentations of 13-year-old boys communing with nature are reminiscent of Hourd (1949) and Marshall (1963). However, his two-part programme provided teachers with a structured and progressive framework for poetry writing. The framework consisted of three strands: form, content and evaluation. By following this structure Powell hoped students of all abilities would develop more acute and lucid forms of expression while benefiting from the 'humanising influence' (Powell, 1968: 5) of poetry on their daily routines. At several points in his text Powell commented that every English teacher should be a writer (a suggestion which is also explored in Chapter 2 of this book). He believed that assuming this role would not only enable teachers to appreciate the demands of the writing process but would also instil in the students a greater respect for their teacher.

The teacher's role was again explored by John Mole (1973). For him poems were 'rooms' and the poetry teacher was someone who would help a student to 'recognise the room he is moving in. How he should behave there is not for me, but for the poem to teach' (Mole, 1973: 191). Mole preferred a formal approach to the writing process, noting the irony of the relaxed feel in a classroom where everyone was writing to the rules. Mole cited Kenneth Koch's work as an influence on his own practice. Koch's accounts of teaching poetry in a New York public school in *Wishes, Lies and Dreams* (1970) and *Rose, Where Did You Get that Red?* (1973) had an impact on writing in schools on both sides of the Atlantic. Koch wanted to stir the genre from its classroom dormancy so that children could participate in the 'mystery' of poetry and harness their 'natural talent' (Koch, 1970: 29–30). He used a series of loose poetic forms such as repeated opening phrases, contrasting pairs of lines and lists of metaphors as models with his classes. Koch's work is still referred to by some teachers and poets (including Yates, 1999) as a valuable source of ideas although others find the use of 'formula poems' (Marsh, 1988: 65) limits students to producing very similar work (Andrews, 1991: 73). I think Koch's approach can provide very useful starting points for teaching and learning to write poetry. Like all models, they are there to be adapted, and ultimately rejected, once the teacher/novice writer has grown in confidence.

Robert Witkin's live wire

In contrast to these three teacher-poets, Robert Witkin was less optimistic about the teacher's role in a rational objective education system. He urged that education should: 'rediscover a real concern with subject-reflexive action. Subject-reflexive action is the foundation of an intelligence of feeling. It is the process whereby Being is transformed and thereby transcends its former relationship to the world' (Witkin, 1974: 29). Most teachers within this system were regarded by Witkin as playing safe, refusing to 'handle the live wire of feeling' (ibid.: 62). Witkin argued that English teachers concentrated too much on the written product which emerged after a stimulus has been used: they did not nurture a thinking environment in their classrooms or fertilise the soil in which a student's 'sensate impulse' (ibid.: 45) could thrive. If teachers did not prepare this ground, but merely concentrated on the plant/idea/draft once it has emerged, Witkin warned they would be kept fully occupied with weeding and might not notice there were very few flowers in the garden. As has been shown in Chapter 2, there is a strong link between developing drafting skills and establishing a thinking environment in the classroom.

For Witkin the conflict between the goals of self-expression and personal development and the demands of the formal examination system were problematic: he recognised the dilemma English was faced with in being regarded as a service subject. A number of writers in the field of English teaching, including Bernard Harrison, Patrick Creber, Michael Benton and Debra Myhill have been influenced by Witkin's ideas. Harrison and Gordon aimed to move Witkin's ideas forward by asking 'ought we to realise, not so much that there is an intelligence *of* feeling (*pace* Witkin 1974) as that we need in all learning to be intelligent *about* feeling, about personal experience.' (Harrison and Gordon, 1983: 266). Creber, who was Harrison's PhD supervisor, also stressed the importance of 'the thinking climate of the classroom' (Creber, 1990: 79). Another of Creber's former students, Debra Myhill concluded that Witkin's investigations into the psychology of the creative processes 'should free teachers to enter into the writing of poetry rather more blinkered than blind, and moreover to feel empowered to take an active role in the stimulation and encouragement of the process' (Myhill, 1986:19).

Redefining English

By the early 1970s a process of redefinition of English had begun which sprang from a 'concern for what language is and the many purposes for which we use it' (Britton, 1973: 23). Britton believed that English teachers were increasingly recognising that their responsibilities stretched across the whole language spectrum. A new terminology was beginning to emerge which would eventually help to shape the language of the English National Curriculum Orders 20 years later. Britton was one researcher in a team which investigated the 'Development of Writing Abilities' at the London Institute of Education. The team's purpose was to 'create a model which would enable us to characterise all mature written utterances and then go on to trace the developmental steps that led to them' (Britton et al., 1975: 6). They considered the similarities between children's writing and speech, labelling the 'verbalisation of the speaker's immediate preoccupation and mood of the moment' as 'expressive language' (ibid. 82). Britton had previously defined the features of 'spectator' and 'participant' roles in language (Britton, 1970: 105) and described expressive language as 'a kind of matrix' (Britton, 1973: 24) of a flexible nature from which transactional and poetic language developed. As expressive language moved towards the poetic he saw it as becoming 'more shaped and organised, heightening or intensifying the implicit' (Britton, 1970: 177).

Transactional language was considered the language for getting things done whereas poetic language was thought to have no purpose beyond existing 'for its own sake' (Britton et al., 1975: 88). There were real difficulties with the attempts to label all types of mature language. The developmental steps for the poetic mode were unexplored: the emphasis was placed on exemplifying transactional levels (Davies, 1986). Andrew Wilkinson considered the team's work was noteworthy for its attempts to classify writing in terms of cognitive operations rather than of literary criticism. However, he argued that differing audience perceptions of written texts could affect the classification process. He likened this to 'trying to fit them into one of two boxes and then closing the lid before they jump out again' (Wilkinson, 1986: 29). (In a similar vein, the subjectivity of the reader within the assessment of poetry is important to acknowledge and has been explored in Chapter 6.)

The Bullock Report

The concept of language across the curriculum was a key feature of the Bullock Report (DES, 1975). The report, entitled *A Language for Life*, recognised a new movement in English teaching and devoted minimal space to poetry teaching (just over three pages). A grand acknowledgement of the 'great educative power' of poetry was coupled with concerns about the 'dispiriting' attitude of students who had 'no intention of reading more poetry after leaving school' (DES, 1975: 137). Bullock observed the unpopularity of poetry amongst a general public who saw it as 'something rather odd, certainly outside the current of normal life; it is either numinous, and therefore rarely to be invoked, or an object of comic derision' (ibid.: 135). However, the report largely endorsed the shift in the curriculum: literature now formed but one strand of English teaching and was no longer considered as dominant as it once had been.

The methods of the Progressive or Creative Writing movement, which still permeated many classrooms, were challenged by the Bullock Committee. It queried the range of writing on offer. This range was often seen to be limited to the purely personal. Poetry was frequently used in a thematic way to explore experience without in depth consideration of the words on the page.

Effective resourcing of the curriculum was also an issue. In a move on from Newsom (Newsom Committeee, 1963), Bullock suggested that subject specialists should offer guidance about suitable teaching materials. Teachers should use subtle approaches to draw out students' responses to texts rather than to encourage parroted responses or an idea that there were right answers. The committee viewed this approach as particularly necessary for poetry, noting that while some students were being given 'enviable' experiences of poetry, 'at the other extreme some children rarely encountered poetry of any kind' (DES, 1975: 135).

After Bullock, David Holbrook took a stand against the report's functional approach to language, citing examples of poetry writing sessions he had led which were 'to do with forms of mysterious indwelling ... English as an art' (Holbrook, 1979: 147). He was seen to be as much 'out of step' (Ball, 1985: 79) in this post-Bullock period as those who insisted on the importance of 'popular culture' in English teaching. Questions about culture, ownership and purpose were being asked at this time and poetry teaching was perceived as a 'precarious business as we move into the 1980s' (Oakley, 1981: 24).

The problem with poetry

In *Developments in English Teaching* Michael Saunders remarked on the pupil-centred nature of the poetry work he had observed in a number of Nottinghamshire secondary schools. In at least one school he found that 'learning by doing is made to apply even to the rarefied pursuit of poetry appreciation' (Saunders, 1976: 53). However, Michael Benton was less optimistic. He noted the 'scant attention' paid to poetry by Bullock and feared that 'poetry survives in the gaps if at all' (Benton, 1978: 114). For

Benton poetry was one of the 'Cinderellas' of the English curriculum, leaving the ball early with drama. He questioned teachers' praxis and the idea that poetry was dutifully taught by teachers who were 'using strategies more appropriate to the cognitive areas of the curriculum' (Benton, 1978: 113). He briefly touched on poetry's problem as being connected with its 'risky' nature (Benton, 1978: 114).

The word 'problem' was to become more closely connected with poetry through Mathieson (1980) and Andrews (1991). After attending a Department of Education and Science (DES) regional conference on poetry, Mathieson reflected on how teachers held examinations responsible for the difficulties they encountered with poetry. For Mathieson this view deflected attention from other concerns which educators might have about the genre. However she did recognise the 'heavy price' (Mathieson, 1980: 39) being paid by Certificate of Secondary Education (CSE) candidates in the practical criticism examinations some of them had to sit. The hand of the 'Cambridge School' on the examination system in England and Wales was clearly being felt in schools. One poet, Adrian Mitchell refused to give permission for any of his work to be used 'in connection with any examination whatsoever' (Mitchell, 1982: 1). The place of poetry within public examinations and the effect that this has on teachers' and pupils' perceptions of poetry remain significant issues for the English curriculum in the twenty-first century.

For Anthony Oakley the main problem with poetry was the familiar theme of a lack of interest shown by both teachers and students. He argued that this lack of interest stemmed from the negative/uncertain attitudes of teachers, the unenlightened practice in schools and was a result of the 'hotch potch' (Oakley, 1981: 77) of advice available to teachers. He perceived that too much credence was being given to the work of professional writers (such as Hughes) who had little classroom experience. In his view the only real attempt to 'systemise' (ibid.: 77) poetry teaching had emerged from the work of practising teachers. Oakley preferred the inclusive approach offered to poetry teachers in Sandy Brownjohn's work. The latter undoubtedly offers the more fail safe option and excellent suggestions for beginning writing. However Hughes's *Poetry in the Making* (1967) gives greater scope for the imagination to take flight. Both approaches have a valid and important place within the repertoire of poetry teaching approaches which practitioners can draw on.

Oakley cited *Touchstones* (Benton and Benton, 1969) as an example of one of the excellent anthologies available for classroom use but was concerned that secondary school teachers should not become overdependent on such texts as they represented 'someone else's tastes and choices' (Oakley, 1981: 77). The extensive use of anthologies was also of concern to the Assessment Performance Unit (APU). In an observation which echoed Inglis's earlier findings on students' poetry choices, the APU document inferred that the 'widespread use of anthologised material' (DES, 1982: 151) had a narrowing influence on students' poetry reading preferences. It noted that students often nominated single poems (especially Wilfred Owen's 'Dulce et Decorum est') as their preferred reading.

Surveys on poetry teaching

Oakley presented a rationale for 'demystifying' poetry via the use of six interlinked dimensions or approaches:

(a) meeting poems;
(b) presenting poems;
(c) sharing poems;
(d) comprehending poems;
(e) considered responses to poems;
(f) collecting and finding poems (Oakley, 1981: 78).

Oakley's largely quantitative survey of the teaching of poetry to children of 10 to 13 years in the East Dorset region was critical of teachers, in the schools surveyed, who were not widely read in poetry for children or contemporary texts on poetry teaching. He also portrayed some staff as stubbornly refusing to improve their expertise in this area.

Oakley's survey was followed by research in a similar field by Harrison and Gordon (1983) and Peter Benton (1984; 1986). Harrison and Gordon's survey raised questions about the seriousness with which poetry was treated in secondary schools at this time. The authors considered poetry had an inspirational role to play in a child's education. They argued that children would gain more from poetry if their teachers enjoyed it too. They believed 'attention needs to be given to methods and quality of poetry teaching' (Harrison and Gordon, 1983: 277). Like Oakley, they wanted teachers to be encouraged to participate in a desired increased in-service provision on teaching the genre.

Peter Benton's 'Teaching poetry: the rhetoric and the reality' (1984) reported on a survey of teachers to discover 'how far we know what we are doing in poetry teaching in the 1980s' (Benton, 1984: 320). The subsequent *Pupil, Teacher, Poem* (Benton, 1986) reported these findings more extensively. He outlined 33 stated difficulties with teaching poetry volunteered by respondents. Major concerns included:

• 'overcoming pupils' inbuilt distaste for poetry';
• 'lack of experience/knowledge on the part of the teacher';
• 'switching pupils off' poetry (Benton, 1986: 10).

Benton was surprised to see these statements occurring most frequently among secondary teachers. He suggested Bullock's view of poetry as 'something odd, certainly outside the current of normal life' (DES, 1975: 135) also prevailed among a number of English teachers.

Like Oakley (1981) and Tunnicliffe (1984) Benton raised concerns about teacher training. He stressed the lasting power of each teacher's memories of her own experience of poetry at school. Benton outlined two extremes of initial teacher training in poetry. These were the rare lecture, which failed to meet trainees' needs, and the 'inspirational' (Benton, 1986: 12) training by tutors who both alerted their students to the possibilities for practical presentation of poetry in the classroom and widened their experience of the genre. Benton considered the assumptions made by tutors about their students' 'knowledge, understanding and liking for poetry' (Benton, 1986: 13) concluding that these assumptions were often far from the truth. He feared that students' limited knowledge/dislike of poetry, which could be traced back to their own school days, would be inherited by future students unless a positive attempt was made to break the vicious circle.

Alongside his two surveys, Peter Benton (1986) used transcripts of taped student discussions about poems. (These discussions had taken place without teachers present.) He explored the ways in which poetry taught thoughtlessly could lead to a 'public exposure of pupils' (Benton, 1986: 67) when a trusting atmosphere was needed in a classroom to draw out a personal response. His conclusions promoted the value of unaided talk about poetry. Benton also questioned both the constant need for a written product in poetry lessons and the over reliance on the stimulus/response approach. He raised issues about access to the genre, stating that 'robust' (Benton, 1986: 65) poetry was often still placed on a 'pedestal' (Benton, 1986: 6) or treated as a problem rather than as a pleasurable experience in which all students and teachers could share. As a means of reinforcing his conclusions, the remainder of the text contained suggested teaching strategies for individual or small group work with poetry. These included ideas about annotation, rereading, discussion, cloze and sequencing activities, which would become very familiar to many English teachers in the subsequent decade.

Process model of writing

During the 1980s consideration of writing and the writing curriculum predominated in professional publications and debates about English teaching. An emphasis was placed on prose writing of different types. A process model of writing emerged, drawn from Graves's influential investigation of young children's writing in New Hampshire. (This is explored more fully in Chapter 2.) Graves saw writing as consisting of a number of separate stages (from the initial drafting process, through conferencing, editing and, finally, publication). The 'scaffolding conferences' (Graves, 1983: 280) held between teacher and student-writer(s) could focus on any element of the writing (including punctuation and selection for publication). The students were 'apprentice authors writing for real audiences' (Maybin, 1994: 188). Graves saw teachers as having a kind of moral obligation to write themselves. He was also very concerned that students should be encouraged to develop their own voices as 'most writers rent their pieces and their teachers own them' (Graves, 1981: 7). It is interesting to see how these metaphors of ownership occur in a later HMI document on *Teaching Poetry in the Secondary School* (DES, 1987).

Many of Graves's ideas were also considered by the National Writing Project (1985–89) and were subsequently incorporated in the National Curriculum. Established by the Schools Curriculum Development Committee in 1985, the aim of the National Writing Project was to 'develop and extend the competence and confidence of children and young adults to write for a range of purposes and a variety of audiences, in a manner that enhances their growth as individuals, their powers of self-expression, their skill as communicators and their facility as learners' (National Writing Project, 1990b: 7). Under its auspices, projects were developed to focus on a variety of writing processes and contexts. These included: writing partnerships between home, school and community; workshops given by Gareth Owen and other poets; writing with computers; a focus on the place of language diversity in writing. Ironically the experimental, cross-curricular nature of much of the work was happening at a time when subject boundaries within the developing core curriculum were being tightened (National Writing Project, 1991).

Genre

The genre theorists of this time were also instrumental in the debate about 'the contexts for writing that different activities provide' (Czerniewska, 1992: 145). Gunther Kress was one of the few critics to adopt a 'sociocultural view of writing' (Rosen, 1992: 121). Kress noted the irony that creative writing was the most highly valued form of writing in school yet the least useful in the adult world. For Kress and Australian critics, like Martin (1984) and Rothery (1984), students needed to achieve an understanding of genres as part of their socialisation: 'denying access to the genre means denying them access to the subject' (Maybin, 1994: 193). Kress 'gloomily' (Rosen, 1992: 121) recognised a young writer's creativity would be subordinated to the demands of the norms of the genre: 'The child learns to control the genre but, in the process the genre comes to control the child' (Kress, 1982: 11). Some critics argued that teaching about genre could lead to uncritical teacher transmission of genre structures and limited engagement with the writing process or focus on how a child's writing might develop. However the impact of genre theory on curriculum innovations emphasised the need for classroom consideration of how language structures worked together with issues of audience and purpose in writing (Czerniewska, 1992).

Sandy Brownjohn

Although theoretical texts focused on genre and process at this time, at classroom level a number of texts including Brownjohn (1980; 1982; 1989), Pirrie (1987), Hayhoe and Parker (1988) and Michael Rosen (1989) offered teachers approaches to the teaching of writing poetry devised by practitioners. Sandy Brownjohn's method was to play games with language and form. A primary school teacher herself, she was encouraged to write down her ideas about poetry teaching by Ted Hughes (Brownjohn, 1999). She depicted teachers as 'desperate to come to grips with teaching poetry' but uncertain 'where to start' (Brownjohn, 1994: 7). To this effect she devised a three-part scheme, stretching over three terms. The scheme started with wordgames, moved on to introduction of forms and concluded with the use of a range of subjects once the students were 'fairly well-versed in the craft' (Brownjohn, 1994: 11). After attempting this approach, and writing alongside their students, Brownjohn hoped teachers would have the confidence to strike out on their own. Both primary and secondary school teachers latched on to her 'replicable' (Andrews, 1991: 71), clear and direct methods as a lifeline (Benton, 1986; Sedgwick, 1987).

Jill Pirrie

Another teacher, Jill Pirrie, was also writing about her own practice at this time. Her *On Common Ground* (1987) recorded the secrets behind her students' frequent successes in poetry competitions. Her approach was based primarily on developing close observational skills so that her students could write with 'precision and honesty' (Andrews, 1991: 70). It has been said that poetry competition judges easily recognised a poem written in Pirrie's classroom because of its strongly individual and startling nature (Blishen, 1993: 11). The thinking silence of this classroom was described as 'miraculous' (Pye, 1994: 36). These religious connotations might be said to echo Benton's notions of 'grace' (Benton, 1986: 2), but Pye insisted that Pirrie's miracles were 'secular and repeatable' (Pye, 1994: 36). In the second edition of *On Common Ground* (published in the light of the newly

established National Curriculum) Pirrie suggested new strategies for teachers which asserted poetry 'as the unifying idiom' (Pirrie, 1994: 1) in
empowering students to develop their mastery of language.

Michael Rosen

Like Brownjohn and Pirrie, Michael Rosen used examples of students'
work, in his case alongside his own poetry, to demonstrate the idea of 'Oral
Writing' (Rosen, 1989: 42). This was a subject which his father Harold had
first explored with Britton et al. in 1975. Drawing on Auden and Garrett's
description of poetry as 'memorable speech' (Auden, and Garrett, 1935: i)
he expressed a desire for students to use 'oral knowledge' (Rosen, 1989: 38)
in the writing process. This involved them in writing in ways which
reflected the spoken word. He argues that such an approach enables young
writers to draw on prior knowledge rather than to 'concoct or translate'
their poems (ibid.: 43). Rosen was critical both of Brownjohn's work as
starting from an adult literary standpoint and of process writing (*pace*
Graves) as producing poems which were 'devoid of feelings' (ibid.: 31). For
Rosen storytelling (including gossip), reading aloud and drama were more
appropriate routes to success with poetry.

The above texts have been compared with recipes (Andrews, 1991;
Sedgwick, 1987). Each has an instructional nature and feature examples of
the poetic dishes which could be conjured up. As recipes they reflect the
characters of their chefs: Brownjohn a 'personality teacher' (Brownjohn,
1994: 7); Pirrie 'an austere but friendly don' (Pye, 1994: 38) and Michael
Rosen a children's writer who considers that others sometimes view him
as a charlatan for the 'Bits' and 'Stuff' he writes (Rosen, 1989: 9). How fail-
safe their methods actually are depends on how readily teachers can
recreate their authors' successes in their own classrooms with their own
sets of ingredients.

The thrust of critical attention in these texts was on enabling teachers
of 8–13-year-olds to teach poetry writing. Texts exploring approaches to
reading and/or responding to poetry were not nearly so prevalent at a
classroom level. The thorny question of teaching poetry under exam conditions was also not touched on. It was not until the mid-1990s, following
the arrival of the National Curriculum, that publishers would firmly focus
their attention on producing practical materials for teaching the read-
ing/study of poetry to 14-year-olds and above.

Teaching Poetry in the Secondary School: An HMI View

In 1987 the viewpoint expressed in *Teaching Poetry in the Secondary School:
An HMI View* was that poetry had a centrality within English 'because of the

quality of language at work on experience that it offers us' (DES, 1987: 3). This publication was concerned with the neglect of poetry. It stressed the need for a range of speaking, listening, reading and writing activities in order to restore the severed connections between language and literature which, the authors thought, left literature as 'a form of knowledge to be examined' (DES, 1987: 4). Benton's transcript of students' unaided discussion about Hughes' poem 'The Warm and the Cold' was reprinted here as an example of the value of exploratory talk in successful poetry teaching.

The image this document presented of poets working 'at the frontier of language' (DES, 1987: 1) must have been daunting for some teachers, especially given the stated expectations for their own practice. Teachers were to have a responsibility to provide models for poetry writing which were 'not stranded in stale and sterile forms' (DES, 1987: 29). Her Majesty's Inspectorate advocated that practitioners should be able to draw on their own wide experience of reading, and perhaps even writing, poetry in order to able to: 'recognise a voice the pupil owns and to be able to distinguish it from one that has been rented for the occasion, and to be alert to those moments in a child's writing when there is an important shift in capability and consciousness' (DES, 1987: 29).

One suspects Robert Hull (whose work is explored in Chapter 2) would have been just the kind of teacher whose practice the HMI were envisaging. In his stimulating and extensive discussion of the use of models in his own classroom he observed: 'in a sense imitation is always there ... The teacher is thrown back on her resources as a reader in order to respond to whatever her pupils may have drawn into their writing from the poems they use as models' (Hull, 1988: 144).

For Andrews the DES document made grand claims for poetry as the 'jewel in the crown of the verbal arts' (Andrews, 1991: 128). However, he felt it represented a 'rearguard action' (Andrews, 1991: 129) in the run-up to the 1988 Education Reform Act and the establishment of National Curriculum Orders for English.

The year after this DES publication, the Kingman Committee, with its remit to define the objectives for the teaching of English language, made little reference to poetry in its report beyond remarking that 'an appreciation of poetry and prose, old and new, requires and influences a knowledge about language – its forms, variations, development and powers of concision' (DES, 1988: 41). Kingman's supporting examples did include some specific poetry activities such as: writing limericks; discussions of unusual features of e.e. cummings's language; explanations of sentence/discourse structure in Donne's verse paragraphs.

The proposals for the National Curriculum (1989), under the chairmanship of Brian Cox, came close on Kingman's heels. (Its inception and subsequent revisions of the National Curriculum are explored in

Chapter 1.) For Andrews the document offered encouragement in its reference to a wide range of cultural traditions and specific activities in the Speaking and Listening, and Reading targets. Conversely it had limitations in that there was no real sense of the distinctive discourse of poetry (Andrews, 1991). Andrews viewed the decision not to include a specific poetry strand as having an 'ominous ring to it ... if no one is going to be required to write poetry, few teachers will try it' (ibid.: 7).

In some respects the above comment still applies over a decade later. The English curriculum cries out for a better balance. It has been shown in Chapter 1 that there are very specific assessment objectives which refer to writing poetry within the National Literacy Strategy in primary schools. However, the lack of specific references to writing poetry within the secondary English curriculum often leads to its avoidance and the selection of prose text types in preference. In addition, the requirement to read and write about poetry in public examinations is viewed by many teachers as an increasingly heavy burden. By making a stronger link between reading and writing this burden can be lightened. As I have shown, much can be learned about the author's craft by adopting a range of drafting strategies, utilising ICT resources, exploring poets' drafts and experimenting with their methods. These methods may also inform examination study. Through working alongside writers, students and teachers can themselves become more confident and engaged readers, writers and assessors of poetry.

Appendix I: The Ghazal

Ghazals were first written in Persia, and since the sixteenth century the ghazal has been the most popular verse form in Urdu. The traditional subject matter of ghazals is wistful or thwarted love seen through the eyes of a male lover. Images of gardens, nature, turtle doves and cruel beloveds often feature. Classical ghazal poetry is usually introspective and nature is only considered as providing a backdrop to human existence, e.g.: 'Mistakenly hoping they can catch a glimpse of you,/ the flowers rush to bloom, one after another' (Ghalib, translations from Ghalib are from Mirza [1992]). Modern ghazals have moved away from this subject matter to concern themselves with a whole range of subjects. It is the form itself which is now perhaps of most interest.

A ghazal is a collection of couplets (although some translators change the ghazal structure to three- or five-line verses). There is no limit on how many couplets a ghazal may have although there are usually at least five. Each couplet (called a *she'r*) contains a separate thought, and can often be disconnected from other couplets in the collection. A she'r can be a poem in its own right. The rhyme scheme and metre are the common formal devices. The rhyme scheme is usually as follows: aa ba ca da ea fa ga, etc. The rhyme may either consist of only one final element, a final rhyming syllable called *qafiyah*, or two, a qafiyah followed by a *radif* (a word or phrase repeated without any change whatsoever). As with any poetic form, there are ghazals which do not follow all the rules. The first couplet of the ghazal, in which both lines rhyme, is called the *matla*. The following is an example of a matla by Ghalib (d. 1869):

har qadam duri-e manzil hai numayanN mujh-se
meri raftar-se bhage hai biyabaN mujh-se

Each step shows how remote the destination is.
The wilderness runs away from me at my speed.

In the last couplet of the poem, called the *maqta*, the poet traditionally mentions his or her real or literary name (*takhallus*). This changes the poem from being a universal one to a text with a more individual focus. In Urdu ghazals have no titles but many translated into English have been given them. More recently poets of other languages, especially Punjabi, Sindhi, Pashto and Bengali in Pakistan and Punjabi, Sindhi, Gujarati and Hindi in India have taken up the form. The poems remain popular today particularly through their use in Indian and Pakistani cinema.

Other useful terms to know

Mushaira: a group or gathering of poets. These take place in any area where Urdu is widely spoken and there are a number of Mushaira groups in the UK. Readings from the ghazal genre usually predominate. Mushairas can last many hours, or even days, because poets are keen to perform and if the audience like a particular couplet they will shout out for it to be repeated (often many times over).

Nazms: traditionally anything which is not a ghazal. This term can be used to cover new genres in Urdu poetry as well as prose poems, free verse and many different rhyming forms.

Appendix 2: Some recommended Poetry Texts for Key Stage 3 Readers

This list is *not* exhaustive but would provide a good basis for a Key Stage 3 poetry box. It includes a mixture of single collections and anthologies. As students are developing their awareness of the writer's craft, it is important that they gain a sense of the difference between a single author collection of poetry and anthologies which are arranged by theme, style, period or in other ways. The suggestions should enable young readers to develop their reading and understanding of poetry further and build on their primary school experience.

Single collections

Ahlberg, Allan (2001) *Friendly Matches*. London: Viking Penguin.

Berry, James (1996) *Playing a Dazzler*. London: Penguin.

Berry, James (2002) *A Nest Full of Stars*. London: Macmillan.

Causley, Charles (1996) *Collected Poems for Children*. London: Macmillan.

Duffy, Carol Ann (1999) *Meeting Midnight*. London: Faber and Faber.

Dunmore, Helen (1994 – second edition in press) *Secrets*. London: The Bodley Head.

Eliot, T.S. illus. Gorey (1982) *Old Possum's Book of Practical Cats*. London: Faber and Faber.

Hardy, Thomas (1997) *Selected Poems*. London: Everyman.

Heaney, Seamus (1966) *Death of a Naturalist*. London: Faber and Faber.

Heaney, Seamus (1999) *Beowulf*. London: Faber and Faber.

Holub, Miroslav (1987) *The Fly*. Newcastle upon Tyne: Bloodaxe.

Kay, Jackie (1994) *Three's Gone*. London: Blackie.

Lear, Edward (2001) Jackson, Holbrook (ed.) *The Complete Nonsense of*

Edward Lear. London: Faber and Faber.

Macrae, Lindsay (2000) *How to Avoid Kissing your Parents in Public*. London: Penguin.

McCabe, Brian (1999) *Body Parts*. Manchester: Carcanet.

McMillan, Ian (2001) *The Very Best of Ian McMillan*. London: Macmillan.

McNaughton, Colin (1990) *Who's Been Sleeping in my Porridge?* London: Walker.

Milligan, Spike (1981) *Unspun Socks from a Chicken's Laundry*. London: Penguin.

Morgan, Edwin (1985) *Selected Poems*. Manchester: Carcanet.

Owen, Gareth (2002) *The Fox on the Roundabout*. Second edition. Oxford: Lions Publishing.

Patten, Brian (2000) *Juggling with Gerbils*. London: Penguin.

Popa, Vasko (1997) *Collected Poems*. London: Anvil.

Scannell, Vernon (2001) *The Very Best of Vernon Scannell*. London: Macmillan.

Sorescu, Marin (1987) *The Biggest Egg in the World*. Newcastle upon Tyne: Bloodaxe.

Sweeney, Matthew (1995) *Fatso in the Red Suit and Other Poems*. London: Faber and Faber.

Tennyson, Alfred, Lord, illust. Charles Keeping (1996). *The Lady of Shalott*. Oxford: Oxford University Press.

Thomas, Edward (1997) *Selected Poems*. London: Everyman.

Turner, Steve (1996) *The Day I Fell Down the Toilet*. Oxford: Lion Publishing.

Zephaniah, Benjamin (1994) *Talking Turkeys*. London: Penguin.

Anthologies

Adams, Pat (ed.) (1986) *With a Poet's Eye*. London: Tate Gallery Publications.

Agard, John and Nichols, Grace (eds) (1994) *A Caribbean Dozen*. London: Walker.

Benson, Gerard (ed.) (1994) *Does W trouble You?* London: Viking.

Benson, Gerard, Chernaik, Judith and Herbert, Cicely (eds) (1994). *Poems from the Underground*. London: Cassell.

Benton, Michael and Peter (eds) (1998). *New Touchstones 11–14*. London: Hodder & Stoughton.

Cope, Wendy (ed.) (1989) *Is that the New Moon?* London: Lions Teen Tracks, Collins.

Foster, John (ed.) (1986) *Spaceways*. Oxford: Oxford University Press.

Foster, John (ed.) (1999) *Word Whirls and Other Shape Poems*. Oxford:

Oxford University Press.

Fuller, John (ed.) (2000) *The Oxford Book of Sonnets*. Oxford: Oxford University Press.

Fusek Peters, Andrew (ed.) (1999) *Sheep Don't Go to School*. Newcastle upon Tyne: Bloodaxe.

Gent, Robert (ed.) (1996) *Poems for the Beekeeper*. Nottingham: Five Leaves Publications.

Harrison, Michael (ed.) (2001) *A Book of Very Short Poems*. Oxford: Oxford University Press.

Harrison, Michael and Stuart-Clark, Christopher (eds) (2001). *The Oxford Treasury of Classic Poems*. Second edition. Oxford: Oxford University Press.

Harvey, Anne (ed.) (1987) *In Time of War*. London: Blackie.

Harvey, Anne (ed.) (1996) *Criminal Records*. London: Penguin.

Heaney, Seamus and Hughes, Ted (eds) (1982) *The Rattlebag*. London: Faber and Faber.

Magee, Wes (ed.) (1991) *Madtail, Miniwhale*. London: Penguin.

McGough, Roger (1983) (ed.) *Sky in the Pie*. London: Penguin.

McMillan, Ian (ed.) (1989) *Against the Grain*. Walton-on-Thames: Nelson.

Mitchell, Adrian (ed.) (1993) *The Orchard Book of Poems*. London: Orchard.

Moses, Brian (ed.) (2002) *Are We Nearly There Yet?* London: Macmillan.

Neill, Heather (ed.) (1999) *The TES Book of Young Poets*. London: Times Supplements Limited.

Nicholls, Judith (ed.) (1993) *Earthways, Earthwise*. Oxford: Oxford University Press.

O'Brien, Sean (ed.) (1998) *The Firebox: Poetry in Britain and Ireland after 1945*. London: Picador.

Rice, John (ed.) (2001) *Scottish Poems*. London: Macmillan.

Richardson, Paul, Watson, Ken and Gill, Margaret (eds) (1998) *Snapshots of Planet Earth*. Oxford: Oxford University Press.

Rosen, Michael (ed.) (n.d.) *A Different Story*. London: English and Media Centre.

Rosen, Michael (ed.) (1991) *A World of Poetry*. London: Kingfisher.

Styles, Morag and Cook, Helen (eds) (1990) *Ink-slinger*. London: A & C Black.

Sweeney, Matthew (ed.) (2001) *The New Faber Book of Children's Verse*. London: Faber and Faber.

Waters, Fiona (ed.) (1996) *Glitter When you Jump*. London: Macmillan.

Waters, Fiona (ed,) (2001) *Poems Then and Now: Poetry Collection 3*. London: Evans.

Wilson, Raymond (ed.) (1995) *The Nine O'Clock Bell*. London: Penguin.

Books about writing

Brownjohn, Sandy (2002) *The Poet's Craft – a Handbook of Rhyme, Metre and Verse*. London: Hodder & Stoughton.

Hughes, Ted (1967) *Poetry in the Making*. London: Faber and Faber.

Mitchell, Adrian (1993) *The Thirteen Secrets of Poetry*. Hove: Macdonald Young Books.

Young Poetry Pack – a lively pack of materials written for young writers produced by the Poetry Society.

Bibliography

Abbs, Peter (1982) *English within the Arts*. London: Hodder and Stoughton.

Andrews, Richard (1983) *Into Poetry*. East Grinstead: Ward Lock.

Andrews, Richard (1991) *The Problem with Poetry*. Buckingham: Open University Press.

AQA (2002) *Delegate pack for Spring Term Introductory Meetings 2002, GCSE English and English Literature Specification A*. Guildford: AQA.

Arts Council of England (1998) *The Policy for Poetry of the English Arts Funding System*. London: Arts Council of England.

Atkinson, Ann, Cashdan, Liz, Michael, Livi and Pople, Ian (2001) 'Analysing the aesthetic: a new approach to developing criteria for assessment of creative writing in higher education, *Writing in Education* (21), Winter: 26–8.

Atkinson, Judith (1995) 'How do we teach pre-twentieth century literature?', in R. Protherough and P. King (eds), *The Challenge of the English National Curriculum*. London: Routledge. pp 48–64.

Auden, W.H. and Garrett, John (1935) *The Poet's Tongue*. London: Bell.

Bain, Richard (1999) 'Hypertexting', *Secondary English Magazine*, 2, February: (3) 20–4.

Baldwin, M. (1959) *Poetry without tears*. London: Routledge and Kegan Paul.

Ball, S., Kenny, A. and Gardner, D. (1990) 'Literacy, politics and the teaching of English' in I. Goodson and P. Medway, (eds) *Bringing English to Order*. Lewes: Falmer Press. pp. 47–86.

Ball, Stephen J. (1985) 'English for the English since 1906', in I. Goodson (ed.) *Social Histories of the Secondary Curriculum*. Lewes: Falmer Press.

Bangert-Drowns, R. (1993) 'The word processor as an instructional tool: a meta-analysis of word processing in writing instruction', *Review of Educational Research*, 63 (1): 69–94.

Barrell, R.C. Barrie and Hammett, Roberta F. (1999) 'Hypermedia as a medium for textual resistance', *English in Education*, 33 (3): 21–31.

Barrs, Myra and Cork, Valerie (2001) *The Reader in the Writer*. London: CLPE.

Baugh, David (2002) 'Bring a touch of life and soul to your lessons', *TES Online*, 4 January, p. 52.

Benton, Michael (1978) 'Poetry for children: a neglected art', *Children's Literature in Education*, 9 (3): 111–26.

Benton, Michael (1984) 'The methodology vacuum in teaching literature', *Language Arts*, 61 (3): 265–75.

Benton, Michael (1990) 'The importance of poetry in children's learning', *CLE Working Papers 1*, pp. 27–36.

Benton, Michael (1995) 'The discipline of literary response: approaches to poetry with L2 students', *Educational Review*, 47 (3): 333–42.

Benton, Michael and Benton, Peter (1969) *Touchstones 1–5*: London: Hodder and Stoughton.

Benton, Michael and Benton, Peter (1990) *Examining Poetry*. London: Hodder and Stoughton.

Benton, Michael and Fox, Geoff (1985) *Teaching Literature Nine to Fourteen*. Oxford: Oxford University Press.

Benton, Michael, Teasey, John, Bell, Ray and Hurst, Keith (1988) *Young Readers Responding to Poems*. London: Routledge.

Benton, Peter (1984) 'Teaching poetry: the rhetoric and the reality', *Oxford Review of Education*, 10 (3): 319–27.

Benton, Peter (1986) *Pupil, Teacher, Poem*. London: Hodder and Stoughton.

Benton, Peter (1999) 'Unweaving the rainbow: poetry teaching in the secondary school I', *Oxford Review of Education*, 25 (4): pp 521–31.

Benton, Peter (2000) 'The conveyor belt curriculum: poetry teaching in the secondary school II', *Oxford Review of Education*, 26 (1): 81–93.

Bereiter, C. and Scardamalia, M. (1982) 'From conversation to composition: the role of instruction in a developmental process', in R. Glaser. (ed.) *Advances in Instructional Psychology*. Hillsdale, NJ: Lawrence Erlbaum Associates.

Bereiter, C. and Scardamalia, M. (1983) 'Does learning to write have to be so difficult?' in A. Freedman, I. Pringle and J. Yalden (eds), *Learning to Write: First Language/Second Language*. Harlow: Longman.

Bereiter, C. and Scardamalia, M. (1987) *The Psychology of Written Composition*. Hillsdale, NJ: Lawrence Erlbaum Associates.

Berliner, Wendy (1992) 'The bunker mentality', *Guardian Education*. 7: 4.

Bibby, Bob and Priest, Sue (2000) *Sharing Poems at KS2*. Sheffield: NATE.

Black, P. (1998) *Testing: Friend or Foe?* London: Falmer Press.

Bleiman, B. (1995) *The Poetry Pack*. London: English and Media Centre.

Blishen, Edward (1993) Foreword in J. Pirrie, (ed.), *Apple Fire*. Newcastle upon Tyne: Bloodaxe.

Blunkett, David (2000) *Poetryclass*. London: DfEE and the Poetry Society.

Bolter, D. (1991) *Writing Space: The Computer, Hypertext and the History of Writing*. Hillsdale, NJ. Lawrence Erlbaum Associates.

Britton, James (1970) *Language and Learning*. London: Penguin.

Britton, James (1973) 'How we got here', in N. Bagnall (ed.) *New Movements in the Study and Taching of English*. London: Temple Smith.

Britton, James, Burgess, Tony, Martin, Nancy, McLeod, Alex and Rosen, Harold (1975) *The Development of Writing Abilities 11–18*. London: Schools Council Research Studies, Macmillan.

Brownjohn, Sandy (1980) *Does It Have to Rhyme?* London: Hodder and Stoughton.

Brownjohn, Sandy (1982) *What Rhymes with 'Secret'?* London: Hodder and Stoughton.

Brownjohn, Sandy (1989) *The Ability to Name Cats*. London: Hodder and Stoughton.

Brownjohn, Sandy (1994) *To Rhyme or Not to Rhyme?* London: Hodder and Stoughton.

Brownjohn, Sandy (1999) 'Inspired by Ted', *Times Educational Supplement*, 11 June: 18–19.

Buzan, T. (1974) *Use your head*. London: BBC.

Carter, Dennis (1998) *Teaching Poetry in the Primary School*. London: David Fulton.

Carter, James (2000) *Rap it Up*. Birmingham: Questions Publishing.

Carter, James (2001) *Creating Writers*. London: Routledge Falmer.

Chandler, Daniel (1987) 'Are we ready for word processors', *English in Australia*, 79, March. 11–17.

Chatterjee, D., Fletcher, S. and Sultan Kazmi, B. (1997) *A Little Bridge*. Hebden Bridge: Pennine Pens.

Clegg, A.B. (1964) *The Excitement of Writing*. London: Chatto and Windus.

Cochrane-Smith, M. (1991) 'Word processing and writing in elementary classrooms: a critical review of related literature', *Review of Educational Research*, 61 (1): 107–55.

Creber, P. (1990) *Thinking English Through*. Buckingham: Open University Press.

Czerniewska, Pam (1992) *Learning About Writing*. Oxford: Blackwell.

D'Arcy, Pat (1989) *Making Sense, Shaping Meaning*. Portsmouth, NH: Boynton Cook/Heinemann.

D' Arcy, Pat (2000) *Two Contrasting Paradigms for the Teaching and Assessment of Writing*. Sheffield: NAAE/NAPE/NATE.

Dauite, C. (1983) 'The computer as stylus and audience', *College Composition and Communication*, 34 (2): 134–45.

Davies, Diana (1986) 'The mapping of writing', in A. Wilkinson *The Quality of Writing*. Buckingham: Open University Press.

Delpit, L. (1988) 'The silenced dialogue: power and pedagogy in education of other people's children, *Harvard Education Review*, 58 (3): 280–98.

DES (1975) *A Language for Life* (Bullock Report). London: HMSO.

DES (1982) *Language Performance in Schools (APU)*. London: HMSO.

DES (1987) *Teaching Poetry in the Secondary School: An HMI View*. London: HMSO.

DES (1988) *Report of the Committee of Inquiry into the Teaching of English Language* (Report of the Kingman Committee). London: HMSO.

DES (1989) *English for Ages 5 to 16: Proposals of the Secretary of State for Education and Science and the Secretary of State for Wales* (Cox Report). York: National Curriculum Council.

DES (1990) *English in the National Curriculum* (No. 2). London: HMSO.

DfE (1993) *English for Ages 5 to 16: Proposals of the Secretary of State for Education and Science and the Secretary of State for Wales*. London: HMSO.

DfE (1995) *English in the National Curriculum*. London: HMSO.

DfEE (1998) *The National Literacy Strategy – Framework for Teaching*. London: HMSO.

DfEE (2000) *Grammar for Writing*. London: HMSO.

DfEE (2001a) *Key Stage 3 National Strategy: Framework for Teaching English Years 7, 8 and 9*. London: HMSO.

DfEE (2001b) *English Department Training 2001*. London: HMSO.

DfEE and QCA (1999) *English: The National Curriculum for England*. London: HMSO.

Dias, Patrick and Hayhoe, Michael (1988) *Developing Response to Poetry*. Buckingham: Open University Press.

Dixon, John (1967) *Growth through English*. Oxford: Oxford University Press.

Driver, C.J. (1977) 'Marking poems', *The Use of English*, 28/3: 4–9.

Dunn, Douglas (1994) 'Writing things down', in C.B. McCully (ed.), *The Poet's Voice and Craft.* Manchester: Carcanet. 84–103.

Dunn, Jennifer, Styles, Morag and Warburton, Nick (1987) *In Tune with Yourself.* Cambridge: Cambridge University Press.

Dymoke, Sue (1994) 'Writers into school: the Jackie Kay experience', in B.T. Harrison (ed.), *The Literate Imagination.* London: David Fulton. pp. 178–86.

Dymoke, Sue (2000a) 'The teaching of poetry in secondary schools'. Unpublished PhD thesis, University of Nottingham.

Dymoke, Sue (2000b) 'Taking stock of poetry', *Secondary English Magazine.* 4 (2): December: 28–32.

Dymoke, Sue (2001) 'Taking poetry off its pedestal: the place of poetry writing in an assessment-driven curriculum, *English in Education,* 35 (3) Autumn: 32–41.

Dymoke, Sue (2001a) *Badger Key Stage 3 Literacy Starters Y7 Word Level.* Stevenage: Badger Publishing.

Dymoke, Sue (2001a) *Badger Key Stage 3 Literacy Starters Y8 Word Level.* Stevenage: Badger Publishing.

Dymoke, Sue (2002) 'The dead hand of the exam', *Changing English,* 9 (1): 85–93.

Dymoke, Sue (2002a) *Badger Key Stage 3 Literacy Starters Y9 Word Level,* Stevenage: Badger Publishing.

Eliot, T.S. (1971) *The Waste Land: A Facsimile and Transcript of the Original Drafts,* ed. Valerie Eliot. London: Faber and Faber.

Fenton, J. (2001) *The Strength of Poetry.* Oxford: Oxford University Press.

Ferguson, Mike (1999) *Poems in your Pocket: Imaginative Approaches to GCSE Poetry (Teachers Guide).* Harlow: Pearson Education.

Fleming, Michael (1996) 'Poetry teaching in the secondary school: the concept of difficulty', in L. Thompson, (ed.), *The Teaching of Poetry – European Perspectives.* London: Cassell.

Fletcher, Chris (ed.) (2000) *Chapter and Verse: 1000 Years of English Literature.* London: British Library.

Frater, Graham (1993) 'Back to the future', *Education,* 22 January: 51.

Furlong, Terry, Venkatakrishnan, Hamsa and Brown, Margaret (2001) *Key Stage 3 National Strategy : An Evaluation of the Strategies for Literacy and Mathematics Interim Report.* London: ATL.

Goodwyn, Andrew (2000) *English in the Digital Age.* London: Cassell Education.

Goody, Joan (1995) *Opening New Worlds.* Sheffield: NATE.

Goody, Joan, with Thomas, Kit (2000) *Multicultural Literature in the Classroom.* Sheffield: NATE.

Graves, Donald (1981) 'Renters and owners', *English Magazine* (8): 4–7.

Graves, Donald (1983) *Writing: Teachers and Children at Work.* London: Heinemann.

Hackman, Sue and Marshall, Barbara (1995) *Into Literature.* London: Hodder and Stoughton.

Hall, Donald (1985) Interview (in 1959) with T.S. Eliot, in G. Plimpton (ed.), *Poets at Work: the Paris Review Interviews.* New York: Viking Penguin. pp. 26–45.

Harrison, Bernard T. (1994a) 'Freedom within the framework: nurturing the imagination in the National Curriculum', *Curriculum,* 15 (2): 104–11.

Harrison, Bernard T. (ed.) (1994b) *The Literate Imagination.* London: David Fulton.

Harrison, Bernard and Gordon, Heather (1983) 'Metaphor is thought: does Northtown need poetry?', *Educational Review,* 35 (3): 265–78.

Harrison, Michael and Stuart-Clark, Christopher (1992) *Writing Poems Plus.* Oxford: Oxford University Press.

Harvey, A. (1982) *The Language of Love*. London: Blackie and Sons.

Harvey, A. (1994) *Criminal Records*. London: Viking.

Harvey, Anne (ed.) (1999) *Adlestrop Revisited*. Stroud: Sutton Publishing.

Hayhoe, Mike and Parker, Stephen (1988) *Words as Large as Apples*. Cambridge: Cambridge University Press.

Heaney, Seamus (1980) 'Feeling into words', in S. Heaney, *Preoccupations – Selected Prose 1968–1978*. London: Faber and Faber.

Heaney, S. (1989) *The Redress of Poetry* (inaugural lecture given on 28 October 1989 at Oxford University). Oxford: Clarendon Press.

Heaney, Seamus (1995) *The Redress of Poetry*. London: Faber and Faber.

Heaney, Seamus and Hughes, Ted (1982) *The Rattle Bag*. London: Faber and Faber.

Holbrook, David (1961a) *Iron, Honey, Gold, (Vols I and II)*. Cambridge: Cambridge University Press.

Holbrook, David (1961b) *English for Maturity*. Cambridge: Cambridge University Press.

Holbrook, David (1964) *English for the Rejected*. Cambridge: Cambridge University Press.

Holbrook, David (1979) *English for Meaning*. Slough: NFER.

Hollander, John (1961) *Introduction to Ben Jonson*. Laurel Poetry Series. New York: Dell Publishing.

Holub, M. (1987) 'Poem Technology' *The Fly*. Newcastle upon Tyne: Bloodaxe.

Hourd, Marjorie (1949) *The Education of the Poetic Spirit*. London: Heinemann.

Hughes, Ted (1967) *Poetry in the Making*. London: Faber and Faber.

Hull, Robert (1988) *Behind the Poem*. London: Routledge.

Hull, Robert (2001) 'What hope for children's poetry?', *Books for Keeps*, (126), January: 10–13.

Inglis, Fred (1969) *The Englishness of English Teaching*. Harlow: Longman.

Johnson, Amryl (1987) 'Essay', in L. Ngcobo, (ed.), *Let it Be Told*. London: Pluto Press. 35–45.

Kay, Jackie (1994) *Three's Gone*. London: Blackie.

Keats, John (1970) *Odes 1820 Facsimile edition*, ed. R. Gittings. London: Heinemann.

Keegan, Victor (2001) 'Text message poetry competition', *Guardian On-line*. http://www.guardian.co.uk.

Kelves, Barbara (1985) Interview (in 1971) with Anne Sexton, in G. Plimpton (ed.), *Poets at Work: The Paris Review Interviews*. New York: Viking Penguin.

Knight, R. (1995) 'The Revised Order for English' (editorial), *The Use of English*, 46 (3): 193–204.

Knight, Roger (1996) *Valuing English: Reflections on the National Curriculum*. London: David Fulton.

Koch, Kenneth (1970) *Wishes, Lies and Dreams*. New York: Harper and Row.

Koch, Kenneth (1973) *Rose, Where Did You Get that Red?* New York: Vintage.

Kress, Gunther (1982) *Learning to Write*. London: Routledge and Kegan Paul.

Langdon, M. (1961) *Let the Children Write*. London: Longman.

Lawrence, D.H. (1929) Preface to *Chariot of the Sun* by Harry Crosby, in E.D. Macdonald (ed.), *Phoenix*. London: Heinemann. p. 255.

Leavis, F.R. and Thompson, Denys (1933) *Culture and Environment*. London: Chatto and Windus.

Lensmire T.J. (1994) *When Children Write: Critical Re-visions of the Writing Workshop*. New York: Teachers College Press.

Leonard, Tom (1988) 'On the teaching of Poetry', *Teaching English*, 21 (1): 4–7.

Levenson, Christopher (1992) 'Magical forms in poetry', in E.G. Ingersoll (ed.) *Margaret Atwood: Conversations*. London: Virago. pp. 20–6.

Lunzer, E. and Gardner, K. (1984) *Learning from the Written Word*. Edinburgh: Oliver and Boyd.

Marsh, George (1988) *Teaching through Poetry*. London: Hodder and Stoughton.

Marshall, Bethan (2000) *English Teachers – The Unofficial Guide: Researching the Philosophies of English Teachers*. London: Routledge Falmer.

Marshall, Sybil (1963) *An Experiment in Education*. Cambridge: Cambridge University Press.

Martin, J.R. (1984) 'Types of writing in infants and primary school', *Proceedings of Macarthur Institute of Higher Education, Reading Language Symposium*, 5: Reading, Writing and Spelling. Cited in Czerniewska, Pam (1992) *Learning About Writing*. Oxford: Blackwell.

Mathieson, Margaret (1980) 'The Problem of Poetry', *Use of English*, Spring: 36–43.

Maybin, Janet (1994) 'Teaching writing: process or genre?', in S. Brindley, (ed.), *Teaching English*. London: Routledge.

McCully, C.B. (ed.) (1994) *The Poet's Voice and Craft*. Manchester: Carcanet.

McMillan, Ian (ed.) (1989) *Against the Grain*. London: Nelson.

McMillan, Ian (2002) *The Invisible Villain*. London: Macmillan.

Millum, T. and Warren, C. (2001) *Twenty Things to Do with a Word Processor*. Kegworth: Resource Education.

Mirza, Y. (1992) *Translation of the Selected Verses of Ghalib's Urdu Ghazals*. New Delhi: Ghalib Institute.

Mitchell, Adrian (1982) *For Beauty Douglas Collected Poems 1953–1979*. London: Allison and Busby.

Mole, John (1973) 'The teacher and the postmistress', in N. Bagnall (ed.), *New Movements in the study and teaching of English*. London: Temple Smith. pp. 189–205.

Morgan, Edwin (1994) 'The poet's voice and craft', in C.B. McCully (ed.), *The Poet's Voice and Craft*. Manchester: Carcanet.

Moses, Brian (2001) Welcome to the Ssssnake Hotel. London: Macmillan.

Muir, Edwin (1962) *The Estate of Poetry*. London: Hogarth Press.

Myhill, Debra (1986) 'Finding a voice: a study of approaches to poetry composition', unpublished MPhil thesis, University of Exeter.

Myhill, Debra (2001) 'Writing: crafting and creating', *English in Education*, 35 (3), Autumn: 13–20.

NATE Drama Committee (2001) *Cracking Drama 5–16*. Sheffield: NATE.

National Writing Project (1990a) *Responding to and Assessing Writing*. London: School Curriculum Development Committee, Thomas Nelson.

National Writing Project (1990b) *Ways of Looking*. London: School Curriculum Development Committee, Thomas Nelson.

National Writing Project (1991) *Changing Practice – a History of the National Writing Project 1985–1989*. York: National Curriculum Council.

Newbolt Committee (1921) The Teaching of English in England. London: HMSO.

NEAB (1996) *NEAB Anthology*. Manchester: NEAB.

NEAB (1998a) *Report on the GCSE Examination 1998*. Manchester: NEAB.

NEAB (1998b) *English Paper 2 Tier H*, 5 June. Manchester: NEAB.

Newman, Michael (1985) Interview (in 1973) with W.H. Auden, in G. Plimpton (ed.), *Poets at Work: The Paris Review Interviews*. New York: Viking Penguin.

Newsom Committee (1963) *Half our Future* (Newsom Report). London: HMSO.

Nicholls, Judith (1990) 'Verse and verbiage', *Times Educational Supplement*, 11 May: B27.

Oakley, Anthony (1981) 'A survey of the teaching of poetry to children between the ages of ten to thirteen in forty three primary, middle and secondary schools in the East Dorset area', unpublished MA Ed dissertation, University of Southampton.

OCR (2002) *GCSE in English (Opening Minds)*. Cambridge: Cambridge, Oxford and RSA Examinations.

P.N. Review (1999) 'Editorial' *P.N. Review*, (129), September/October: 1.

Pirrie, Jill (1987) *On Common Ground*. London: Hodder.

Pirrie, Jill (1994) *On Common Ground* (second edition). Godalming: WWF.

Pirrie, Jill (1999) 'The astonishment of being', *Use of English*, 50 (3): 204 –13.

Plimpton, G. (ed.) (1985) *Poets at Work: The Paris Review Interviews*. New York: Viking Penguin.

Poulson, Louise (1998) *The English Curriculum in Schools*. London: Cassell.

Powell, Brian (1968) *English through Poetry Writing*. London: Heinemann.

Protherough, Robert and King, Peter (eds) (1995) *The Challenge of the English National Curriculum*. London: Routledge.

Pugh, Sheenagh (1999) 'Tutorial', in S. Pugh, *Selected Poems*. Bridgend: Seren.

Pye, Jim (1994) 'Catching a mind', Jill Pirrie's English Teaching, *Use of English*, 46 (1): 36–52.

QCA (1998) *Standards at Key Stage 3 English: Report on the 1997 National Curriculum Assessments for 14-year-olds*. London: Qualifications and Curriculum Authority.

QCA (1999) *Improving Writing at Key Stages 3 and 4*. London: Qualifications and Curriculum Authority.

QCA (2002) *Assessment Objectives for GCSE 2004* (published in each GCSE English specification for 2004).

Riley, Jeni and Reedy, David (2000) *Developing Writing for Different Purposes*. London: Paul Chapman Publishing.

Rose, June and Scafe, Suzanne (1997) 'Interrupting the literature lesson', *Changing English*, 4 (1), March: 123–30.

Rosen, Harold (1992) 'The politics of writing', in K. Kimberly, M. Meek and J. Miller (eds), *New Readings: Contributions to an Understanding of Literacy*. London: A & C Black. pp. 119–30.

Rosen, Michael (1989) *Did I Hear You Write?* London: Andre Deutsch (second edition, 1998, Nottingham: Five Leaves Publications).

Rosenblatt, Louise M. (1978) *The Reader, the Text, the Poem*. Carbondale, IL: Southern Illinois University Press.

Rothery, J. (1984) 'The development of genres – primary to junior secondary school', in *Deakin University Course Study Guide: Children Writing*. Victoria: Deakin University.

Sansom, Peter (1994) *Writing Poems*. Newcastle upon Tyne: Bloodaxe Books.

Sarton, May (1995) *Writings on Writing*. London: Women's Press.

Saunders, Michael (1976) *Developments in English Teaching*. London: Open Books.

Sedgwick, Fred (1987) 'The Green Fire: poems about the beginning of poems', *Cambridge Journal of Education*, 17 (2), Spring: 114–20.

SCAA (1997) *Key Stage 3 English Paper 1 Levels 4-7*. London: SCAA.

Scardamalia, M, Bereiter, C. and Lamon, M. (1994) 'The CISLE Project: trying to bring the classroom into the world 3', in K. McGilly (ed.), *Classroom Lessons: Integrating Cognitive Theory and Classroom Practice*. Cambridge: Bradford/MIT. pp. 210–28.

Shayer, David (1972) *The Teaching of English in Schools 1900–70*. London: Routledge and Kegan Paul.

Simpson, Peter (1999) *Original Writing*. London: Hodder and Stoughton.

Smith, Alistair (1996) *Accelerated Learning in the Classroom*. Stafford: Network Educational Press.

Smith, F. (1982) *Writing and the Writer*. London: Heinemann.

Smith, John and Elley, Warwick (1998) *How Children Learn to Write*. London: Paul Chapman Publishing.

Smith, Vivienne (2000) 'Give yourself a hug', in H. Anderson and M. Styles (eds), *Teaching through Texts*. London: Routledge. pp. 13–28.

Snyder, Ilana (1993) 'Writing with word processors: a research overview', *Educational Research*, 35, Spring: 49–68.

Stafford, William (1986) 'A course in creative writing', in W. Stafford, *You Must Revise Your Life*. Ann Arbor, MI: University of Michigan Press.

Steiner, George (1978) *On Difficulty and Other Essays*. Oxford: Oxford University Press.

Stibbs, Andrew (1981) 'Teaching poetry', *Children's Literature in Education*, 12 (1): 39–50.

Stibbs, A. (1995) 'The specialness of poetry', *English in Education*, 29 (3): 14–19.

Thomas, Peter (2000) 'Mid-term Report', *Secondary English Magazine*, 3 (4): 27–31.

Travers, M. (1984) 'The Poetry teacher: behaviour and attitudes' in *Research in the Teaching of English*, 18(4) 367–384.

Tunnicliffe, Stephen (1984) *Poetry Experience*. London: Methuen.

Tweddle, Sally (1993) 'Developing Tray as an assessment tool', in NATE English and New Technologies Committee, *Developing English: Approaches to IT*. Sheffield: NATE.

Tweddle, Sally, Adams, Anthony, Clark, Stephen, Scrimshaw, Peter and Walton, Shona (1997) *English for Tomorrow*. Buckingham: Open University Press.

Vincent, J. (2001) 'The role of visually rich technology in facilitating children's writing', *Journal of Computer Assisted Learning*, 17: 242–50.

Wade, Barrie and Sidaway, Sue (1990) 'Poetry in the curriculum: a crisis of confidence', *Educational Studies*, 16 (1): 75–83.

Whitehead, Frank (1966) *The Disappearing Dias*. London: Chatto and Windus.

Wiliam, D. (1998) 'The validity of teachers' assessments'. Paper presented at 22nd annual conference of the International Group for the Psychology of Mathematics Education, Stellenbosch, South Africa.

Wilkinson, Andrew (ed.) (1986) *The Quality of Writing*. Buckingham: Open University Press.

Wilson, Andrew (2001) Guardian Unlimited, 29 March, http://www.guardian.co.uk

Wilson, Antony (ed.), with Sian Hughes (1998) *The Poetry Book for Primary Schools*. London: Poetry Society.

Witkin, R. (1974) *The Intelligence of Feeling*. London: Heinemann.

WJEC (2002) GCSE English Specification for 2004. Cardiff: WJEC.

Yates, Cliff (1999) *Jumpstart: Poetry in the Secondary School*. London: Poetry Society.

Yates, Cliff (ed.) (2001) *Oranges: Poems from the Maharishi School*. Ormskirk: Maharishi School Press.

Author Index

Subject Index